Everyman, I will go with thee,
and be thy guide

Dance to the music of
Yours Charles

Izaak Walton

THE COMPLETE ANGLER
OR
THE CONTEMPLATIVE MAN'S
RECREATION

Edited by
JONQUIL BEVAN
Department of English Literature
University of Edinburgh

EVERYMAN
J. M. DENT · LONDON
CHARLES E. TUTTLE
VERMONT

Introduction, Chronology, Note on the Text and all endmatter
© J.M.Dent 1993
Reprinted 1995

This edition first published 1993

J.M.Dent
Orion Publishing Group, Orion House
5 Upper St Martin's Lane, London WC2H 9EA

and

Charles E. Tuttle
28 South Main Street, Rutland, Vermont 05701, USA

Printed in Great Britain by The Guernsey Press Co. Ltd, Guernsey, C.I.

British Library Cataloguing-in-Publication Data
for this title is available upon request

ISBN 0 460 87281 8

CONTENTS

NOTE ON THE AUTHOR AND EDITOR

IZAAK WALTON was born at Stafford in 1593 into a widespread family, with whom he always remained in touch. He went early to London, to live with his sister and her husband, a prosperous merchant in whose footsteps Walton followed. He was much influenced by his vicar there, John Donne, and married into a family – the Cranmers – who had close personal ties with Richard Hooker ('the Anglican Thomas Aquinas'); Walton, later (1665), was to write his *Life*. His first *Life* was that of Donne (1640), followed by the *Life* of Sir Henry Wotton (1651). *The Complete Angler* appeared in 1653; Walton continued to revise it extensively until 1676. After *Hooker*, Walton wrote (in 1670) a *Life* of George Herbert 'to please myself' (the other *Lives* had been commissioned); and he completed the series with another ecclesiastical *Life*, of Bishop Sanderson (1678). During the interregnum Walton bought (quite modest) property near his native Stafford; the nucleus of this, at Shallowford, is now the Izaak Walton Cottage Museum Trust. An assiduous servant of the Church of England (although a somewhat sceptical Royalist), Walton shared in the post-Restoration fortune of his party. He became the steward of his old friend George Morley, who, as Bishop of Winchester (1662), enjoyed the richest see in England. Walton died at Winchester in 1683, and his tombstone may be seen there, in Prior Silkstead's chapel.

JONQUIL BEVAN was born in Brecon, Wales. She was educated at the Godolphin and Latymer School, London, and at Lady Margaret Hall, Oxford. After a year as part-time research assistant to Dame Helen Gardner, she took up a post at Edinburgh University, where she has remained; she is now a Reader there. In 1983 she published an old-spelling edition of *The Compleat Angler* (both 1653 and 1676 editions) with the Clarendon Press, and in 1988 published a short study of the book. She is now engaged, with L. G. Black, in editing Walton's *Lives* for the Clarendon Press.

CHRONOLOGY OF WALTON'S LIFE

CHRONOLOGY OF HIS TIMES

Year	Literary Context	Historical Events
1593	Marlowe killed G. Herbert born	Henri IV changes religion
1597	Bacon's *Essays* pub.	Essex's Azores Expedition
1613	Crashaw, Jeremy Taylor born	Princess Elizabeth m. Elector Palatine
1618	Ralegh executed Cowley born	Beginning of Thirty Years War
1626	Sandys's trans. of Ovid Donne's *Five Sermons* pub. Bacon dies	Second Parliament
1630	Drayton's *Muses' Elysium* pub.	'Great Migration' to New Zealand
1631	Great Tew circle starts Drayton dies Dryden born	Laud enforces conformity
1633	G. Herbert dies *The Temple* pub.	Migration to New England
1639	Fuller's *Holy War* pub.	First Bishops' War
1640	Carew's *Poems*, Jonson's *Works*, Harvey's *Synagogue*, pub.	Second Bishops' War Strafford and Laud impeached
1643	Browne's *Religio Medici* pub.	Episcopacy abolished
1644	Milton's *Areopagitica* pub.	Covenant imposed
1647	Cleveland's *Poems*, Cowley's *The Mistress*, Beaumont and Fletcher, pub.	King given up to Parliament; escapes to Isle of Wight
1648	Herrick's *Hesperides* pub.	Army seizes King, enters London
1651	Vaughan's *Olor Iscanus*, Donne's *Essays in Divinity*, *Letters*; Hobbes's *Leviathan*, Taylor's *Holy Dying*, pub.	Charles II crowned at Scone Battle of Worcester Confiscation of Royalist estates

Year	Age	Life
1653	60	Publishes *The Complete Angler* (in May)
1655	62	Buys property near Stafford 2nd much expanded edn of *The Complete Angler*
1660	67	Publishes pastoral eclogue to celebrate the Restoration Apptd steward to G. Morley, Dean of Christ Church, Oxford; moves with him to Worcester
1661	68	Third edn of *The Complete Angler*, again revised
1662	69	Wife dies; moves with Morley to Winchester
1665	72	Publishes *Life of Richard Hooker*
1668	75	Fourth (unrevised) edn of *The Complete Angler*
1670	77	Publishes *Life of George Herbert*; publishes collected *Lives*
1675	82	Second edn of collected *Lives*
1676	83	Fifth edn of *The Complete Angler*, thoroughly revised; Charles Cotton adds Part II
1678	85	Publishes *The Life of Bishop Sanderson*
1680	87	? Publishes anon. *Love and Truth* ?
1683	90	Publishes an edn of Chalkhill's *Thealma and Clearchus* Dies, 15 December; buried Winchester Cathedral
1718		Canon Isaac Walton gives his share of his father's books to Salisbury Cathedral Library

Year	Literary Context	Historical Events
1653	Newcastle's *Philosophical Fancies*, pub.	Protectorate established Legislation against Anglicans West Indian colonies secured
1655	Denham's *Cooper's Hill*, Marvell's *First Anniversary*, pub.	
1660	Lovelace's *Lucasta*, Dryden's *Astraea Redux*, Donne's *XXVI Sermons*, Milton's *Ready and Easy Way*, pub.	Restoration of Charles II Founding of Royal Society
1661	Dryden's *To his Sacred Majesty* pub.	Coronation; Savoy Conference
1662	Butler's *Hudibras*, Fuller's *Worthies* pub.	Charles m. Catherine of Braganza
1665	Dryden's *The Indian Emperor* perf.	Second Dutch War; Plague
1668	Dryden's *Essay of Dramatic Poesy* pub.	Triple Alliance
1670	Milton's *History of Britain* pub.	Cabal formed
1675	Wycherley's *Country Wife* perf.	Edict against Nonconformists
1676	Wycherley's *Plain Dealer* perf.	Charles concludes secret treaty with Louis XIV
1678	Bunyan's *Pilgrim's Progress* pub.	Treaty of Nijmegen
1680	Rochester's *Poems* pub.	Shaftesbury indicts Duke of York
1683	Oldham's *Poems*, Dryden's trans. of Plutarch's *Lives* pub.	Rye House Plot; the Thames freezes in the Great Frost

INTRODUCTION

Izaak Walton began writing as a biographer, publishing in 1640 the *Life* of his friend John Donne, poet and Dean of St Paul's; the *Life* of their friend Sir Henry Wotton followed in 1651. The intervening decade was turbulent: by the mid-1640s the Presbyterians were in power and the Anglican Church under threat. In 1649 the King was beheaded. The *Lives* of Donne and Wotton can be seen, from their first publication, as retrospective, demonstrating aspects of what Walton found best in the old Anglican Church. By 1651 that church was so beleaguered that ejected members of its clergy were reduced to corresponding secretly, under assumed names.[1] The battle of Worcester dashed the last hopes of Royalists, and life became even more difficult for Anglicans; there was anxious discussion about whether episcopacy could survive.

The 1650s were no time for Izaak Walton's kind of biography. Instead, *The Complete Angler* appeared in 1653, reappearing, much revised, in 1655. Not until the Restoration did Walton return to biography, with a *Life* of Richard Hooker (theologian) in 1665, of George Herbert (poet and priest) in 1670, and of Bishop Robert Sanderson in 1678. These *Lives* add to the ecclesiastical picture which Walton's earlier biographies had begun, and in 1670 Walton printed a collected edition of *Lives*, reprinted in 1675. When the *Life of Bishop Sanderson* (1678) is added, we have a portrayal of the Church, from deacon to bishop, illustrating Church work through preaching, teaching, theology, and pastoral care.[2] After the Restoration Walton continued to revise *The Complete Angler*, so that from 1661 one sees him developing his biographical project with one hand while continuing to enlarge and reshape *The Complete Angler* with the other.

The Complete Angler was written when measures which punished private families who harboured Anglican priests or used the Book of Common Prayer made it difficult for men like

Walton to speak openly. True, the *Angler* is a practical fishing-manual, designed to provide instruction, as well as humour, entertainment, and song; but it has a further, encoded purpose. This purpose may be more clearly seen if we consider what kind of man Walton was.

Izaak Walton was baptised at Stafford on 21 September 1593.[3] His father died in 1597 and his mother remarried the following year, and Walton moved early to London, where his sister, Anne, was married to Thomas Grinsell, a rich London linen-draper in the parish of St Dunstan's-in-the-West. Walton was apprenticed to Grinsell, and became a freeman of the Ironmongers' Company on 12 November 1618.[4] The Ironmongers' Company was a close, often intermarried, society, with its own charities for members and their families. Walton must have known that John Donne's father had been a prominent Ironmonger.[5] Yet Walton, like Grinsell, was not in business as an ironmonger; he was a linen-draper.[6]

In 1624 John Donne, Dean of St Paul's, became vicar of St Dunstan's-in-the-West, and Izaak Walton's parish priest. The two men had probably already met.[7] Donne exerted a powerful influence: Walton was to describe himself, after Donne's death, as his 'Convert' and Donne's thought dominates the rest of Walton's long life. Henry King, at this time a canon of St Paul's, tells us that Walton knew Donne well enough to be present at his deathbed in 1631.[8] Some have thought it surprising that a friendship could exist between the Dean of St Paul's and a humble tradesman,[9] but Walton was Donne's equal, both socially and financially. Ties with the clergy were strengthened when Walton married, in 1626, the great-great-niece of Thomas Cranmer, Archbishop of Canterbury (the Cranmers retained close connections with the senior members of the Church) and were strengthened further when one of the junior clergy in the parish, appointed by Donne, married Walton's niece, Sarah Grinsell.[10]

He was Henry Valentine, and his earliest printed sermon, preached at Paul's Cross while he was still at St Dunstan's, displays Donne's influence clearly.[11] His and Walton's elegies on Donne are adjacent in Donne's *Poems* (1633).[12] Two of Valentine's later sermons exert, in turn, a marked influence on Walton's *Angler*.[13] Walton and Valentine shared an admiration for Donne, and their friendship not only indicates that Walton, through Valentine, may have been closer to Donne in these years than some historians have cared to admit; it also helps explain Walton's commitment to the Anglican Church. No doubt Walton also met some of Valentine's clerical friends, such as Gilbert Sheldon.

John Donne had entrusted his sermons, prepared for posthumous publication, to Henry King (King was later to call upon Walton's witness that this was so); this occasioned the writing of the *Life of Donne*. Originally a prefatory *Life* was to be written by Sir Henry Wotton, and Izaak Walton was to be his research assistant.[14] This was discussed when Walton visited Sir Henry at Eton, while the two men went angling together along the banks of the Thames.[15] But Sir Henry died before the *Life of Donne* had been written, and Walton, with a professed sense of his own unworthiness, stepped into the gap lest the sermons should be published 'and want the *Authors Life*'.[16] By the time Izaak Walton published the *Life of Donne* (1640), he had acquired an extensive acquaintance among the clergy of the Church of England. The book's publication doubtless helped increase it.

But long before 1640 he was acquainted with the clergyman whose friendship he was to retain throughout his life and in whose household, in 1683, he was to die: George Morley. In 1670 Walton dedicated his collected *Lives* to Morley, explaining 'if I had been fit for this Undertaking, it would not have been by acquir'd Learning or Study, but by the advantage of forty years friendship, and thereby the hearing of and discoursing with your Lordship, which hath inabled me to make the relation of these Lives passable in an eloquent and captious age.'[17]

Walton is notoriously unreliable about dates, and it may be objected that we have here only his own testimony for his and Morley's 'forty years friendship'. But Morley surely read this open letter, and Walton clearly would not have stated to him in it facts about their friendship which both men knew to be untrue. If we trust Walton's date, he first met George Morley in 1630. As this is the year in which Morley's friend Gilbert Sheldon was responsible for preferring Walton's nephew, Henry Valentine, to his new living, it seems a not improbable date.

After Donne, Morley was perhaps the strongest influence in Walton's life, and during their later years their fortunes were intertwined. To know something of Morley and his circle is to

know much of Walton's loyalties and affiliations and to understand where he stood in 1653, when *The Complete Angler* first
appeared. Probably, as Morley and others of his friends did,
Walton, in the 1630s, had misgivings about the King's conduct,
and that of his extremist Archbishop of Canterbury. But when
it came to direct conflict, Walton and his friends adhered to the
cause which they saw as that of rightful law as well as of their
church.[18] So Walton was a Royalist. In 1651 he risked imprisonment, possibly death, by secretly conveying part of the Garter
regalia, abandoned in the flight after the battle of Worcester,
from Stafford to a Royalist prisoner in the Tower of London.
This prisoner promptly escaped, and returned the Lesser George
to the exiled Charles II.[19] We learn from this that Walton was
known and trusted among Royalists in the area about his native
Stafford; and as it would seem to be madness to smuggle an
important piece of Royalist regalia into the Tower unless one
already knew that the recipient was due to escape to France,
Walton must have been privy to the Royalists' counsels.

While some Royalists went into exile, Walton stayed in
England. But he remained openly Anglican, despite the legal
penalties. When, on 7 September 1651, his son Isaac was born,
he was christened, illicitly, that same evening 'by Mr Thruscros
in my house at Clerkenwell'.[20] In 1652 Walton contributed a
commendatory verse to Edward Sparke's provocatively Anglican
Scintillula altaris. And Walton made his contribution to the
well-being of his fellow-Anglicans and fellow-Royalists through
his own writings. As we shall see, *The Complete Angler* unob-
trusively, but firmly, asserts their values. What other services
Walton performed for the Anglican and Royalist cause during
the dark days of the interregnum we do not know; Henry King
later remembered 'the constant experience of your Love even in
the worst of the late sad times'.[21]

In 1660, at the Restoration, George Morley was reinstalled in
his canonry at Christ Church, Oxford, and rewarded for his
long services. He became Dean of Christ Church, then Bishop
of Worcester. Morley seems immediately to have appointed
Walton as his business agent: in 1660 Walton was at Christ
Church, signing for Morley's stipend, and he then followed
Morley to Worcester where he acted as the Bishop's steward.[22]
There, in 1662, Walton's second wife died and was buried in
the Cathedral. She was Anne Ken and her younger half-brother

was Thomas Ken, who had been educated at Winchester College and was now at New College, reading for the Church; he was eventually to become Bishop of Bath and Wells, and is known today as the author of the hymn 'Awake, my soul, and with the sun'.

Later in 1662, Morley was translated to Winchester and Walton moved with him, presumably still as his steward, taking with him his two children, fourteen-year-old Anne and eleven-year-old Isaac. Six years later young Isaac Walton went to Morley's old college at Oxford, Christ Church. His tutor there was Richard Allestree, who had acted throughout the interregnum as a Royalist agent until his imprisonment in Lambeth Palace in 1660; Izaak Walton presented to him several of the different editions of his Lives, and these are still at Christ Church.[23] By 1678 young Isaac Walton, like his uncle, was in holy orders; he became a canon of Salisbury Cathedral. He was to remain at Salisbury all his life and presented his share of his father's books to Salisbury Cathedral Library.[24] At Winchester, meanwhile, Izaak Walton's daughter Anne married William Hawkins, a canon, like her uncle Thomas Ken, of Winchester Cathedral, and vicar of Droxford. Walton divided his last years between Droxford, the canonry at Winchester, and Bishop Morley's town house in Chelsea and palace at Farnham Castle. Walton died at Winchester in 1683 and Morley died in the following year; both old friends are buried in Winchester Cathedral.

It would be misleading to attempt to associate Izaak Walton's Complete Angler with any particular literary group; there is no reason to suppose he set out to produce a work of literature. He was, it is true, a poet, like many of his contemporaries, and here we can say that his taste was old-fashioned, as he himself knew: when he praises the poetry of Christopher Marlowe (who died in 1593, the year of his own birth) and Sir Walter Ralegh (died 1618) he concedes that 'they were old fashioned Poetry, but choicely good, I think much better than the strong lines that are now in fashion in this critical age' (Angler, p. 57). By 'strong lines' he means the heavily accented, terse, colloquial lines of such of his contemporaries as Donne. And later, when he does find a poem of Donne's to praise, a parody of Marlowe, he states that it was 'made to show the world that he could make soft and smooth Verses when he thought smoothness worth his labour' (p. 127). His taste in prose is also old-fashioned; when he is writing 'high' prose, as in the elaborately fashioned paragraphs on pp. 56, 82 and 144, his immediate model is the *Arcadia* of Sir Philip Sidney, first published in 1590. His 'low' style is partly based on sermon-prose, partly on the vernacular prose of play-texts and other popular literature, partly too (to judge from his surviving letters) on the rhythms of his own speech, much influenced by the Bible and by proverbs. He exemplifies, in short, ordinary contemporary taste, not the elitist taste of the Court and its hangers-on.

But Walton can be associated with a particular intellectual group: those believers in moderation often described as the Great Tew circle. These men frequently met at the house of Lucius Carey, Viscount Falkland, some twenty miles from Oxford. They included George Morley, Edward Hyde (later Lord Clarendon), Robert Sanderson (whose *Life* Walton was later to write), Gilbert Sheldon (mentioned in the Angler (p. 137), subsequently Archbishop of Canterbury, to whose patronage, in 1630, Henry Valentine owed his preferment), Henry Hammond, William Chillingworth, John Hales and others. Discussions at Great Tew evolved a tolerant belief that all things necessary to salvation are, by definition, non-controversial; religious dispute and acrimony is, therefore, an unnecessary irrelevance. Refusal to be drawn into unnecessary dispute, together with a pronounced sense of community, are characteristics of *The Complete Angler* (Gilbert Sheldon belonged to a real-life Brotherhood of the Angle, and Anglers are an obvious metaphor in Walton's book for Anglicans). It is interesting that the majority of the writers who contributed elegies to the first edition of the *Poems* of John Donne in 1633 were members of the Great Tew circle; Walton's and Valentine's names, as we have seen, were among them.

The Civil War scattered the Great Tew circle. Falkland was killed in battle in 1643; William Chillingworth died in prison in 1644; fellows of Oxford colleges were ejected from their fellowships, and most of the clergy among them were also ejected from their livings. Some lived in hiding, on the charity of friends, writing and publishing in defence of an increasingly forlorn cause; Morley went into exile, corresponding with the others under the name of 'Jasper Gower'. Hyde went into exile too. What survives of Sheldon's correspondence makes fascinating reading: it is principally he, Hammond, and Morley who keep the Church alive. We find an ejected canon of Christ Church, Robert Payne, writing to Sheldon:

> I heare from H[enry]. H[ammond]. that our brother Sand[erson] hath bene there, for a week, very cheerfull, which addes one scruple more to my envy or melancholy ... yet I am sometimes relieved by the kinde visitts of my acquaintance, and one of yours is now here, a brother of the Angle.[25]

Walton was a brother of the Angle, who knew Sheldon, Hammond, and Sanderson at this date (7 October 1650), but we do not know if Payne is referring to him. What does seem clear is that such men, and many others of their persuasion, were the earliest target audience of The Complete Angler.

There was a well-established tradition of writing about angling by the time that Izaak Walton began. The subject had been treated by classical authors, although Walton made use, in the main, of writers in English. It can be shown that he is directly indebted to at least seven writers on angling from 1577 onwards, most of them interdependent and most, more or less, in a tradition of angling manual that goes back to the Treatyse of Fysshynge wyth an Angle which appeared in the second edition of the Book of St Albans (1496). It is to the Treatyse tradition that Walton owes the order in which he deals with his fish, his list of twelve artificial flies (the jury that will condemn the trout), and the debate at the beginning between the Hunter, the Falconer and the Angler, together with their praise of the elements of Earth, Air and Water, on or in which their sports are pursued.[26] Nor was Walton solely indebted to printed sources to buttress his own store of practical experience: he also used notes of 'secrets' obtained from friends. What immediate sources lay before him as he wrote is not entirely possible to determine: the evidence suggests that he had formed his own manuscript compilation, or angling 'commonplace-book', and used this to supplement printed books and, perhaps, manuscripts.

Walton's most interesting printed angling source lay largely outside the Treatyse tradition: this was William Samuel's Arte of Angling (1577). Its special interest lies less in its angling content than in the fact that it is constructed as a lively dialogue between two characters, Piscator and Viator, and contains several scenes which have their counterparts in *The Complete Angler*.

It is possible that, even without Samuel's book, Walton might have thought for himself of casting *The Complete Angler* in dialogue. Dialogue was a traditional form for manuals of instruction, and this was particularly well known from the popular school textbook, Erasmus's *Colloquies*. One of Walton's earliest admirers draws a parallel between the *Colloquies* and the *Angler*.[27] Perhaps, too, Walton was influenced by the experience he had, shared with increasing numbers after the Puritans largely succeeded in closing the public theatres, of reading plays rather than witnessing them in performance.

I have mentioned the possibility that Walton used an angling commonplace-book; people were taught at school to compile these personal anthologies, and a number of them have come down to us. Perhaps Walton worked from more than one, for it seems possible that he may also be drawing on his own commonplace-book of verse. There are three dozen verse-quotations in the *Angler*, mostly of poems, although eight sets of verses are sung rather than spoken. Most of the songs are sung to well-known tunes, some of which have survived,[28] but the music for the Catch on pp. 145–6 was composed specially for Walton by Henry Lawes, Milton's friend, and Walton saw to it that the music was printed in the editions published during his own lifetime. With his songs and poems, the engraved illustrations of fish, and the little inset dramatic scenes, Walton has provided us with multimedia entertainment of a highly original and experimental kind.

Part of the charm of *The Complete Angler* lies in its casual, holiday mood. When Piscator overtakes Auceps and Venator to enjoy their company, they are strangers to him; his generous sociability remains a dominant theme in the book. Neither he nor Venator has any very clear plans which cannot be altered. Piscator gives up a day of fishing to the otter-hunt; Venator then gives up the rest of his holiday to learn angling. Piscator's original intention to spend the night at Trout-hall changes when he learns that Peter will be at Bleak-hall; he thereupon decides to lodge there too. Rain interrupts angling, and Peter diverts half the day to playing at shovel-board; nor does Peter's intention of getting up before breakfast come to anything: he is still asleep when Piscator and Venator set off for the day.

This seeming inconsequence masks a very careful structure. The narrative follows a classic pattern: 'There and Back Again', as Tolkien subtitled *The Hobbit*. A group of citizens has escaped from London for a few days, and will return back to the world of work and grime:

> *As one who long in populous city pent,*
> *Where houses thick and sewers annoy the air,*
> *Forth issuing on a summer's morn to breathe*
> *Among the pleasant villages and farms*
> *Adjoined, from each thing met conceives delight,*
> *The smell of grain, or tedded grass, or kine,*
> *Or dairy, each rural sight, each rural sound . . .*[29]

This is the essence of pastoral escape. The exactness, though, with which Walton traces Piscator's journey, belies fantasy: it may easily be followed on a map. Landmarks – Tottenham Hill, the gates of Theobalds, the Thatched House (an actual inn at Hoddesdon) – can be identified. Mr Sadler, owner of the otter-dogs, was a real person.

Walton has also worked out a timetable: the First Day (chapter I); the Second Day (first half of chapter II); the Third Day (middle of chapter II and chapters III, IV, and part of chapter V); the Fourth Day (most of chapter V until nearly the end of chapter XVI); the Fifth Day (the end of chapter XVI to the end of the last chapter, XXI).

In addition to its log-book structure, the *Angler* has another formal pattern: there are three richly written passages in which individuals, first Piscator and finally Venator, lose themselves in what seems almost an out-of-body experience (pp. 56, 82 and 144). Each passage is preceded by retreat to the shelter of a tree: a literary device which Walton's earliest readers would have recognised as a transition to pastoral mode, because of the famous opening lines of Virgil's First Eclogue: 'Tityrus, resting under the shelter of a broad beech tree, you contemplate the woodland muse with your slender pipe.'[30]

These serious passages, others which equate fishers with the scriptural Fishers of Men (the Apostles), and numerous short

passages which claim for anglers special moral virtues, are all
part of what Walton is teaching. It is the reader, of course, not
Venator, who is his real pupil. Tuition in angling is not to be
underestimated : fish are never thrown back in this book : they
are food, God's provision for the patient and skilled, and alms
for the poor. But the essential qualities of the angler are inner
ones : 'Study to be quiet'.[31]

The Complete Angler has been neglected by recent critics,
although its popularity with the general public has little dimin-
ished. The problem seems to be how to fit the book into one of
the clearly recognisable categories either of fashionable literary
theory, or of the historical interpretation of seventeenth-century
political thought.

In the eighteenth and nineteenth centuries, *The Complete
Angler* was a phenomenally successful book, and this very
popularity militated against it. Early in the twentieth century,
when 'metaphysical' poetry was rediscovered, the *Angler* seemed
insufficiently 'difficult'; and no one could apply the term
'metaphysical' to its prose, as they could to that of Browne or
Traherne. The qualities which were claimed for it – freshness,
nostalgia, rural simplicity – were associated with the outmoded
Georgian style. And no subsequently fashionable label easily
contains it : one could hardly, for example, claim it as a feminist
text.

If the *Angler* has ever been credited with any political thought,
this, too, has been seen to be on the 'wrong' side. An over-
simple reading of the seventeenth century as the Age of the
English Revolution, the reading prevalent in the last fifty years,
will dismiss the *Angler* because it cannot be seen as a cry for
radical political change. Walton is described instead, even by so
acute a critic as John Carey, as 'an unscrupulous High-Church
propagandist'.[32] He ought not, of course, to be rejected so
thoughtlessly. Rather, his affiliation with Great Tew; his admiration for the Puritan preacher Richard Sibbes; the open
meadows and common highways of his landscape (which may
be contrasted with the Puritan Marvell's aristocratically
enclosed country-house poem, 'Appleton House'); his reflec-
tions on the communistic society of beggars (below, p. 83); the
exchange of goods and services symbolised by the shared fish –

all these should give pause before too hasty a judgement is made.

Finally, *The Complete Angler*'s place in the history of narrative fiction remains to be assessed. The book is not a romance; it is not a novel; what is it? What reading skills did it expect of its first audience? What influence does this highly popular book exert on the earliest novels which are so shortly to follow it? Perhaps the critical neglect has been benign; there are many questions waiting to be answered by the reader who can bring to this unusual and delightful book a fresh, unprejudiced eye.

NOTES

1 Gilbert Sheldon (later Archbishop of Canterbury) thought at one time that they should correspond in code, but his correspondents were reluctant: 'it costs so much time to write or to interpret' (BL MS Harl. 6942, fol. 70).

2 Cf. David Novarr, *The Making of Walton's Lives* (New York, 1958), pp. 366–7 (although I do not accept Novarr's claim that the Sanderson *Life* was a substitute for a *Life* of Bishop Morley); John Butt, 'Izaak Walton as Biographer', in *Pope, Dickens and Others* (Edinburgh, 1969), pp. 56 ff., demonstrates the irony with which Walton modifies what would otherwise be a 'too Theophrastan consistency'.

3 We do not know exactly when Walton was born; a tradition arose that the date on which he was to make his will, 9 August, was his birthday, but it is unlikely that his baptism (at St Mary's, Stafford) was delayed so long. The best account of Walton's life is A. M. Coon's unpublished Cornell University thesis, 'The Life of Izaak Walton' (1938).

4 'Isack Walton, late apprentice to Thomas Grinsell was now admitted and sworne a free brother of this [the Ironmongers'] Companie.' Guildhall Library, MS 16, 967/3, f. 139ᵛ.

5 John Donne's father had been apprentice to Mrs Lewin, widow of the Company's Master, and was co-executor of her will, which established an important Ironmongers' Company charity; and in 1574 he was the Ironmongers' Warden.

6 This was a luxury trade. A lay subsidy roll for Chancery Lane in 1625 (PRO E179/147/537) provides Grinsell's and Walton's addresses; in 1640 Thomas Grinsell appointed Izaak Walton and Henry Valentine to be overseers of his will (PRO Prob 11/193).

7 Walton may have met Donne through Samuel Page as early as 1613, when the dedication to 'Iz. Wa.' of verse published by S.P., *The Love of Amos and Laura*, appeared. This credits 'Iz. Wa.' with poems of his own, since it claims that if he, rather than S.P., had written the book it would be better. S.P. has been identified as Samuel Page, a member, with Donne, Ben Jonson, Michael Drayton and others, of the Mermaid Tavern poets. So it seems Walton at twenty, was a poet (he wrote and published verse throughout his life) and moved on the fringes of literary London society. In addition to a possible connection through Samuel Page, Donne and Walton had both been involved in the affair of the will of Nicholas Hare: see Jonquil Bevan, *Izaak Walton's The Compleat Angler: The Art of Recreation* (Brighton and New York, 1988), p. 7.

8 'An Elegy on Dr. Donne', dated 7 April 1631, in *Lives*, ed. George Saintsbury (Oxford, 1927), pp. 87–9 (this elegy was undated at its first appearance in John Donne, *Poems* (1633), pp. 382–4); letter from Henry King in *Lives*, ed. cit., p. 15.

9 'He [Dr Johnson] observed, that "it was wonderful that Walton, who was in a very low situation in life, should have been familiarly received by so many great men, and that at a time when the ranks of society were kept more separate than they are now." He supposed that Walton had then given up his business as a linen-draper and sempster' (James Boswell, *Life of Johnson*, ed. R. W. Chapman (Oxford, 1904; reprinted 1960), p. 627).

10 Bevan, *Izaak Walton's The Compleat Angler*, pp. 7–10; more detail is in the same author's 'Henry Valentine, John Donne, and Izaak Walton', *Review of English Studies*, n.s., xi, no. 158 (1989), pp. 179–201.

11 The title-page reads: 'Noahs Dove: or a prayer for the peace of Jerusalem. Delivered in a sermon at Pauls Crosse, Decemb. 31. 1626. by H. Valentine, Master in Arts, and Lecturer at Saint Donstans in the West. London . . . for John Marriot, . . . 1627.' For Izaak Walton's association with John and Richard Marriot, see Jonquil Bevan, 'Izaak Walton and his Publisher', *The Library*, 5th ser., xxxii, no. 4 (December 1977), pp. 344–59. For some account of the sermon and its relations to Donne's sermons, see Bevan, 'Henry Valentine, John Donne, and Izaak Walton'.

12 John Donne, *Poems* (1633), pp. 379–84.

13 The first two of Valentine's *Foure Sea-Sermons* (1635) show some striking parallels with *The Complete Angler*.

14 *Lives*, ed. Saintsbury, p. 15. Walton might have come to know Sir Henry first through Henry Valentine, because of the connections they shared with the Fanshawe family; there was clearly an overlap of friendships. Sir Henry's tie with his native Kent meant that he also knew some of Walton's relations-in-law.

15 Sir Henry Wotton, *Life and Letters*, ed. Logan Pearsall Smith (Oxford, 1907; reprinted 1966), ii, pp. 376–7, 404–5. In one of these letters to Walton Wotton refers to Donne as 'our ever-memorable friend' (ii, p. 404).

16 *Lives*, ed. cit., p. 21.

17 *Lives* (1670), A3ᵛ; *Lives*, ed. cit., p. 3.

18 It is significant that the 'Eclogue' Walton wrote to celebrate the Restoration of Charles II in 1660 has the refrain 'We have our Laws, and have our King', placing the restoration of the Law before that of the King; and writing, in 1678, of the execution of the Archbishop of Canterbury, he emphasises that the Archbishop was 'by an unknown law condemned to die'.

19 Elias Ashmole, *The Institution ... of the Order of the Garter* (1672), p. 228.

20 Timothy Thruscros (or Thurscross) was an Anglican priest who flouted the law by officiating in private congregations. The entry about the birth and christening of young Isaac Walton is in his father's copy of the Book of Common Prayer (1639 edition) which is now in the British Library, pressmark C.61.k.5.

21 Izaak Walton, *Lives*, ed. Saintsbury, p. 14.

22 Walton's name appears in the Cathedral records authorising payment for materials needed for the rebuilding of the Cathedral fabric. For Walton at Oxford see W. G. Hiscock, *A Christ Church Miscellany* (1946), pp. 10–11; for Walton at Worcester see Canon Clement Price, *Times Literary Supplement* (14 August 1919), p. 437.

23 Robert S. Bosher, *The Making of the Restoration Settlement* (1951), pp. 30, 88, 89, 94, 98–9, 105, 284; *The Letter-Book of John Viscount Mordaunt 1658–1660*, ed. Mary Coate for the Camden Society (1945), p. 16; I am indebted to Mr Paul Morgan who first told me of the Allestree books at Christ Church.

24 Miss Suzanne Eward, Librarian and Keeper of the Muniments at Salisbury Cathedral, has discovered an entry in the Salisbury Communars' Accounts for October 1718 to October 1719 that shows that Canon Walton had presented his books to the Cathedral Library in the year before his death.

25 For the above two paragraphs about Great Tew, see Bevan, *Izaak Walton's The Compleat Angler*, pp. 13, 17–28.

26 See Izaak Walton, *The Compleat Angler*, ed. Jonquil Bevan (Oxford, 1983), Introduction, pp. 15–21.

27 See below, p. 217.

28 See Appendix.

29 Milton, *Paradise Lost*, IX. 445–51.

30   Tityre, tu patulae recubans sub tegmine fagi
            silvestrem tenui Musam meditaris avena.

For a discussion of these three passages and their significance in the
book as a whole, see Bevan, *Izaak Walton's The Compleat Angler*,
pp. 51–4, 128–30.

31 1 Thessalonians 4:11; the words with which the *Angler* concludes.

32 John Carey, 'Sixteenth- and Seventeenth-Century Prose', in *English
Poetry and Prose 1540–1674*, ed. Christopher Ricks, Sphere History of Literature (London, 1970; revised 1986; 1987).

NOTE ON THE TEXT

The version of *The Complete Angler* which first appeared in print, in May 1653, was quite brief. It opened with two characters, Piscator and Viator. The second edition (1655) was much expanded; Viator became Venator, and the character of Auceps was added. The book was further revised for its publication in 1661 (second issue, 1664). The fourth edition of 1668 was not seen through the press by the author; there is evidence that this publication was rushed out to make some money, after the Great Fire of 1666 had devastated the book industry in London. The fifth edition of 1676, again carefully revised and supervised by Walton, was the last edition to appear in his lifetime. It provides the text for this edition.

The spelling has been modernised and, on one occasion, the text has been translated: Lake Como has been substituted for the obscure Lake Lurian. But the original punctuation and use of italics and capitals has been carefully retained. These often provide a guide to phrasing and emphasis. In the middle of the seventeenth century punctuation was in transition from rhetorical punctuation to modern grammatical punctuation. Rhetorical punctuation marks where breaths and pauses should come (commas and colons, etc., are like quavers and semibreves etc. in music). The exception is the occurrence of marks of punctuation within closing parentheses or brackets; these have been moved outside, in accordance with modern convention.

The first part.

PART. I.

BEING A

DISCOURSE

OF

Rivers, Fiſh-ponds, Fiſh and Fiſhing.

Written by *IZAAK WALTON*.

The Fifth Edition much corrected and enlarged.

LONDON,
Printed for Richard Marriott. 1676.

FACSIMILE OF THE TITLE PAGE TO THE FIFTH
EDITION OF PART I, 1676

To the Right worshipful
JOHN OFFLEY
Of *Madeley* Manor in the County
of *Stafford*, Esq;
My most honoured Friend.

SIR,

I Have made so ill use of your former favours, as by them to be encouraged to entreat that they may be enlarged to the *Patronage* and *protection* of this Book; and I have put on a modest confidence, that I shall not be denied, because it is a Discourse of *Fish* and *Fishing*, which you know so well, and both love and practise so much.

You are assured (though there be ignorant men of another belief) that *Angling* is an *Art*; and you know that *Art* better than others; and that this is truth is demonstrated by the fruits of that pleasant labour which you enjoy when you purpose to give rest to your mind, and divest your self of your more serious business, and (which is often) dedicate a day or two to this *Recreation*.

At which time if *common Anglers* should attend you, and be eye witnesses of the success, not of your *fortune* but your *skill*, it would doubtless beget in them an emulation to be like you, and that emulation might beget an industrious diligence to be so; but I know it is not attainable by common capacities. And there be now many men of great *wisdom*, *learning* and *experience* which love and practise this *Art*, that know I speak the truth.

Sir, This pleasant curiosity of Fish and Fishing, (of which you are so great a Master) has been thought worthy the *Pens* and *Practices* of divers in other Nations, that have been reputed men of great *Learning* and *Wisdom*, and amongst those of this Nation, I remember Sir *Henry Wotton* (a dear lover of this Art) has told me that his intentions were to write a Discourse of the Art, and in praise of *Angling*, and doubtless he had done so, if

death had not prevented him; the remembrance of which hath
often made me sorry, for if he had lived to do it, then the
unlearned *Angler* had seen some better Treatise of this Art, a
Treatise that might have proved worthy his perusal, which
5 (though some have undertaken) I could never yet see in English.

But mine may be thought as *weak*, and as *unworthy* of
common view; and I do here freely confess, that I should rather
excuse my self, than censure others, my own Discourse being
liable to so many exceptions; against which you (Sir) might
10 make this one, *That it can contribute nothing to your Knowledge*. And lest a longer Epistle may diminish your pleasure, I
shall make this no longer than to add this following Truth, *That
I am really*,

SIR,

15   *Your most affectionate Friend,
                    and most humble Servant,*
                    Iz. Wa.

To all Readers of this Discourse, but especially to the honest *ANGLER*.

I Think fit to tell thee these following truths; That I did neither undertake, nor write, nor publish, and much less own, this Discourse to please my self: and having been too easily drawn to do all to please others, as I proposed not the gaining of credit by this undertaking, so I would not willingly lose any part of that to which I had a just title before I begun it, and do therefore desire and hope, if I deserve not commendations, yet, I may obtain pardon.

And though this Discourse may be liable to some Exceptions, yet I cannot doubt but that most Readers may receive so much pleasure or profit by it, as may make it worthy the time of their perusal, if they be not too grave or too busy men. And this is all the confidence that I can put on concerning the merit of what is here offered to their consideration and censure; and if the last prove too severe, as I have a liberty, so I am resolved to use it and neglect all sour Censures.

And I wish the Reader also to take notice, that in writing of it I have made my self a recreation of a recreation; and that it might prove so to him, and not read dull and tediously, I have in several places mixed (not any scurrility, but) some innocent, harmless mirth; of which, if thou be a severe, sour-complexioned man, then I here disallow thee to be a competent judge; for Divines say, There are offences given, and offences not given but taken.

And I am the willinger to justify the pleasant part of it, because though it is known I can be serious at seasonable times, yet the whole discourse is, or rather was, a picture of my own disposition, especially in such days and times as I have laid aside business, and gone a-fishing with honest Nat. and R. Roe; but they are gone, and with them most of my pleasant hours, even as a shadow, that passeth away, and returns not.

And next let me add this, that he that likes not the book should like the excellent picture of the Trout, and some of the other fish; which I may take a liberty to commend, because they concern not my self.

Next let me tell the Reader, that in that which is the more

useful part of this Discourse, *that is to say, the observations of
the* nature *and* breeding, *and* seasons, *and* catching *of Fish, I am
not so simple as not to know, that a captious Reader may find
exceptions against something said of some of these; and there-*
5 *fore I must entreat him to consider, that experience teaches us
to know, that several Countries alter the time, and I think
almost the manner, of fishes breeding, but doubtless of their
being in season; as may appear by three Rivers in* Monmouth-
shire, *namely* Severn, Wye, *and* Usk, *where* Camden (Brit. f.
10 633.) *observes, that in the River* Wye, *Salmon are in season
from* Sept. *to* April, *and we are certain, that in* Thames *and*
Trent, *and in most other Rivers they be in season the six hotter
months.*

Now for the Art of catching fish, *that is to say, how to make*
15 *a man that was none, to be an Angler by a book: he that
undertakes it shall undertake a harder task, than Mr* Hales *(a
most valiant and excellent Fencer) who in a printed book (called,*
A private School of Defence) *undertook to teach that art or
science, and was laughed at for his labour. Not but that many*
20 *useful things might be learned by that book, but he was laughed
at, because that art was not to be taught by words, but practice:
and so must Angling. And note also, that in this Discourse I do
not undertake to say all that is known, or may be said of it, but
I undertake to acquaint the Reader with many things that are*
25 *not usually known to every Angler; and I shall leave gleanings
and observations enough to be made out of the experience of all
that love and practise this recreation, to which I shall encourage
them. For Angling may be said to be so like the* Mathematics,
that it can never be fully learned; at least not so fully, but that
30 *there will still be more new experiments left for the trial of other
men that succeed us.*

*But I think all that love this game may here learn something
that may be worth their money, if they be not poor and needy
men; and in case they be, I then wish them to forbear to buy it;*
35 *for I write not to get money, but for pleasure, and this Discourse
boasts of no more; for I hate to promise much, and deceive the
Reader.*

*And however it proves to him, yet I am sure I have found a
high content in the search and conference of what is here offered*
40 *to the Reader's view and censure: I wish him as much in the
perusal of it, and so I might here take my leave, but will stay a*

little and tell him, that whereas it is said by many, that in fly-fishing for a Trout, *the Angler must observe his* 12 *several flies for the twelve months of the year; I say, he that follows that rule, shall be as sure to catch fish, and be as wise, as he that makes Hay by the fair days in an Almanac, and no surer; for those very flies that use to appear about and on the water in one month of the year, may the following year come almost a month sooner or later; as the same year proves colder or hotter; and yet in the following Discourse I have set down the twelve flies that are in reputation with many Anglers, and they may serve to give him some observations concerning them. And he may note that there are in* Wales *and other Countries, peculiar flies, proper to the particular place or Country; and doubtless, unless a man makes a fly to counterfeit that very fly in that place, he is like to lose his labour, or much of it: But for the generality, three or four flies neat and rightly made, and not too big, serve for a* Trout *in most Rivers all the Summer. And for* Winter *fly-fishing it is as useful as an Almanac out of date. And of these (because as no man is born an artist, so no man is born an Angler) I thought fit to give thee this notice.*

When I have told the Reader, that in this fifth Impression there are many enlargements, gathered both by my own observation, and the communication with friends, I shall stay him no longer than to wish him a rainy evening to read this following Discourse; *and that (if he be an honest Angler) the East wind may never blow when he goes a-Fishing.*

                                                    I.W.

THE
COMPLETE ANGLER,

OR, THE
Contemplative MAN'S
RECREATION.

PART I.

CHAP. I.

A Conference betwixt an Angler, *a* Falconer, *and a* Hunter, *each commending
his Recreation.*

> PISCATOR. A
> VENATOR. V
> AUCEPS. H

Pisc. You are well overtaken, Gentlemen, a good morning to
you both; I have stretched my legs up *Tottenham-hill* to
overtake you, hoping your business may occasion you towards
Ware whither I am going this fine, fresh *May* morning.

Venat. Sir, I for my part shall almost answer your hopes, for
my purpose is to drink my morning's draught at the *Thatched
House* in *Hoddesdon*, and I think not to rest till I come thither,
where I have appointed a friend or two to meet me: but for this
Gentleman that you see with me, I know not how far he intends
his journey; he came so lately into my company, that I have
scarce had time to ask him the question.

Auceps. Sir, I shall by your favour bear you company as far
as *Theobalds*, and there leave you, for then I turn up to a
friend's house who mews a Hawk for me, which I now long to
see.

Venat. Sir, we are all so happy as to have a fine, fresh, cool morning, and I hope we shall each be the happier in the others' company. And Gentlemen, that I may not lose yours, I shall either abate or amend my pace to enjoy it ; knowing that (as the Italians say) *Good company in a Journey makes the way to seem the shorter*.

Auceps. It may do so Sir, with the help of good discourse, which methinks we may promise from you that both look and speak so cheerfully : and for my part I promise you, as an invitation to it, that I will be as free and openhearted, as discretion will allow me to be with strangers.

Ven. And Sir, I promise the like.

Pisc. I am right glad to hear your answers, and in confidence you speak the truth, I shall put on a boldness to ask you Sir, Whether business or pleasure caused you to be so early up, and walk so fast, for this other Gentleman hath declared he is going to see a Hawk, that a friend mews for him.

Ven. Sir mine is a mixture of both, a little business and more pleasure, for I intend this day to do all my business, and then bestow another day or two in hunting the *Otter*, which a friend that I go to meet, tells me, is much pleasanter than any other chase whatsoever ; howsoever I mean to try it ; for tomorrow morning we shall meet a pack of Otter dogs of *noble Mr Sadler's* upon *Amwell hill*, who will be there so early, that they intend to prevent the Sun-rising.

Pisc. Sir, my fortune has answered my desires, and my purpose is to bestow a day or two in helping to destroy some of those villainous vermin, for I hate them perfectly, because they love fish so well, or rather, because they destroy so much ; indeed so much, that in my judgment all men that keep *Otter-dogs* ought to have pensions from the King to encourage them to destroy the very breed of those base *Otters*, they do so much mischief.

Ven. But what say you to the Foxes of the Nation, would not you as willingly have them destroyed ? for doubtless they do as much mischief as *Otters* do.

Pisc. Oh Sir, if they do, it is not so much to me and my fraternity as those base Vermin the *Otters* do.

Auc. Why Sir, I pray, of what Fraternity are you, that you are so angry with the poor *Otters* ?

Pisc. I am (Sir) a brother of the *Angle*, and therefore an enemy to the *Otter* : for you are to note, that we Anglers all love one

another, and therefore do I hate the *Otter* both for my own and
for their sakes who are of my brotherhood.

Ven. And I am a lover of Hounds; I have followed many a
pack of dogs many a mile, and heard many merry huntsmen
make sport and scoff at Anglers.   5

Auc. And I profess my self a Falconer, and have heard many
grave, serious men pity them, 'tis such a heavy, contemptible,
dull recreation.

Pisc. You know Gentlemen, 'tis an easy thing to scoff at any
Art or Recreation; a little *wit* mixed with ill nature, confidence   10
and *malice* will do it; but though they often venture boldly, yet
they are often caught even in their own trap, according to that
of *Lucian*, the father of the family of Scoffers:

> Lucian *well skilled in scoffing, this hath writ,*
> *Friend, that's your folly which you think your wit:*   15
> *This you vent oft, void both of wit and fear,*
> *Meaning another, when, your self you jeer.*

If to this you add what *Solomon* says of Scoffers, that they
are an abomination to mankind, let him that thinks fit scoff on,
and be a Scoffer still, but I account them enemies to me, and to   20
all that love virtue and Angling.

And for you that have heard many grave serious men pity
Anglers; let me tell you Sir, there be many men that are by
others taken to be serious and grave men, which we contemn
and pity. Men that are taken to be grave, because Nature hath   25
made them of a sour complexion, money-getting-men, men that
spend all their time first in getting, and next in anxious care to
keep it; men that are condemned to be rich, and then always
busy or discontented: for those poor-rich-men, we Anglers pity
them perfectly, and stand in no need to borrow their thoughts   30
to think our selves so happy. No, no, Sir, we enjoy a contentedness above the reach of such dispositions, and as the learned
and ingenuous* *Montaigne* says like himself freely, *When my*
Cat and I entertain each other with mutual apish tricks (as
playing with a garter) who knows but that I make my Cat more   35
sport than she makes me? shall I conclude her to be simple, that
has her time to begin or refuse to play as freely as I my self

* *in Apol. for Ra. Sebond.*

have? Nay, who knows but that it is a defect of my not
understanding her language (for doubtless Cats talk and reason
with one another) that we agree no better: and who knows but
that she pities me for being no wiser, than to play with her, and
5 *laughs and censures my folly for making sport for her when we*
two play together?

Thus freely speaks *Montaigne* concerning Cats, and I hope I
may take as great a liberty to blame any man, and laugh at him
too let him be never so grave, that hath not heard what Anglers
10 can say in the justification of their Art and Recreation; which I
may again tell you is so full of pleasure, that we need not
borrow their thoughts to think our selves happy.

Venat. Sir, you have almost amazed me, for though I am no
scoffer, yet I have (I pray let me speak it without offence) always
15 looked upon Anglers as more patient and more simple men,
than I fear I shall find you to be.

Pisc. Sir, I hope you will not judge my earnestness to be
impatience: and for my *simplicity*, if by that you mean a
harmlessness, or that simplicity which was usually found in the
20 primitive Christians, who were (as most Anglers are) quiet men,
and followers of peace; men that were so simply-wise, as not to
sell their Consciences to buy riches, and with them vexation and
a fear to die; If you mean such simple men as lived in those
times when there were fewer Lawyers; when men might have
25 had a Lordship safely conveyed to them in a piece of Parchment
no bigger than your hand, (though several sheets will not do it
safely in this wiser age) I say Sir, if you take us Anglers to be
such simple men as I have spoke of, then my self and those of
my profession will be glad to be so understood: But if by
30 simplicity you meant to express a general defect in those that
profess and practise the excellent Art of Angling, I hope in time
to disabuse you, and make the contrary appear so evidently,
that if you will but have patience to hear me, I shall remove all
the Anticipations that discourse, or time, or prejudice have
35 possessed you with against that laudable and ancient art; for I
know it is worthy the *knowledge* and *practice* of a wise man.

But (Gentlemen) though I be able to do this, I am not so
unmannerly as to engross all the discourse to my self; and
therefore, you two having declared your selves, the one to be a
40 lover of *Hawks*, the other of *Hounds*, I shall be most glad to
hear what you can say in the commendation of that recreation

which each of you love and practise; and having heard what you can say, I shall be glad to exercise your attention with what I can say concerning my own Recreation and Art of Angling, and by this means, we shall make the way to seem the shorter: and if you like my motion, I would have Mr *Falconer* to begin. 5

Auc. Your motion is consented to with all my heart, and to testify it, I will begin as you have desired me.

And first, for the Element that I use to trade in, which is the Air, an Element of more worth than weight, an Element that doubtless exceeds both the Earth and Water; for though I 10 sometimes deal in both, yet the Air is most properly mine, I and my Hawks use that most, and it yields us most recreation; it stops not the high soaring of my noble generous *Falcon*; in it she ascends to such an height, as the dull eyes of beasts and fish are not able to reach to; their bodies are too gross for such high 15 elevations: in the Air my troops of Hawks soar up on high, and when they are lost in the sight of men, then they attend upon and converse with the gods, therefore I think my *Eagle* is so justly styled *Jove's servant in Ordinary*: and that very *Falcon*, that I am now going to see deserves no meaner a title, for she 20 usually in her flight endangers her self, (like the son of *Dædalus*) to have her wings scorched by the Sun's heat, she flies so near it, but her mettle makes her careless of danger, for she then heeds nothing, but makes her nimble Pinions cut the fluid air, and so makes her high-way over the steepest mountains and deepest 25 rivers, and in her glorious career looks with contempt upon those high Steeples and magnificent Palaces which we adore and wonder at; from which height I can make her to descend by a word from my mouth (which she both knows and obeys) to accept of meat from my hand, to own me for her Master, to go 30 home with me, and be willing the next day to afford me the like recreation.

And more; this Element of Air which I profess to trade in, the worth of it is such, and it is of such necessity, that no creature whatsoever, not only those numerous creatures that feed on the 35 face of the Earth, but those various creatures that have their dwelling within the waters, every creature that hath life in its nostrils stands in need of my Element. The Waters cannot preserve the Fish without Air, witness the not breaking of Ice in an extreme Frost; the reason is, for that if the inspiring and 40 expiring Organ of any animal be stopped, it suddenly yields to

Nature, and dies. Thus necessary is Air to the existence both of
Fish and Beasts, nay, even to Man himself; that Air or breath of
life with which God at first inspired Mankind, he, if he wants it,
dies presently, becomes a sad object to all that loved and beheld
5 him, and in an instant turns to putrefaction.

Nay more, the very birds of the air (those that be not Hawks)
are both so many, and so useful and pleasant to mankind, that I
must not let them pass without some observations: They both
feed and refresh him; feed him with their choice bodies, and
10 refresh him with their Heavenly voices. I will not undertake to
mention the several kinds of Fowl by which this is done; and
his curious palate pleased by day, and which with their very
excrements afford him a soft lodging at night. These I will pass
by, but not those little nimble Musicians of the air, that warble
15 forth their curious Ditties, with which Nature hath furnished
them to the shame of Art.

As first the *Lark*, when she means to rejoice; to cheer her self
and those that hear her, she then quits the earth, and sings as
she ascends higher into the air, and having ended her Heavenly
20 employment, grows then mute and sad to think she must
descend to the dull earth, which she would not touch but for
necessity.

How do the *Black-bird* and *Throstle* with their melodious
voices bid welcome to the cheerful Spring, and in their fixed
25 Months warble forth such ditties as no art or instrument can
reach to?

Nay, the smaller birds also do the like in their particular
seasons, as namely the *Laverock*, the *Tit-lark*, the little *Linnet*,
and the honest *Robin*, that loves mankind both alive and dead.

30 But the *Nightingale* (another of my Airy Creatures) breathes
such sweet loud music out of her little instrumental throat, that
it might make mankind to think Miracles are not ceased. He
that at midnight (when the very labourer sleeps securely) should
hear (as I have very often) the clear airs, the sweet descants, the
35 natural rising and falling, the doubling and redoubling of her
voice, might well be lifted above earth, and say; Lord, what
Music hast thou provided for the Saints in Heaven, when thou
affordest bad men such music on Earth!

And this makes me the less to wonder at the many *Aviaries* in
40 *Italy*, or at the great charge of *Varro* his *Aviary*, the ruins of
which are yet to be seen in *Rome*, and is still so famous there,

that it is reckoned for one of those Notables which men of foreign Nations either record, or lay up in their memories when they return from travel.

This for the birds of pleasure, of which very much more might be said. My next shall be of Birds of Political use; I think 'tis not to be doubted that Swallows have been taught to carry Letters betwixt two Armies. But 'tis certain that when the Turks besieged *Malta* or *Rhodes* (I now remember not which 'twas) *Pigeons* are then related to carry and recarry Letters. And Mr G. *Sandys* in his Travels (fol. 269.) relates it to be done betwixt *Aleppo* and *Babylon*. But if that be disbelieved, 'tis not to be doubted that the *Dove* was sent out of the Ark by *Noah*, to give him notice of Land, when to him all appeared to be Sea; and the *Dove* proved a faithful and comfortable messenger. And for the Sacrifices of the Law, a pair of *Turtle Doves* or young *Pigeons* were as well accepted as costly *Bulls* and *Rams*. And when God would feed the Prophet *Elijah*, (1 *King*. 17.) after a kind of miraculous manner he did it by *Ravens*, who brought him meat morning and evening. Lastly, the Holy Ghost when he descended visibly upon our Saviour, did it by assuming the shape of a *Dove*. And, to conclude this part of my discourse, pray remember these wonders were done by birds of the Air, the Element in which they and I take so much pleasure.

There is also a little contemptible winged Creature (an Inhabitant of my Aerial Element) namely, the laborious *Bee*, of whose *Prudence*, *Policy* and regular Government of their own Commonwealth I might say much, as also of their several kinds, and how useful their honey and wax is both for meat and Medicines to mankind; but I will leave them to their sweet labour, without the least disturbance, believing them to be all very busy at this very time amongst the herbs and flowers that we see nature puts forth this *May* morning.

And now to return to my Hawks from whom I have made too long a digression; you are to note, that they are usually distinguished into two kinds; namely, the long-winged and the short-winged Hawk: of the first kind, there be chiefly in use amongst us in this Nation,

The *Gerfalcon* and *Jerkin*
The *Falcon* and *Tiercel-gentle*
The *Laner* and *Laneret*
The *Bockerel* and *Bockeret*

The *Saker* and *Sacaret*
The *Merlin* and *Jack Merlin*
The *Hobby* and *Jack*
There is the *Stelletto* of *Spain*
5   The Blood red *Rook* from *Turkey*
The *Waskite* from *Virginia*
And there is of short-winged Hawks,
The *Eagle* and *Iron*
The *Goshawk* and *Tiercel*
10 The *Sparrowhawk* and *Musket*
The French *Pye* of two sorts
These are reckoned Hawks of note and worth, but we have also
of an inferior rank,
The *Stanyel*, the *Ringtail*.
15 The *Raven*, the *Buzzard*.
The forked *Kite*, the bald *Buzzard*.
The *Hen-driver*, and others that I forbear to name.

Gentlemen, If I should enlarge my discourse to the observation
of the *Aeries*, the *Brancher*, the *Ramish Hawk*, the *Haggard*,
20 and the two sorts of *Lentners*, and then treat of their several
Aeries, their *Mewings*, rare order of casting, and the renovation
of their *Feathers*; their reclaiming, dieting, and then come to
their rare stories of practice; I say, if I should enter into these,
and many other observations that I could make, it would be
25 much, very much pleasure to me: but lest I should break the
rules of Civility with you, by taking up more than the proportion
of time allotted to me, I will here break off, and entreat you, Mr
Venator, to say what you are able in the commendation of
Hunting, to which you are so much affected, and if time will
30 serve, I will beg your favour for a further enlargement of some
of those several heads of which I have spoken. But no more at
present.

Venat. Well Sir, and I will now take my turn, and will first
begin with a commendation of the earth, as you have done most
35 excellently of the Air, the Earth being that Element upon which
I drive my pleasant, wholesome, hungry trade. The Earth is a
solid, settled Element; an Element most universally beneficial
both to man and beast: to men who have their several Recreations upon it, as Horse-races, Hunting, sweet smells, pleasant
40 walks. The Earth feeds man, and all those several beasts that
both feed him, and afford him recreation: What pleasure doth

man take in hunting the stately *Stag*, the generous *Buck*, the *Wild Boar*, the cunning *Otter*, the crafty *Fox*, and the fearful *Hare*? And if I may descend to a lower Game, what pleasure is it sometimes with Gins to betray the very vermin of the earth? as namely, the *Fitchew*, the *Fulimart*, the *Ferret*, the *Pole-cat*, the *Mould-warp*, and the like creatures that live upon the face, and within the bowels of the earth. How doth the earth bring forth *herbs*, *flowers* and *fruits*, both for *physic* and the *pleasure* of mankind? and above all, to me at least, the fruitful *Vine*, of which, when I drink moderately, it clears my brain, cheers my heart, and sharpens my wit. How could *Cleopatra* have feasted *Mark Antony* with eight Wild Boars roasted whole at one Supper, and other meat suitable, if the earth had not been a bountiful mother? But to pass by the mighty *Elephant*, which the earth breeds and nourisheth, and descend to the least of creatures, how doth the earth afford us a doctrinal example in the little *Pismire*, who in the Summer provides and lays up her Winter provision, and teaches man to do the like! The earth feeds and carries those horses that carry us. If I would be prodigal of my time and your patience, what might not I say in commendations of the earth? That puts limits to the proud and raging *Sea*, and by that means preserves both man and beast that it destroys them not, as we see it daily doth those that venture upon the Sea, and are there shipwrecked, drowned, and left to feed Haddocks; when we that are so wise as to keep our selves on *earth*, *walk*, and *talk*, and *live*, and *eat*, and *drink*, and go a-*hunting*: of which recreation I will say a little, and then leave Mr *Piscator* to the commendation of Angling.

Hunting is a game for Princes and noble persons; it hath been highly prized in all Ages; it was one of the qualifications that *Xenophon* bestowed on his *Cyrus*, that he was a Hunter of wild beasts. Hunting trains up the younger Nobility to the use of manly exercises in their riper age. What more manly exercise than *hunting the Wild Boar*, the *Stag*, the *Buck*, the *Fox* or the *Hare*? How doth it preserve health, and increase strength and activity?

And for the Dogs that we use, who can commend their excellency to that height which they deserve? How perfect is the Hound at *smelling*, who never leaves or forsakes his first scent, but follows it through so many changes and varieties of other scents, even over, and in the water, and into the earth? What

music doth a pack of Dogs then make to any man, whose heart
and ears are so happy as to be set to the tune of such
instruments? How will a right *Greyhound* fix his eye on the
best *Buck* in a *herd*, single him out, and follow him, and him
5 only through a whole herd of Rascal game, and still know and
then kill him? For my Hounds I know the language of them,
and they know the language and meaning of one another as
perfectly as we know the voices of those with whom we
discourse daily.

10   I might enlarge myself in the commendation of *Hunting*, and
of the noble Hound especially, as also of the docibleness of *dogs*
in general; and I might make many observations of Land-
creatures, that for composition, order, figure and constitution,
approach nearest to the completeness and understanding of
15 man; especially of those creatures which *Moses* in the Law
permitted to the Jews, (which have cloven Hoofs and chew the
Cud) which I shall forbear to name, because I will not be so
uncivil to Mr *Piscator*, as not to allow him a time for the
commendation of *Angling*, which he calls an Art; but doubtless
20 'tis an easy one: and Mr *Auceps*, I doubt we shall hear a watery
discourse of it, but I hope 'twill not be a long one.

    Auc. And I hope so too, though I fear it will.

    Pisc. Gentlemen; let not prejudice prepossess you. I confess
my discourse is like to prove suitable to my Recreation, *calm*
25 and *quiet*; we seldom make the Welkin to roar, we seldom take
the name of God into our mouths, but it is either to praise him
or pray to him; if others use it vainly in the midst of their
recreations, so vainly as if they meant to conjure, I must tell
you, it is neither our fault nor our custom; we, we protest
30 against it. But, pray remember I accuse no body; for as I would
not make a *watery* discourse, so I would not put too much
vinegar into it; nor would I raise the reputation of my own Art
by the diminution or ruin of another's. And so much for the
Prologue to what I mean to say.

35   And now for the *Water*, the Element that I trade in. The *water*
is the eldest daughter of the Creation, the Element upon which
the Spirit of God did first move, the Element which God
commanded to bring forth living creatures abundantly; and
without which those that inhabit the Land, even all creatures
40 that have breath in their nostrils must suddenly return to
putrefaction. *Moses* the great Law-giver and chief Philosopher,

skilled in all the learning of the Egyptians, who was called the friend of God, and knew the mind of the Almighty, names this Element the first in the Creation; this is the Element upon which the Spirit of God did first move, and is the chief Ingredient in the Creation: many Philosophers have made it to comprehend all the other Elements, and most allow it the chiefest in the mixtion of all living creatures.

There be that profess to believe that all bodies are made of *water*, and may be reduced back again to water only: they endeavour to demonstrate it thus:

Take a *Willow* (or any like speedy growing plant) newly rooted in a box or barrel full of earth, weigh them all together exactly when the tree begins to grow, and then weigh all together after the tree is increased from its first rooting to weigh an hundred pound weight more than when it was first rooted and weighed; and you shall find this augment of the tree to be without the diminution of one dram weight of the earth. Hence they infer this increase of wood to be from water of rain, or from dew, and not to be from any other Element. And they affirm, they can reduce this wood back again to water; and they affirm also the same may be done in any *animal* or *vegetable*. And this I take to be a fair testimony of the excellency of my Element of Water.

The *Water* is more productive than the *Earth*. Nay, the earth hath no fruitfulness without showers or dews; for all the *herbs*, and *flowers*, and *fruit* are produced and thrive by the water; and the very Minerals are fed by streams that run under ground, whose natural course carries them to the tops of many high mountains, as we see by several springs breaking forth on the tops of the highest hills; and this is also witnessed by the daily trial and testimony of several Miners.

Nay, the increase of those creatures that are bred and fed in the water, are not only more, and more miraculous, but more advantageous to man; not only for the lengthening of his life, but for the preventing of sickness; for 'tis observed by the most learned Physicians, that the casting off of Lent and other Fish-days, (which hath not only given the Lie to so many learned, pious, wise Founders of Colleges, for which we should be ashamed) hath doubtless been the chief cause of those many putrid, shaking, intermitting Agues, unto which this Nation of ours is now more subject than those wiser Countries that feed

on Herbs, Salads, and plenty of Fish; of which it is observed in
History, that the greatest part of the world now do. And it may
be fit to remember that *Moses* (*Lev.* 11. 9. *Deut.* 14. 9.)
appointed Fish to be the chief diet for the best Common-wealth
5 that ever yet was.

And it is observable not only that there are *fish*, (as namely
the *Whale*) three times as big as the mighty Elephant, that is so
fierce in battle; but that the mightiest Feasts have been of Fish.
The *Romans* in the height of their glory have made Fish the
10 mistress of all their entertainments; they have had Music to
usher in their *Sturgeon*, *Lampreys*, and *Mullet*, which they
would purchase at rates rather to be wondered at than believed.
He that shall view the Writings of *Macrobius* or *Varro*, may be
confirmed and informed of this, and of the incredible value of
15 their Fish and fish-ponds.

But, Gentlemen, I have almost lost my self, which I confess I
may easily do in this Philosophical Discourse; I met with most
of it very lately (and I hope happily) in a conference with a most
learned Physician, Dr *Wharton*, a dear Friend; that loves both
20 me and my Art of Angling. But however I will wade no deeper
in these mysterious Arguments, but pass to such Observations
as I can manage with more pleasure, and less fear of running
into error. But I must not yet forsake the Waters, by whose help
we have so many known advantages.

25 And first (to pass by the miraculous cures of our known
Baths) how advantageous is the *Sea* for our daily Traffic;
without which we could not now subsist! How does it not only
furnish us with food and Physic for the bodies, but with such
Observations for the mind as ingenious persons would not
30 want!

How ignorant had we been of the beauty of *Florence*, of the
Monuments, *Urns*, and *Rarities* that yet remain in, and near
unto old and new *Rome* (so many as it is said will take up a
year's time to view, and afford to each of them but a convenient
35 consideration); and therefore it is not to be wondered at, that
so learned and devout a Father as St *Jerome*, after his wish to
have seen Christ in the flesh, and to have heard St *Paul* preach,
makes his third wish, to *have seen Rome in her glory*; and that
glory is not yet all lost, for what pleasure is it to see the
40 Monuments of *Livy*, the choicest of the Historians: of *Tully*,
the best of Orators; and to see the Bay-trees that now grow out

of the very Tomb of *Virgil*! These to any that love Learning must be pleasing. But what pleasure is it to a devout Christian to see there the humble house in which St *Paul* was content to dwell; and to view the many rich *Statues* that are there made in honour of his memory! nay, to see the very place in which St 5 *Peter* and he lie buried together? These are in and near to *Rome*. And how much more doth it please the pious curiosity of a Christian to see that place on which the blessed Saviour of the world was pleased to humble himself, and to take our nature upon him, and to converse with men: to see Mount *Sion*, 10 *Jerusalem*, and the very Sepulchre of our Lord Jesus! How may it beget and heighten the zeal of a Christian to see the Devotions that are daily paid to him at that place! Gentlemen, lest I forget my self I will stop here, and remember you, that but for my Element of water the Inhabitants of this poor Island must remain 15 ignorant that such things ever were, or that any of them have yet a being.

Gentlemen, I might both enlarge and lose my self in such like Arguments; I might tell you that Almighty God is said to have spoken to a *Fish*, but never to a *Beast*; that he hath made a 20 *Whale* a Ship to carry and set his Prophet *Jonah* safe on the appointed shore. Of these I might speak, but I must in manners break off, for I see *Theobalds* house. I cry you mercy for being so long, and thank you for your patience.

Auceps. Sir, my pardon is easily granted you: I except against 25 nothing that you have said; nevertheless, I must part with you at this Park-wall, for which I am very sorry; but I assure you Mr *Piscator*, I now part with you full of good thoughts, not only of your self, but your Recreation. And so Gentlemen, God keep you both. 30

Pisc. Well, now Mr *Venator* you shall neither want time nor my attention to hear you enlarge your Discourse concerning Hunting.

Venat. Not I Sir, I remember you said that *Angling* it self was of great Antiquity, and a perfect Art, and an Art not easily 35 attained to; and you have so won upon me in your former discourse, that I am very desirous to hear what you can say further concerning those particulars.

Pisc. Sir, I did say so, and I doubt not but if you and I did converse together but a few hours, to leave you possessed with 40 the same high and happy thoughts that now possess me of it;

not only of the Antiquity of *Angling*, but that it deserves commendations, and that it is an Art, and an Art worthy the knowledge and practice of a wise man.

Venat. Pray Sir, speak of them what you think fit, for we have
5 yet five miles to the *Thatched-House*, during which walk, I dare promise you my patience, and diligent attention shall not be wanting. And if you shall make that to appear which you have undertaken, first, that it is an Art, and an Art worth the learning, I shall beg that I may attend you a day or two a-fishing, and
10 that I may become your Scholar, and be instructed in the Art it self which you so much magnify.

Pisc. O Sir, doubt not but that *Angling* is an Art; is it not an Art to deceive a *Trout* with an artificial Fly? a *Trout*! that is more sharp sighted than any Hawk you have named, and more
15 watchful and timorous than your high mettled *Merlin* is bold? and yet, I doubt not to catch a brace or two tomorrow, for a friend's breakfast: doubt not therefore, Sir, but that *Angling* is an Art, and an Art worth your learning: the Question is rather, whether you be capable of learning it? for *Angling* is somewhat
20 like *Poetry*, men are to be born so: I mean, with inclinations to it, though both may be heightened by discourse and practice, but he that hopes to be a good *Angler* must not only bring an inquiring, searching, observing wit; but he must bring a large measure of hope and patience, and a love and propensity to the
25 Art it self; but having once got and practised it, then doubt not but *Angling* will prove to be so pleasant, that it will prove to be like Virtue, *a reward to it self.*

Venat. Sir, I am now become so full of expectation that I long much to have you proceed; and in the order that you
30 propose.

Pisc. Then first, for the *antiquity* of *Angling*, of which I shall not say much, but only this; Some say it is as ancient as *Deucalion's* Flood: others that *Belus*, who was the first Inventor of Godly and virtuous Recreations, was the first Inventor of
35 *Angling*: and some others say (for former times have had their disquisitions about the Antiquity of it) that *Seth*, one of the Sons of *Adam*, taught it to his Sons, and that by them it was derived to posterity: others say, that he left it engraven on those pillars which he erected, and trusted to preserve the knowledge of the
40 *Mathematics*, *Music*, and the rest of that precious knowledge, and those useful Arts which by God's appointment or allowance

and his noble industry were thereby preserved from perishing in *Noah's* flood.

These, Sir, have been the opinions of several men, that have possibly endeavoured to make *Angling* more ancient than is needful, or may well be warranted; but for my part, I shall content my self in telling you that Angling is much more ancient than the Incarnation of our Saviour; for in the Prophet *Amos* mention is made of *fish-hooks*; and in the Book of *Job* (which was long before the days of *Amos*, for that book is said to be writ by *Moses*) mention is made also of fish-hooks, which must imply Anglers in those times.

But, my worthy friend, as I would rather prove my self a *Gentleman* by being *learned* and *humble, valiant*, and *inoffensive, virtuous*, and *communicable*, than by any fond ostentation of riches, or wanting those virtues my self, boast that these were in my Ancestors (and yet I grant that where a noble and ancient descent and such merits meet in any man, it is a double dignification of that person): So if this Antiquity of *Angling* (which for my part I have not forced) shall like an ancient family, be either an honour or an ornament to this virtuous Art which I profess to love and practise, I shall be the gladder that I made an accidental mention of the antiquity of it; of which I shall say no more but proceed to that just commendation which I think it deserves.

And for that I shall tell you, that in ancient times a debate hath risen, (and it remains yet unresolved) Whether the happiness of man in this world doth consist more in *Contemplation* or *Action*?

Concerning which some have endeavoured to maintain their opinion of the first, by saying, *That the nearer we Mortals come to God by way of imitation, the more happy we are*. And they say, *That God enjoys himself only by a contemplation of his own infiniteness, Eternity, Power and Goodness*, and the like. And upon this ground many Cloisteral men of great learning and devotion prefer *Contemplation* before *Action*. And many of the fathers seem to approve this opinion, as may appear in their Commentaries upon the words of our Saviour to *Martha, Luke* 10. 41, 42.

And on the contrary, there want not men of equal authority and credit, that prefer *action* to be the more excellent, as namely *experiments in Physic, and the application of it, both for the*

ease and prolongation of man's life; by which each man is
enabled to act and do good to others; either to serve his
Country, or do good to particular persons; and they say also,
That action is Doctrinal, and teaches both art and virtue, and is
5 *a maintainer of human society*; and for these, and other like
reasons to be preferred before *contemplation*.

Concerning which two opinions I shall forbear to add a third
by declaring my own, and rest my self contented in telling you
(my very worthy friend) that both these meet together, and do
10 most properly belong to the most *honest, ingenuous, quiet*, and
harmless art of *Angling*.

And first, I shall tell you what some have observed, (and I
have found it to be a real truth) that the very sitting by the
River's side is not only the quietest and fittest place for *contem-*
15 *plation*, but will invite an Angler to it: and this seems to be
maintained by the learned *Peter du Moulin*, who (in his Discourse of the fulfilling of Prophecies) observes, that when God
intended to reveal any future events or high notions to his
Prophets, he then carried them either to the *Deserts* or the
20 *Seashore*, that having so separated them from amidst the press
of *people* and *business*, and the cares of the world, he might
settle their minds in a quiet repose, and there make them fit for
Revelation.

And this seems also to be intimated by the Children of *Israel*,
25 (*Psal.* 137.) who having in a sad condition banished all mirth
and music from their pensive hearts, and having hung up their
then mute Harps upon the Willow-trees growing by the Rivers
of *Babylon*, sat down upon those banks bemoaning the ruins of
Sion, and contemplating their own sad condition.

30 And an ingenuous *Spaniard* says, *That Rivers and the Inhabitants of the watery Element were made for wise men to
contemplate, and fools to pass by without consideration.* And
though I will not rank my self in the number of the first, yet give
me leave to free my self from the last, by offering to you a short
35 contemplation, first of *Rivers*, and then of *Fish*; concerning
which I doubt not but to give you many observations that will
appear very considerable: I am sure they have appeared so to
me, and made many an hour pass away more pleasantly, as I
have sat quietly on a flowery Bank by a calm River, and
40 contemplated what I shall now relate to you.

And first concerning Rivers; there be so many wonders

reported and written of them, and of the several Creatures that be bred and live in them; and, those by Authors of so good credit, that we need not to deny them an historical Faith.

As namely of a River in *Epirus*, that puts out any lighted Torch, and kindles any Torch that was not lighted. Some Waters being drunk cause madness, some drunkenness, and some laughter to death. The River *Selarus* in a few hours turns a rod or wand to stone: and our *Camden* mentions the like in *England*, and the like in *Lochmere* in *Ireland*. There is also a River in *Arabia*, of which all the sheep that drink thereof have their wool turned into a Vermilion colour. And one of no less credit than *Aristotle*, tells us of a merry River, (the River *Elusina*) that dances at the noise of music, for with music it bubbles, dances and grows sandy, and so continues till the music ceases, but then it presently returns to its wonted calmness and clearness. And *Camden* tells us of a Well near to *Kirkby* in *Westmorland*, that ebbs and flows several times every day: and he tells us of a River in *Surrey* (it is called *Mole*) that after it has run several miles, being opposed by hills, finds or makes it self a way under ground, and breaks out again so far off, that the Inhabitants thereabout boast, (as the *Spaniards* do of their River *Anas*) that they feed divers flocks of sheep upon a Bridge. And lastly, for I would not tire your patience, one of no less authority than *Josephus* that learned Jew, tells us of a River in *Judea*, that runs swiftly all the six days of the week, and stands still and rests all their *Sabbath*.

But I will lay aside my Discourse of Rivers and tell you some things of the Monsters, or Fish, call them what you will, that they breed and feed in them. *Pliny* the Philosopher says, (in the third Chapter of his ninth Book) that in the *Indian Sea*, the fish called the *Balæna* or *Whirl-Pool* is so long and broad, as to take up more in length and breadth than two Acres of ground, and of other fish of two hundred cubits long; and that in the River *Ganges*, there be Eels of thirty foot long. He says there, that these Monsters appear in that Sea only, when the tempestuous winds oppose the Torrents of Waters falling from the Rocks into it, and so turning what lay at the bottom to be seen on the waters' top. And he says, that the people of *Cadara* (an Island near this place) make the Timber for their houses of those Fish-bones. He there tells us, that there are sometimes a thousand of these great Eels found wrapped, or interwoven together. He tells

us there, that it appears that Dolphins love music, and will
come, when called for, by some men or boys, that know and use
to feed them, and that they can swim as swift as an Arrow can
be shot out of a Bow, and much of this is spoken concerning the
5 *Dolphin*, and other Fish, as may be found also in learned Dr
Casaubon's Discourse of Credulity, and Incredulity, printed by
him about the year 1670.

I know, we Islanders are averse to the belief of these wonders :
but, there be so many strange Creatures to be now seen (many
10 collected by *John Tradescant*, and others added by my friend
Elias Ashmole Esq; who now keeps them carefully and meth-
odically at his house near to *Lambeth* near *London*) as may get
some belief of some of the other wonders I mentioned. I will tell
you some of the wonders that you may now see, and not till
15 then believe, unless you think fit.

You may there see the *Hog-fish*, the *Dog-fish*, the *Dolphin*,
the *Cony-Fish*, the *Parrot-fish*, the *Shark*, the *Poison-fish*, *sword-
fish*, and not only other incredible fish ! but you may there see
the *Salamander*, several sorts of *Barnacles*, of *Solan Geese*, the
20 *bird* of *Paradise*, such sorts of *Snakes*, and such *birds-nests*, and
of so various forms, and so wonderfully made, as may beget
wonder and amusement in any beholder : and so many hundreds
of other rarities in that Collection, as will make the other
wonders I spake of, the less incredible ; for, you may note, that
25 the waters are nature's store-house, in which she locks up her
wonders.

But, Sir, lest this Discourse may seem tedious, I shall now give
it a sweet conclusion out of that holy Poet Mr *George Herbert*
his Divine Contemplation on God's Providence.

30   *Lord, who hath praise enough, nay, who hath any ?*
         None can express thy works, but he that knows them ;
         And none can know thy works, they are so many,
         And so complete, but only he that owes them.

         We all acknowledge both thy power and love
35   *To be exact, transcendent and divine ;*
         Who dost so strangely and so sweetly move,
         Whilst all things have their end, yet none but thine.

         Wherefore, most sacred Spirit, I here present
         For me, and all my fellows, praise to thee ;

And just it is that I should pay the rent,
Because the benefit accrues to me.

And as concerning Fish in that Psalm, (*Psal.* 104.) wherein for height of Poetry and Wonders the Prophet *David* seems even to exceed himself, how doth he there express himself in choice Metaphors, even to the amazement of a contemplative Reader, concerning the *Sea*, the *Rivers*, and the *Fish* therein contained? And the great Naturalist *Pliny* says, *That Nature's great and wonderful power is more demonstrated in the Sea than on the Land.* And this may appear by the numerous and various Creatures inhabiting both in and about that Element; as to the Readers of *Gesner, Rondeletius, Pliny, Ausonius, Aristotle,* and others, may be demonstrated. But I will sweeten this Discourse also out of a Contemplation in Divine *Dubartas,*[a] who says,

God quickened in the sea and in the rivers,   15
So many Fishes of so many features,
That in the waters we may see all creatures,
Even all that on the earth are to be found,
As if the world were in deep waters drowned.
For seas (as well as skies) have Sun, Moon, Stars;   20
(As well as air) Swallows, Rooks, and Stares;
(As well as earth) Vines, Roses, Nettles, Melons,
Mushrooms, Pinks, Gillyflowers, and many millions
Of other plants, more rare, more strange than these,
As very fishes living in the seas: 25
As also Rams, Calves, Horses, Hares and Hogs,
Wolves, Urchins, Lions, Elephants and Dogs;
Yea men and Maids, and which I most admire,
The mitred Bishop, and the cowled Friar.
Of which, Examples but a few years since,   30
Were shown the Norway *and* Polonian *Prince.*

These seem to be wonders, but have had so many confirmations from men of learning and credit, that you need not doubt them; nor are the number, nor the various shapes of fishes, more strange or more fit for *contemplation*, than their different natures, inclinations and actions; concerning which I shall beg your patient ear a little longer.

The *Cuttle-fish* will cast a long gut out of her throat, which

[a] *Dubartas in the fifth day.*

(like as an Angler doth his line) she sendeth forth and pulleth in
again at her pleasure, according as she sees some little fish come
near to her; and the *Cuttle-fish* (being then hid in the gravel)
lets the smaller fish nibble and bite the end of it, at which time
5 she by little and little draws the smaller fish so near to her, that
she may leap upon her, and then catches and devours her:[a] and
for this reason some have called this fish the *Sea-Angler*.

And there is a fish called a *Hermit*, that at a certain age gets
into a dead fish's shell, and like a Hermit dwells there alone,
10 studying the wind and weather, and so turns her shell, that she
makes it defend her from the injuries that they would bring
upon her.

There is also a fish called by *Ælian* (in his 9. book of Living
Creatures, Chap. 16.) the *Adonis*, or Darling of the Sea; so
15 called, because it is a loving and innocent fish, a fish that hurts
nothing that hath life, and is at peace with all the numerous
Inhabitants of that vast watery Element: and truly I think most
Anglers are so disposed to most of mankind.

And there are also lustful and chaste fishes, of which I shall
20 give you examples.

And first, what *Dubartas* says of a fish called the *Sargus*;
which (because none can express it better than he does) I shall
give you in his own words, supposing it shall not have the less
credit for being Verse, for he hath gathered this, and other
25 observations out of Authors that have been great and industrious searchers into the secrets of Nature.

> The Adulterous *Sargus doth not only change*
> *Wives every day in the deep streams, but (strange)*
> *As if the honey of Sea-love delight*
> 30 *Could not suffice his ranging appetite,*
> *Goes courting she-Goats on the grassy shore,*
> *Horning their husbands that had horns before.*

And the same Author writes concerning the *Cantharus*, that
which you shall also hear in his own words.

> 35 *But contrary, the constant* Cantharus
> *Is ever constant to his faithful Spouse,*

[a] *Mont. Essays, and others affirm this.*

In nuptial duties spending his chaste life,
Never loves any but his own dear Wife.

Sir, but a little longer, and I have done.

Venat. Sir, take what liberty you think fit, for your discourse
seems to be Music, and charms me to an attention.

Pisc. Why then Sir, I will take a little liberty to tell, or rather
to remember you what is said of *Turtle-Doves*; First, That they
silently plight their troth and marry; and that then, the Survivor
scorns (as the *Thracian women* are said to do) to out-live his or
her mate, and this is taken for a truth, and if the survivor shall
ever couple with another, then not only the living, but the dead,
(be it either the He or the she) is denied the *name* and *honour* of
a true *Turtle-dove*.

And to parallel this Land-Rarity, and teach mankind moral
faithfulness, and to condemn those that talk of Religion, and yet
come short of the moral faith of fish and fowl (Men that violate
the Law affirmed by Saint *Paul* (*Rom.* 2. 14, 15.) to be writ in
their hearts, and which he says, shall at the last day condemn
and leave them without excuse), I pray hearken to what *Dubartas* sings: (for the hearing of such conjugal faithfulness, will be
Music to all chaste ears) and therefore I pray hearken to what
Dubartas sings of the *Mullet*.

> *But for chaste love the* Mullet *hath no peer;*
> *For, if the Fisher hath surprised her fere,*
> *As mad with woe, to shore she followeth,*
> *Prest to consort him both in life and death.*

On the contrary, What shall I say of the *House-Cock*, which
treads any Hen, and then (contrary to the *Swan*, the *Partridge*
and *Pigeon*) takes no care to hatch, to feed or to cherish his own
brood, but is senseless though they perish.

And 'tis considerable, that the Hen (which because she also
takes any *Cock*, expects it not) who is sure the Chickens be her
own, hath by a moral impression her care and affection to her
own Brood more than doubled, even to such a height, that our
Saviour in expressing his love to *Jerusalem* (*Mat.* 23. 37.) quotes
her for an example of tender affection; as his Father had done
Job for a pattern of patience.

And to parallel this *Cock*, there be divers fishes that cast their

Spawn on flags or stones, and then leave it uncovered, and exposed to become a prey, and be devoured by Vermin or other fishes : but other fishes (as namely the *Barbel*) take such care for the preservation of their seed, that (unlike to the *Cock* or the *Cuckoo*) they mutually labour (both the Spawner and the Milter) to cover their Spawn with sand, or watch it, or hide it in some secret place unfrequented by Vermin or by any Fish but themselves.

Sir, these Examples may, to you and others, seem strange ; but they are testified some by *Aristotle*, some by *Pliny*, some by *Gesner*, and by many others of credit, and are believed and known by divers, both of wisdom and experience, to be a Truth ; and indeed are (as I said at the beginning) fit for the contemplation of a most serious and a most pious man. And doubtless this made the Prophet *David* say, *They that occupy themselves in deep waters see the wonderful works of God* : indeed such wonders and pleasures too as the land affords not.

And that they be fit for the contemplation of the most prudent, and pious, and peaceable men, seems to be testified by the practice of so many devout and contemplative men, as the *Patriarchs* and *Prophets* of old ; and of the *Apostles* of our Saviour in our latter times ; of which twelve, we are sure he chose four that were simple Fishermen, whom he inspired and sent to publish his blessed Will to the *Gentiles, and inspired them also with a power to speak all languages, and by their powerful Eloquence to beget faith in the unbelieving Jews : and themselves to suffer for that Saviour whom their forefathers and they had Crucified, and, in their sufferings, to preach freedom from the incumbrances of the Law, and a new way to everlasting life :* this was the employment of these happy Fishermen. Concerning which choice, some have made these Observations :

First that he never reproved these for their Employment or Calling, as he did the *Scribes* and the *Money-changers*. And secondly, he found that the hearts of such men by nature were fitted for contemplation and quietness ; men of mild, and sweet, and peaceable spirits, as indeed most Anglers are : these men our blessed Saviour, (who is observed to love to plant grace in good natures) though indeed nothing be too hard for him, yet these men he chose to call from their irreprovable employment of Fishing, and gave them grace to be his Disciples, and to follow him and do wonders, I say four of twelve.

And it is observable, that it was our Saviour's will, that these our four Fishermen should have a priority of nomination in the Catalogue of his twelve Apostles, (*Mat.* 10.) as namely first St *Peter*, St *Andrew*, St *James* and St *John*, and then the rest in their order.   5

And it is yet more observable, that when our blessed Saviour went up into the Mount, when he left the rest of his Disciples, and chose only three to bear him company at his *Transfiguration*, that those three were all Fishermen. And it is to be believed, that all the other Apostles, after they betook themselves to   10 follow Christ, betook themselves to be Fishermen too; for it is certain that the greater number of them were found together Fishing by Jesus after his Resurrection, as it is recorded in the 21. Chapter of St *John's* Gospel.

And since I have your promise to hear me with patience, I will   15 take a liberty to look back upon an observation that hath been made by an ingenuous and learned man, who observes that God hath been pleased to allow those, whom he himself hath appointed to write his holy Will in holy writ, yet, to express his Will in such Metaphors as their former affections or practice   20 had inclined them to; and he brings *Solomon* for an example, who before his conversion was remarkably carnally-amorous; and after by God's appointment wrote that spiritual Dialogue or holy amorous Love-song (the *Canticles*) betwixt God and his Church; (in which he says his beloved had *Eyes like the fish-*   25 *pools of Heshbon*).

And if this hold in reason (as I see none to the contrary), then it may be probably concluded, that *Moses* (who, I told you before, writ the Book of *Job*) and the Prophet *Amos*, who was a Shepherd, were both Anglers; for you shall in all the Old   30 Testament find Fish-hooks, I think but twice mentioned, namely, by meek *Moses* the friend of God, and by the humble Prophet *Amos*.

Concerning which last, namely the Prophet *Amos*, I shall make but this Observation, That he that shall read the *humble*,   35 *lowly*, *plain style* of that *Prophet*, and compare it with the *high*, *glorious*, *eloquent style* of the Prophet *Isaiah* (though they be both equally true) may easily believe *Amos* to be, not only a Shepherd, but a good natured, plain *Fisherman*.

Which I do the rather believe by comparing the affectionate,   40 loving, lowly, humble Epistles of S. *Peter*, S. *James* and S. *John*, whom we know were all Fishers, with the glorious language and high Metaphors of S. *Paul*, who we may believe was not.

And for the lawfulness of Fishing it may very well be maintained by our Saviour's bidding St *Peter* cast his hook into the water and catch a Fish, for money to pay Tribute to *Caesar*. And let me tell you, that Angling is of high esteem, and of much use in other Nations. He that reads the Voyages of *Ferdinand Mendez Pinto*, shall find, that there he declares to have found a King and several Priests a-Fishing.

And he that reads *Plutarch*, shall find, that Angling was not contemptible in the days of *Mark Antony* and *Cleopatra*, and that they in the midst of their wonderful glory used Angling as a principal recreation. And let me tell you, that in the Scripture, Angling is always taken in the best sense, and that though hunting may be sometimes so taken, yet it is but seldom to be so understood. And let me add this more, he that views the ancient Ecclesiastical Canons, shall find *Hunting* to be forbidden to *Church-men*, as being a turbulent, toilsome, perplexing Recreation; and shall find *Angling* allowed to *Clergy-men*, as being a harmless Recreation, a recreation that invites them to *contemplation* and *quietness*.

I might here enlarge my self by telling you, what commendations our learned *Perkins* bestows on Angling: and how dear a lover, and great a practiser of it our learned Doctor *Whitaker* was, as indeed many others of great learning have been. But I will content my self with two memorable men, that lived near to our own time, whom I also take to have been ornaments to the Art of Angling.

The first is Doctor *Nowel* sometimes* Dean of the Cathedral Church of St. *Paul's* in *London*, where his Monument stands yet undefaced, a man that in the Reformation of Queen *Elizabeth* (not that of *Henry the VIII.*) was so noted for his meek spirit, deep learning, prudence and piety, that the then Parliament and Convocation both, chose, enjoined and trusted him to be the man to make a Catechism for public use, such a one as should stand as a rule for faith and manners to their posterity. And the good old man (though he was very learned, yet knowing that God leads us not to Heaven by many nor by hard questions) like an honest Angler, make that *good, plain, unperplexed*

* 1550.

Catechism which is printed with our good old Service Book. I say, this good man was as dear a lover, and constant practiser of Angling, as any Age can produce; and his custom was to spend besides his fixed hours of prayer, (those hours which by command of the Church were enjoined the Clergy, and voluntarily dedicated to devotion by many Primitive Christians): I say, besides those hours, this good man was observed to spend a tenth part of his time in Angling; and also (for I have conversed with those which have conversed with him) to bestow a tenth part of his Revenue, and usually all his fish, amongst the poor that inhabited near to those Rivers in which it was caught: saying often, *That charity gave life to Religion*: and at his return to his House would praise God he had spent that day free from worldly trouble; both harmlessly, and in a recreation that became a Church-man. And this good man was well content, if not desirous, that posterity should know he was an Angler, as may appear by his Picture, now to be seen, and carefully kept in *Brazen-nose College* (to which he was a liberal Benefactor) in which Picture he is drawn leaning on a Desk with his Bible before him, and, on one hand of him his *lines*, *hooks*, and other *tackling* lying in a round; and on his other hand are his Angle-rods of several sorts: and by them this is written, *That he died 13. Feb. 1601. being aged 95. years, 44. of which he had been Dean of St Paul's Church; and that his age had neither impaired his hearing, nor dimmed his eyes, nor weakened his memory, nor made any of the faculties of his mind weak or useless.* 'Tis said that *angling* and *temperance* were great causes of these blessings, and I wish the like to all that imitate him, and love the memory of so good a man.

My next and last example shall be that under-valuer of money, the late Provost of *Eton* College, Sir *Henry Wotton*, (a man with whom I have often fished and conversed) a man whose foreign employments in the service of this *Nation*, and whose *experience, learning, wit* and *cheerfulness* made his company to be esteemed one of the delights of mankind; this man, whose very approbation of Angling were sufficient to convince any modest censurer of it, this man was also a most dear lover, and a frequent practiser of the art of angling; of which he would say, *'Twas an employment for his idle time, which was then not idly spent*: for angling was after tedious Study, *a rest to his mind, a cheerer of his spirits, a diverter of sadness, a calmer of*

unquiet thoughts, a moderator of passions, a procurer of contentedness : and *that it begat habits of* peace *and* patience *in those that professed and practised it.* Indeed, my friend, you will find angling to be like the virtue of Humility, which has a
5 calmness of spirit, and a world of other blessings attending upon it.

   Sir, This was the saying of that learned man, and I do easily believe that *peace,* and *patience,* and a calm *content* did cohabit in the cheerful heart of Sir *Henry Wotton,* because I know that
10 when he was beyond seventy years of age, he made this description of a part of the present pleasure that possessed him, as he sat quietly in a Summer's evening on a bank a-Fishing; it is a description of the Spring, which, because it glided as soft and sweetly from his pen, as that river does at this time by
15 which it was then made, I shall repeat it unto you.

        This day dame Nature seemed in love :
        The lusty sap began to move ;
        Fresh juice did stir th' embracing Vines,
        And birds had drawn their Valentines,
20   *The jealous* Trout, *that low did lie,*
        Rose at a well dissembled fly ;
        There stood my friend with patient skill,
        Attending of his trembling quill.
        Already were the eaves possessed
25   *With the swift Pilgrim's daubed nest :*
        The Groves already did rejoice,
        In Philomel's *triumphing voice :*
        The showers were short, the weather mild,
        The morning fresh, the evening smiled.
30   Joan *takes her neat rubbed pail, and now*
        She trips to milk the sand-red Cow ;
        Where, for some sturdy foot-ball Swain,
        Joan *strokes a* sillabub *or twain.*
        The fields and gardens were beset
35   *With* Tulips, Crocus, Violet,
        And now, though late, the modest Rose
        Did more than half a blush disclose.
        Thus all looks gay, and full of cheer
        To welcome the new liveried year.

40 These were the thoughts that then possessed the undisturbed mind of Sir *Henry Wotton.* Will you hear the wish of another

Angler, and the commendation of his happy life which he also
sings in Verse? *viz. Jo. Davors* Esq.

> *Let me live harmlessly, and near the brink*
> *Of* Trent *or* Avon *have a dwelling place;*
> *Where I may see my quill or cork down sink*   5
> *With eager bite of* Perch, *or* Bleak, *or* Dace:
> *And on the world and my Creator think,*
> *Whilst some men strive ill gotten goods t'embrace;*
> > *And others spend their time in base excess*
> > *Of wine, or worse, in* war and wantonness.   10

> *Let them that list, these pastimes still pursue,*
> *And on such pleasing fancies feed their fill,*
> *So I the* fields *and* Meadows *green may view,*
> *And daily by* fresh Rivers *walk at will,*
> *Among the* Daisies *and the* Violets *blue,*   15
> Red Hyacinth, *and yellow* Daffodil,
> > *Purple* Narcissus *like the morning rays,*
> > *Pale* Ganderglass, *and azure* Culverkeys.

> *I count it higher pleasure to behold*
> *The stately compass of the lofty sky,*   20
> *And in the midst thereof (like burning gold)*
> *The flaming Chariot of the* World's *great eye,*
> *The watery clouds that in the air up rolled,*
> *With sundry kinds of painted colours fly;*
> > *And fair* Aurora *lifting up her head,*   25
> > *Still blushing, rise from old* Tithonus' *bed.*

> *The* hills *and* mountains *raised from the* plains,
> *The* plains *extended level with the* ground,
> *The* grounds *divided into sundry* veins,
> *The* veins *inclos'd with* rivers *running round;*   30
> *These* rivers *making way through nature's chains*
> *With headlong course into the sea profound;*
> > *The raging* sea, *beneath the valleys low,*
> > *Where* lakes *and* rills *and* rivulets *do flow.*

> *The lofty woods, the forests wide and long*   35
> *Adorned with leaves and branches fresh and green,*
> *In whose cool bowers the birds with many a song*
> *Do welcome with their Choir the* Summer's *Queen:*
> *The Meadows fair where* Flora's *gifts among*

> *Are intermixed, with verdant grass between.*
> *The silver-scaled fish that softly swim*
> *Within the sweet brook's crystal, watery stream.*

> *All these, and many more of his Creation*
> 5   *That made the Heavens, the* Angler *oft doth see,*
> *Taking therein no little delectation,*
> *To think how strange, how wonderful they be;*
> *Framing thereof an inward contemplation,*
> *To set his heart from other fancies free;*
> 10   `   `*And whilst he looks on these with joyful eye,*
> *His mind is rapt above the starry Sky.*

Sir I am glad my memory has not lost these last Verses, because they are somewhat more pleasant and more suitable to *May-Day*, than my harsh Discourse, and I am glad your patience hath held out so long, as to hear them and me: for both together have brought us within the sight of the *Thatched-house*: and I must be your Debtor (if you think it worth your attention) for the rest of my promised discourse, till some other opportunity, and a like time of leisure.

Venat. Sir, you have Angled me on with much pleasure to the *Thatched-house*: and I now find your words true *That good company makes the way seem short*, for trust me, Sir, I thought we had wanted three miles of this *House* till you showed it to me: but now we are at it, we'll turn into it, and refresh our selves with a cup of drink and a little rest.

Pisc. Most gladly (Sir) and we'll drink a civil cup to all the *Otter Hunters* that are to meet you tomorrow.

Ven. That we will Sir, and to all the lovers of Angling too, of which number, I am now willing to be one my self, for by the help of your good discourse and company, I have put on new thoughts both of the Art of Angling, and of all that profess it: and if you will but meet me tomorrow at the time and place appointed, and bestow one day with me and my friends in hunting the *Otter*, I will dedicate the next two days to wait upon you, and we two will for that time do nothing but angle, and talk of fish and fishing.

Pisc. 'Tis a match, Sir, I'll not fail you, God willing, to be at *Amwell-hill* tomorrow morning before Sun-rising.

CHAP. II.

Observations of the Otter and Chub.

Venat. My friend *Piscator*, you have kept time with my thoughts, for the Sun is just rising, and I my self just now come to this place, and the dogs have just now put down an *Otter*; look down at the bottom of the hill there in that Meadow, chequered with *water-Lilies*, and *Lady-smocks*, there you may see what work they make; look, look, you may see all busy, men and dogs, dogs and men, all busy.

Pisc. Sir, I am right glad to meet you, and glad to have so fair an entrance into this day's sport, and glad to see so many dogs, and more men all in pursuit of the *Otter*; let's compliment no longer, but join unto them; come honest *Venator*, let's be gone, let's make haste; I long to be doing: no reasonable hedge or ditch shall hold me.

Ven. Gentleman Huntsman, where found you this *Otter*?

Hunt. Marry (Sir) we found her a mile from this place a-fishing; she has this morning eaten the greatest part of this *Trout*; she has only left thus much of it as you see, and was fishing for more; when we came we found her just at it: but we were here very early, we were here an hour before Sun-rise, and have given her no rest since we came; sure she will hardly escape all these dogs and men. I am to have the skin if we kill her.

Ven. Why, Sir, what's the skin worth?

Hunt. 'Tis worth ten shillings to make gloves; the gloves of an *Otter* are the best fortification for your hands that can be thought on against wet weather.

Pisc. I pray, honest Huntsman, let me ask you a pleasant question, do you hunt a beast or a fish?

Hunt. Sir, It is not in my power to resolve you, I leave it to be resolved by the College of *Carthusians*, who have made vows never to eat flesh. But I have heard, the question hath been debated among many great Clerks, and they seem to differ about it; yet most agree that her tail is Fish: and if her body be

Fish too, then I may say, that a Fish will walk upon land, (for an *Otter* does so) sometimes five or six, or ten miles in a night to catch for her young ones, or to glut herself with Fish, and I can tell you that *Pigeons* will fly forty miles for a breakfast,
5 but *Sir*, I am sure the *Otter* devours much Fish, and kills and spoils much more than he eats: And I can tell you, that this Dog-fisher (for so the Latins call him) can smell a Fish in the water an hundred yards from him (*Gesner* says much farther) and that his stones are good against the Falling-sickness: and
10 that there is an herb *Benzoin*, which being hung in a linen cloth near a Fish-pond, or any haunt that he uses, makes him to avoid the place; which proves he can smell both by water and land; and I can tell you there is brave hunting this Water-dog in *Cornwall*, where there have been so many, that our learned
15 *Camden* says, there is a River called *Ottery*, which was so named, by reason of the abundance of *Otters* that bred and fed in it.

And thus much for my knowledge of the *Otter*, which you may now see above water at vent, and the dogs close with him;
20 I now see he will not last long, follow therefore my Masters, follow, for *Sweetlips* was like to have him at this last vent.

Ven. Oh me, all the Horse are got over the River, what shall we do now? shall we follow them over the water?

Hunt. No, *Sir*, no, be not so eager, stay a little and follow me,
25 for both they, and the dogs will be suddenly on this side again, I warrant you: and the *Otter* too, it may be: now have at him with *Killbuck*, for he vents again.

Ven. Marry! so he does, for look he vents in that corner. Now, now *Ringwood* has him: now he's gone again, and has
30 bit the poor dog. Now *Sweetlips* has him; hold him *Sweetlips*! now all the dogs have him, some above and some under water; but now, now he's tired, and past losing: come bring him to me, *Sweetlips*. Look, 'tis a Bitch-*Otter*, and she has lately whelped, let's go to the place where she was *put down*, and not
35 far from it you will find all her young ones, I dare warrant you, and kill them all too.

Hunt. Come, Gentlemen, come all, let's go to the place where we *put down* the *Otter*. Look you, hereabout it was that she kennelled; look you, here it was indeed, for here's her young
40 ones, no less than five; come let's kill them all.

Pisc. No, I pray Sir, save me one, and I'll try if I can make her tame, as I know an ingenuous Gentleman in *Leicestershire* (Mr *Nich. Seagrave*) has done; who hath not only made her tame, but to catch Fish, and do many other things of much pleasure.

Hunt. Take one with all my heart, but let us kill the rest. And now let's go to an honest Ale-house, where we may have a cup of good *Barley-wine*, and sing *Old Rose*, and all of us rejoice together.

Venat. Come my friend, *Piscator*, let me invite you along with us; I'll bear your charges this night, and you shall bear mine tomorrow; for my intention is to accompany you a day or two in Fishing.

Pisc. Sir, your request is granted, and I shall be right glad, both to exchange such a courtesy, and also to enjoy your company.

Venat. Well, now let's go to your sport of Angling.

Pisc. Let's be going with all my heart. God keep you all, Gentlemen, and send you meet this day with another Bitch-Otter, and kill her merrily, and all her young ones too.

Ven. Now, *Piscator*, where will you begin to fish?

Pisc. We are not yet come to a likely place, I must walk a mile further yet, before I begin.

Venat. Well then, I pray, as we walk tell me freely, how do you like your lodging and mine Host and the company? is not mine Host a witty man?

Pisc. Sir, I will tell you presently what I think of your Host; but first I will tell you, I am glad these *Otters* were killed, and I am sorry there are no more *Otter-killers*: for I know that the want of *Otter-killers*, and the not keeping the *Fence months* for the preservation of *fish*, will in time prove the destruction of all *Rivers*; and those very few that are left, that make conscience of the Laws of the Nation, and of keeping days of abstinence, will be forced to eat flesh, or suffer more inconveniences than are yet foreseen.

Venat. Why, Sir, what be those that you call the Fence months?

Pisc. Sir, they be principally three, namely, *March*, *April*, and *May*, for these be the usual months that *Salmon* come out of the Sea to spawn in most fresh Rivers, and their Fry would about a certain time return back to the salt water, if they were not

hindered by *weirs* and *unlawful gins*, which the greedy Fishermen set, and so destroy them by thousands, as they would
(being so taught by nature) change the *fresh* for *salt water*. He
that shall view the wise Statutes made in the 13 of *Edw. the I.*
and the like in *Rich. the III.* may see several provisions made
against the destruction of Fish: and though I profess no knowledge of the Law, yet I am sure the regulation of these defects
might be easily mended. But I remember that a wise friend of
mine did usually say, *That which is everybody's business, is
nobody's business*. If it were otherwise, there could not be so
many Nets and Fish that are under the Statute size, sold daily
amongst us, and of which the *conservators* of the waters should
be ashamed.

But above all, the taking Fish in Spawning time, may be
said to be against nature; it is like the taking the dam on
the nest when she hatches her young: a sin so against nature,
that Almighty God hath in the Levitical Law made a Law
against it.

But the poor Fish have enemies enough beside such unnatural
Fishermen, as namely, the *Otters* that I spake of, the *Cormorant*,
the *Bittern*, the *Osprey*, the *Sea-gull*, the *Heron*, the *Kingfisher*,
the *Gorrara*, the *Pewit*, the *Swan, Goose, Ducks*, and the
Craber, which some call the Water-rat: against all which any
honest man may make a just quarrel, but I will not, I will leave
them to be quarrelled with, and killed by others; for I am not
of a cruel nature, I love to kill nothing but Fish.

And now to your question concerning your Host, to speak
truly, he is not to me a good companion: for most of his conceits
were either Scripture jests, or lascivious jests; for which I count
no man witty, for the Devil will help a man that way inclined,
to the first; and his own corrupt nature (which he always carries
with him) to the latter. But a companion that feasts the company
with *wit* and *mirth*, and leaves out the sin (which is usually
mixed with them) he is the man; and indeed such a companion
should have his charges borne: and to such company I hope to
bring you this night; for at *Trout-hall*, not far from this place,
where I purpose to lodge tonight, there is usually an Angler that
proves good company: and let me tell you, good company and
good discourse are the very sinews of virtue: but for such
discourse as we heard last night, it infects others; the very boys
will learn to talk and swear as they heard mine Host, and

another of the company that shall be nameless; I am sorry the
other is a Gentleman, for less Religion will not save their Souls
than a beggar's; I think more will be required at the last great
day. Well, you know what Example is able to do, and I know
what the Poet says in the like case, which is worthy to be noted   5
by all parents and people of civility:

> ——Many a one
> Owes to his Country his Religion:
> And in another would as strongly grow,
> Had but his nurse or mother taught him so.   10

This is reason put into Verse, and worthy the consideration
of a wise man. But of this no more, for though I love civility, yet
I hate severe censures: I'll to my own art, and I doubt not but
at yonder tree I shall catch a *Chub*, and then we'll turn to an
honest cleanly Hostess, that I know right well; rest our selves   15
there, and dress it for our dinner.

Venat. Oh Sir, a *Chub* is the worst Fish that swims, I hoped
for a *Trout* to my dinner.

Pisc. Trust me, *Sir*, there is not a likely place for a *Trout*
hereabout, and we stayed so long to take our leave of your   20
Huntsmen this morning, that the Sun is got so high, and shines
so clear, that I will not undertake the catching of a *Trout* till
evening; and though a *Chub* be by you and many others
reckoned the worst of *fish*, yet you shall see I'll make it a good
Fish, by dressing it.   25

Ven. Why, how will you dress him?

Pisc. I'll tell you by and by, when I have caught him. Look
you here, Sir, do you see? (but you must stand very close) there
lie upon the top of the water in this very hole twenty *Chubs*: I'll
catch only one, and that shall be the biggest of them all: and   30
that I will do so, I'll hold you twenty to one, and you shall see it
done.

Venat. Aye marry Sir, now you talk like an Artist, and I'll say
you are one, when I shall see you perform what you say you can
do; but I yet doubt it.   35

Pisc. You shall not doubt it long, for you shall see me do it
presently: look, the biggest of these *Chubs* has had some bruise
upon his tail, by a Pike or some other accident, and that looks
like a white spot; that very *Chub* I mean to put into your hands

presently; sit you but down in the shade, and stay but a little while, and I'll warrant you I'll bring him to you.

Venat. I'll sit down and hope well, because you seem to be so confident.

5 *Pisc.* Look you Sir, there is a trial of my skill, there he is, that very *Chub* that I showed you with the white spot on his tail: and I'll be as certain to make him a good dish of meat, as I was to catch him. I'll now lead you to an honest Ale-house where we shall find a cleanly room, *Lavender* in the Windows, and twenty

10 *Ballads* stuck about the wall; there my Hostess (which I may tell you, is both cleanly and handsome and civil) hath dressed many a one for me, and shall now dress it after my fashion, and I warrant it good meat.

Ven. Come Sir, with all my heart, for I begin to be hungry,

15 and long to be at it, and indeed to rest my self too; for though I have walked but four miles this morning, yet I begin to be weary; yesterday's hunting hangs still upon me.

Pisc. Well Sir, and you shall quickly be at rest, for yonder is the house I mean to bring you to.

20 Come Hostess, how do you? Will you first give us a cup of your best drink, and then dress this *Chub*, as you dressed my last, when I and my friend were here about eight or ten days ago? but you must do me one courtesy, it must be done instantly.

25 *Host.* I will do it, Mr *Piscator*, and with all the speed I can.

Pisc. Now Sir, has not my Hostess made haste? and does not the fish look lovely?

Ven. Both, upon my word, Sir, and therefore let's say grace and fall to eating of it.

30 *Pisc.* Well Sir, how do you like it?

Ven. Trust me, 'tis as good meat as I ever tasted: now let me thank you for it, drink to you, and beg a courtesy of you; but it must not be denied me.

Pisc. What is it I pray Sir? you are so modest, that methinks I

35 may promise to grant it before it is asked.

Ven. Why Sir, it is, that from henceforth you would allow me to call you *Master*, and that really I may be your Scholar, for you are such a companion, and have so quickly caught, and so excellently cooked this fish, as makes me ambitious to be your

40 Scholar.

Pisc. Give me your hand; from this time forward I will be

your Master, and teach you as much of this Art as I am able; and will, as you desire me, tell you somewhat of the nature of most of the Fish that we are to angle for; and I am sure I both can and will tell you more than any common *Angler* yet knows.

CHAP. III.

How to fish for, and to dress the Chavender *or* Chub.

Pisc. The *Chub*, though he eat well thus dressed, yet as he is usually dressed, he does not: he is objected against, not only for being full of small forked bones, dispersed through all his body, but that he eats waterish, and that the flesh of him is not firm, but short and tasteless. The *French* esteem him so mean, as to call him *Un Vilain;* nevertheless he may be so dressed as to make him very good meat; as namely, if he be a large Chub, then dress him thus:

First scale him, and then wash him clean, and then take out his guts; and to that end make the hole as little and near to his gills as you may conveniently, and especially make clean his throat from the grass and weeds that are usually in it (for if that be not very clean, it will make him to taste very sour); having so done, put some sweet herbs into his belly, and then tie him with two or three splinters to a spit, and roast him, basted often with Vinegar, or rather verjuice and butter, with good store of salt mixed with it.

Being thus dressed, you will find him a much better dish of meat than you, or most folk, even than Anglers themselves do imagine; for this dries up the fluid watery humour with which all *Chubs* do abound.

But take this rule with you, That a *Chub* newly taken and newly dressed, is so much better than a *Chub* of a day's keeping after he is dead, that I can compare him to nothing so fitly as to Cherries newly gathered from a tree, and others that have been bruised and lain a day or two in water. But the *Chub* being thus used and dressed presently, and not washed after he is gutted (for note that lying long in water, and washing the blood out of any fish after they be gutted, abates much of their sweetness) you will find the Chub being dressed in the blood and quickly, to be such meat as will recompense your labour, and disabuse your opinion.

Or you may dress the *Chavender* or *Chub* thus:

When you have scaled him, and cut off his tail and fins, and washed him very clean, then chine or slit him through the middle, as a salt fish is usually cut, then give him three or four cuts or scotches on the back with your knife, and broil him on
5 *Charcoal, or Wood-coal that are free from smoke, and all the time he is a-broiling baste him with the best sweet Butter, and good store of salt mixed with it; and to this add a little Thyme cut exceeding small, or bruised into the butter.* The Cheven thus dressed hath the watery taste taken away, for which so many
10 except against him. Thus was the Cheven dressed that you now liked so well, and commended so much. But note again, that if this Chub that you eat of, had been kept till tomorrow, he had not been worth a rush. And remember that his throat be washed very clean, I say very clean, and his body not washed after he is
15 gutted, as indeed no fish should be.

Well Scholar, you see what pains I have taken to recover the lost credit of the poor despised *Chub*. And now I will give you some rules how to catch him; and I am glad to enter you into the Art of fishing by catching a *Chub*, for there is no Fish better
20 to enter a young Angler, he is so easily caught, but then it must be this particular way.

Go to the same hole in which I caught my *Chub*, where in most hot days you will find a dozen or twenty *Chevens* floating near the top of the water, get two or three Grasshoppers as you
25 go over the meadow, and get secretly behind the tree, and stand as free from motion as is possible, then put a Grasshopper on your hook, and let your hook hang a quarter of a yard short of the water, to which end you must rest your rod on some bough of the tree, but it is likely the Chubs will sink down towards the
30 bottom of the water at the first shadow of your Rod, for a Chub is the fearfullest of fishes, and will do so if but a bird flies over him, and makes the least shadow on the water; but they will presently rise up to the top again, and there lie soaring till some shadow affrights them again: I say when they lie upon the top
35 of the water, look out the best Chub, (which you setting your self in a fit place, may very easily see) and move your Rod as softly as a Snail moves, to that Chub you intend to catch; let your bait fall gently upon the water three or four inches before him, and he will infallibly take the bait, and you will be as sure
40 to catch him; for he is one of the leather-mouthed fishes, of which a hook does scarce ever lose its hold; and therefore give

him play enough before you offer to take him out of the water. Go your way presently, take my Rod, and do as I bid you, and I will sit down and mend my tackling till you return back.

Ven. Truly, my loving Master, you have offered me as fair as I could wish. I'll go and observe your directions.

Look you, Master, what I have done, that which joys my heart, caught just such another *Chub* as yours was.

Pisc. Marry, and I am glad of it: I am like to have a towardly Scholar of you. I now see, that with advice and practice you will make an *Angler* in a short time. Have but a love to it and I'll warrant you.

Venat. But Master, what if I could not have found a *Grasshopper*?

Pisc. Then I may tell you, that a *black Snail*, with his belly slit, to show his white: or a piece of soft *cheese*, will usually do as well: nay, sometimes a *worm*, or any kind of *fly*, as the *Ant-fly*, the *Flesh-fly*, or *Wall-fly*, or the *Dor* or *Beetle*, (which you may find under a Cow-turd) or a *Bob*, which you will find in the same place, and in time will be a Beetle; it is a short white worm, like to and bigger than a Gentle; or a *Cod-worm*, or a *Case-worm*: any of these will do very well to fish in such a manner. And after this manner you may catch a *Trout* in a hot evening: when as you walk by a Brook, and shall see or hear him leap at flies, then if you get a *Grasshopper*, put it on your hook, with your line about two yards long, standing behind a bush or tree where his hole is, and make your bait stir up and down on the top of the water: you may if you stand close, be sure of a bite, but not sure to catch him, for he is not a leather-mouthed Fish: and after this manner you may fish for him with almost any kind of live fly, but especially with a *Grasshopper*.

Venat. But before you go further, I pray good Master, what mean you by a leather-mouthed Fish?

Pisc. By a leather-mouthed Fish, I mean such as have their teeth in their throat, as the *Chub* or *Cheven*, and so the *Barbel*, the *Gudgeon* and *Carp*, and divers others have; and the hook being stuck into the leather or skin of the mouth of such fish does very seldom or never lose its hold: But on the contrary, a *Pike*, a *Perch*, or *Trout*, and so some other Fish, which have not their teeth in their throats, but in their mouths, (which you shall observe to be very full of bones, and the skin very thin, and little of it) : I say, of these fish the hook never takes so sure hold, but you often lose your fish, unless he have gorged it.

Ven. I thank you, good Master, for this observation; but now what shall be done with my *Chub* or *Cheven*, that I have caught?

Pisc. Marry Sir, it shall be given away to some poor body, for I'll warrant you I'll give you a *Trout* for your supper: and it is a good beginning of your Art to offer your first fruits to the poor, who will both thank God and you for it, which I see by your silence you seem to consent to. And for your willingness to part with it so charitably, I will also teach you more concerning Chub-Fishing: you are to note that in *March* and *April* he is usually taken with worms; in *May*, *June*, and *July* he will bite at any *fly*, or at *Cherries*, or at *Beetles* with their legs and wings cut off, or at any kind of *Snail*, or at the black *Bee* that breeds in clay walls; and he never refuses a Grasshopper on the top of a swift stream, nor at the bottom the young *humble-bee* that breeds in long grass, and is ordinarily found by the Mower of it. In *August*, and in the cooler months a yellow *paste*, made of the strongest cheese, and pounded in a Mortar with a little butter and saffron, (so much of it as being beaten small will turn it to a lemon colour). And some make a paste for the Winter months, at which time the Chub is accounted best, (for then it is observed, that the forked bones are lost, or turned into a kind of gristle, especially if he be baked) of Cheese and Turpentine; he will bite also at a Minnow or Pink, as a Trout will: of which I shall tell you more hereafter, and of divers other baits. But take this for a rule, that in hot weather he is to be fished for towards the mid-water, or near the top; and in colder weather nearer the bottom. And if you fish for him on the top, with a Beetle or any *fly*, then be sure to let your line be very long, and to keep out of sight. And having told you that his Spawn is excellent meat and that the head of a large Cheven, the Throat being well washed, is the best part of him, I will say no more of this Fish at the present, but wish you may catch the next you fish for.

But lest you may judge me too nice in urging to have the Chub dressed so presently after he is taken, I will commend to your consideration how curious former times have been in the like kind.

You shall read in *Seneca* his Natural Questions (*Lib.3.cap.*17.)

that the Ancients were so curious in the newness of their Fish, that that seemed not new enough that was not put alive into the guest's hand; and he says that to that end they did usually keep them living in glass-bottles in their dining-rooms; and they did glory much in their entertaining of friends to have that Fish 5 taken from under their table alive, that was instantly to be fed upon. And he says, they took great pleasure to see their Mullets change to several colours, when they were dying. But enough of this, for I doubt I have stayed too long from giving you some observations of the *Trout*, and how to fish for him, which shall 10 take up the next of my spare time.

CHAP. IV.

Observations of the nature and breeding of the Trout; and how to fish for him. And the Milk-maid's Song.

Pisc. The *Trout* is a fish highly valued both in this and foreign Nations: he may be justly said, (as the old Poets said of wine, and we English say of Venison) to be a generous Fish: a Fish that is so like the *Buck* that he also has his seasons, for it is observed, that he comes in and goes out of season with the *Stag* and *Buck*. *Gesner* says, his name is of a German off-spring, and says he is a fish that feeds clean and purely, in the swiftest streams, and on the hardest gravel; and that he may justly contend with all fresh-water-Fish, as the Mullet may with all Sea-Fish for precedency and daintiness of taste, and that being in right season, the most dainty palates have allowed precedency to him.

And before I go farther in my Discourse, let me tell you, that you are to observe, that as there be some *barren Does*, that are good in Summer, so there be some *barren Trouts* that are good in Winter; but there are not many that are so, for usually they be in their perfection in the month of *May*, and decline with the *Buck*. Now you are to take notice, that in several Countries, as in *Germany* and in other parts, compared to ours, Fish do differ much in their bigness, and shape, and other ways, and so do *Trouts*; it is well known that in the Lake *Leman* (the Lake of *Geneva*) there are *Trouts* taken of three Cubits long, as is affirmed by *Gesner*, a Writer of good credit; and *Mercator* says, the *Trouts* that are taken in the Lake of *Geneva*, are a great part of the Merchandise of that famous City. And you are further to know, that there be certain waters that breed *Trouts* remarkable, both for their number and smallness. I know a little Brook in *Kent* that breeds them to a number incredible, and you may take them twenty or forty in an hour, but none greater than about the size of a *Gudgeon*; There are also in divers Rivers, especially that relate to, or be near to the Sea (as *Winchester*, or the *Thames* about *Windsor*) a little *Trout* called a *Samlet* or *Skegger Trout* (in both which places I have caught twenty or forty at a standing) that will bite as fast and as freely as *Minnows*; these be by some taken to be young *Salmons*, but in those waters they never grow to be bigger than a *Herring*.

There is also in *Kent* near to *Canterbury*, a *Trout* (called there a *Fordwich Trout*) a *Trout* (that bears the name of the Town, where it is usually caught) that is accounted the rarest of Fish; many of them near the bigness of a *Salmon*, but known by their different colour, and in their best season they cut very white; and none of these have been known to be caught with an Angle, unless it were one that was caught by Sir *George Hastings* (an excellent Angler, and now with God) and he hath told me, he thought that *Trout* bit not for hunger but wantonness; and it is the rather to be believed, because both he then, and many others before him, have been curious to search into their bellies, what the food was by which they lived; and have found out nothing by which they might satisfy their curiosity.

Concerning which you are to take notice, that it is reported by good Authors, that *grass-hoppers* and some Fish have no mouths, but are nourished and take breath by the porousness of their Gills, Man knows not how; And this may be believed, if we consider that when the *Raven* has hatched her eggs, she takes no further care, but, leaves her young ones, to the care of the God of Nature, who is said in the *Psalms*, *To feed the young Ravens that call upon him*. And they be kept alive, and fed by a *dew*, or *worms* that breed in their nests, or some other ways that we Mortals know not, and this may be believed of the *Fordwich Trout*, which, as it is said of the *Stork*, that he knows his season, so he knows his times (I think almost his day) of coming into that River out of the Sea, where he lives (and it is like, feeds) nine months of the Year, and fasts three in the River of *Fordwich*. And you are to note, that those Townsmen are very punctual in observing the time of beginning to fish for them; and boast much that their River affords a Trout, that exceeds all others. And just so does *Sussex* boast of several Fish; as namely, a *Selsey Cockle*, a *Chichester Lobster*, an *Arundel Mullet*, and an *Amberley Trout*.

And now for some confirmation of the *Fordwich* Trout, you are to know that this Trout is thought to eat nothing in the fresh water; and it may be the better believed, because it is well known, that *Swallows* and *Bats* and *Wagtails*, which are called half-year birds, and not seen to fly in *England* for six months in the Year (but about *Michaelmas* leave us for a hotter Climate);

yet some of them that have been left behind their fellows, have been found (many thousands at a time) in hollow trees, or clay-Caves, where they have been observed, to live and sleep out the whole Winter without meat;[a] and so *Albertus* observes that there is one kind of *Frog* that hath her mouth naturally shut up about the end of *August*, and that she lives so all the Winter:[b] and though it be strange to some, yet it is known to too many among us to be doubted.

And so much for these *Fordwich trouts*, which never afford an *Angler* sport, but either live their time of being in the fresh water, by their meat formerly gotten in the Sea (not unlike the *Swallow* or *Frog*) or by the virtue of the fresh water only; or as the birds of *Paradise*, and the *Chameleon* are said to live by the *Sun* and the *Air*.

There is also in *Northumberland* a *Trout* called a *Bull-trout*, of a much greater length and bigness, than any in these Southern parts: and there are in many Rivers that relate to the Sea, *Salmon-trouts*, as much different from others, both in shape and in their spots, as we see sheep in some Countries differ one from another in their shape and bigness, and in the fineness of their wool: and certainly, as some pastures breed larger sheep, so do some Rivers, by reason of the ground over which they run, breed larger *Trouts*.

Now the next thing that I will commend to your consideration is, that the *Trout* is of a more sudden growth than other Fish: concerning which you are also to take notice, that he lives not so long as the *Perch* and divers other Fishes do, as Sir *Francis Bacon* hath observed in his History of Life and Death.

And next you are to take notice, that he is not like the *Crocodile*, which if he lives never so long, yet always thrives till his death: but 'tis not so with the Trout, for after he is come to his full growth, he declines in his body, and keeps his bigness or thrives only in his head till his death. And you are to know, that he will about (especially before) the time of his Spawning, get almost miraculously through *Weirs*, and *Flood-gates* against the stream; even, through such high and swift places as is almost incredible. Next, that the *Trout* usually Spawns about *October* or *November*, but in some Rivers a little sooner or later: which is the more observable, because most other fish Spawn in the

[a] *View Sir Fra. Bacon, exper.* 899.
[b] *See Topsel of Frogs.*

Spring or Summer, when the Sun hath warmed both the earth and water, and made it fit for generation. And you are to note, that he continues many months out of season: for it may be observed of the Trout, that he is like the Buck or the Ox, that will not be fat in many months, though he go in the very same pastures that horses do, which will be fat in one month; and so you may observe, that most other Fishes recover strength, and grow sooner fat, and in season than the Trout doth.

And next, you are to note, that till the Sun gets to such a height as to warm the earth and the water, the Trout is sick and lean, and lousy, and unwholesome: for you shall in winter find him to have a big head, and then to be lank, and thin, and lean; at which time many of them have sticking on them Sugs, or *Trout lice*, which is a kind of a worm, in shape like a clove or pin with a big head, and sticks close to him and sucks his moisture; those, I think, the *Trout* breeds himself, and never thrives till he free himself from them, which is when warm weather comes; and then, as he grows stronger, he gets from the dead, still water, into the sharp streams, and the gravel, and there rubs off these worms or lice; and then, as he grows stronger, so he gets him into swifter and swifter streams, and there lies at the watch for any fly or Minnow, that comes near to him; and he especially loves the *May-fly*, which is bred of the *Cod-worm*, or *Caddis*; and these make the Trout bold and lusty, and he is usually fatter and better meat at the end of that month, than at any time of the year.

Now you are to know, that it is observed, that usually the best *trouts* are either red or yellow, though some (as the *Fordwich trout*) be white and yet good; but that is not usual: and it is a note observable, that the female *Trout* hath usually a less head, and a deeper body than the male *Trout*; and is usually the better meat: and note that a hogback, and a little head to either *Trout*, *Salmon*, or any other fish, is a sign that that fish is in season.

But yet you are to note, that as you see some Willows or palm-trees bud and blossom sooner than others do, so some Trouts be in Rivers sooner in season; and as some Hollies or Oaks are longer before they cast their leaves, so are some Trouts in Rivers longer before they go out of season.

And you are to note, that there are several kinds of *Trouts*, but these several kinds are not considered but by very few men, for they go under the general name of *Trouts*: just as Pigeons do in most places; though it is certain there are tame, and wild Pigeons: and of the tame, there be *Helmets* and *Runts* and *Carriers*, and *Croppers*, and indeed too many to name. Nay, the *Royal Society* have found and published lately, that there be thirty and three kinds of Spiders: and yet, all (for aught I know) go under that one general name of *Spider*. And 'tis so with many kinds of Fish, and of *Trouts* especially, which differ in their bigness and shape, and spots, and colour. The great *Kentish Hens* may be an instance, compared to other Hens; And doubtless there is a kind of small Trout, which will never thrive to be big, that breeds very many more than others do, that be of a larger size; which you may rather believe, if you consider, that the little *Wren* and *Titmouse* will have twenty young ones at a time, when usually the noble *Hawk* or the Musical *Throstle* or *Black-bird* exceed not four or five.

And now you shall see me try my skill to catch a Trout, and at my next walking either this evening, or tomorrow morning I will give you direction, how you your self shall fish for him.

Venat. Trust me, Master, I see now it is a harder matter to catch a *Trout* than a *Chub*: for I have put on patience, and followed you these two hours, and not seen a Fish stir, neither at your Minnow nor your Worm.

Pisc. Well Scholar, you must endure worse luck sometime, or you will never make a good Angler. But what say you now? there is a *Trout* now, and a good one too, if I can but hold him, and two or three turns more will tire him: Now you see he lies still, and the sleight is to land him: Reach me that Landing Net: So (Sir) now he is mine own, what say you now? is not this worth all my labour and your patience?

Venat. On my word Master, this is a gallant *Trout;* what shall we do with him?

Pisc. Marry even eat him to supper: We'll go to my Hostess, from whence we came; she told me, as I was going out of door, that my brother *Peter*, a good Angler and a cheerful companion, had sent word he would lodge there tonight, and bring a friend with him. My Hostess has two beds, and, I know, you and I may have the best: we'll rejoice with my brother *Peter* and his friend, tell tales, or sing Ballads, or make a Catch, or find some harmless sport to content us, and pass away a little time without offence to God or man.

Venat. A match, good Master, let's go to that house, for the linen looks white, and smells of Lavender, and I long to lie in a pair of sheets that smell so : let's be going, good Master, for I am hungry again with fishing.

Pisc. Nay, stay a little good Scholar, I caught my last *Trout*
5 with a Worm, now I will put on a Minnow and try a quarter of an hour about yonder trees for another, and so walk towards our Lodging. Look you Scholar, thereabout we shall have a bite presently, or not at all : Have with you (Sir !) o' my word I have hold of him. Oh it is a great loggerheaded *Chub;* Come, hang
10 him upon that Willow twig, and let's be going. But turn out of the way a little, good Scholar, towards yonder high *honeysuckle* hedge : there we'll sit and sing whilst this shower falls so gently upon the teeming earth, and gives yet a sweeter smell to the lovely flowers that adorn these verdant Meadows.

15   Look ; under that broad *Beech-tree*, I sat down, when I was last this way a-fishing, and the birds in the adjoining Grove seemed to have a friendly contention with an Echo, with an Echo whose dead voice seemed to live in a hollow cave, near to the brow of that Primrose-hill ; there I sat viewing the silver-
20 streams glide silently towards their centre, the tempestuous Sea ; yet, sometimes opposed by rugged roots, and pebble stones, which broke their waves, and turned them into foam : and sometimes I beguiled time by viewing the harmless Lambs, some leaping securely in the cool shade, whilst others sported them-
25 selves in the cheerful Sun : and saw others craving comfort from the swollen Udders of their bleating Dams. As I thus sat, these and other sights had so fully possessed my soul with content, that I thought as the Poet has happily expressed it :

> *I was for that time lifted above earth ;*
30 > *And possessed joys not promised in my birth.*

As I left this place, and entered into the next field, a second pleasure entertained me : 'twas a handsome milk-maid that had not yet attained so much age and wisdom as to load her mind with any fears of many things that will never be (as too many
35 men too often do) but she cast away all care, and sung like a *Nightingale* : her voice was good, and the Ditty fitted for it ; 'twas that smooth song, which was made by *Kit. Marlowe*, now at least fifty years ago : and the Milk-maid's Mother sung an answer to it, which was made by Sir *Walter Raleigh* in his younger days.

They were old fashioned Poetry, but choicely good, I think much better than the strong lines that are now in fashion in this critical age. Look yonder! on my word, yonder they both be a-milking again: I will give her the *Chub*, and persuade them to sing those two songs to us.   5

God speed you good woman, I have been a-Fishing, and am going to *Bleak Hall* to my bed, and having caught more Fish than will sup my self and my friend, I will bestow this upon you and your Daughter, for I use to sell none.

Milkw. Marry, God requite you Sir, and we'll eat it cheer-   10
fully: and if you come this way a-Fishing two months hence, a grace of God I'll give you a Sillabub of new Verjuice in a new made Hay-cock, for it, and my *Maudlin* shall sing you one of her best *Ballads*; for she and I both love all *Anglers*, they be such honest, civil, quiet men; in the mean time will you drink a   15
draught of *Red-Cow's milk*, you shall have it freely.

Pisc. No, I thank you, but I pray do us a courtesy that shall stand you and your daughter in nothing, and yet we will think our selves still something in your debt; it is but to sing us a Song, that was sung by your daughter, when I last passed over   20
this Meadow, about eight or nine days since.

Milk. What Song was it, I pray? was it, *Come Shepherds deck your heads*: or, *As at noon* Dulcina *rested*: or, Phillida *flouts me*: or, *Chevy Chase*: or, *Johnny Armstrong*: or, *Troy Town*?   25

Pisc. No, it is none of those: it is a Song that your daughter sung the first part, and you sung the answer to it.

Milk. O, I know it now, I learned the first part in my golden age, when I was about the age of my poor daughter; and the latter part, which indeed fits me best now, but two or three   30
years ago, when the cares of the World began to take hold of me: but you shall, God willing, hear them both, and sung as well as we can, for we both love Anglers. Come *Maudlin*, sing the first part to the Gentlemen with a merry heart, and I'll sing the second, when you have done.   35

The Milk-maid's Song.

Come live with me, and be my Love,
And we will all the pleasures prove
That valleys, groves, or hills, or fields,
Or woods, and steepy mountains yields.   40

Where we will sit upon the Rocks,
And see the Shepherds feed our flocks,
By shallow Rivers, *to whose falls,*
Melodious birds sing Madrigals.

5   *And I will make thee beds of* Roses,
And then a thousand fragrant Posies,
A cap of flowers, and a Kirtle
Embroidered all with leaves of myrtle.

A Gown made of the finest Wool
10   *Which from our pretty Lambs we pull;*
Slippers lined choicely for the cold,
With buckles of the purest gold.

A Belt of Straw and Ivy-buds,
With Coral Clasps, and Amber studs:
15   *And if these pleasures may thee move,*
Come live with me, and be my Love.

Thy silver dishes for thy meat,
As precious as the Gods do eat,
Shall on an Ivory Table be
20   *Prepared each day for thee and me.*

The Shepherds Swains shall dance and sing
For thy delight each May-morning:
If these delights thy mind may move,
Then live with me, and be my Love.

25   *Venat.* Trust me, Master, it is a choice Song, and sweetly sung
by honest *Maudlin.* I now see it was not without cause, that our
good Queen *Elizabeth* did so often wish her self a Milk-maid all
the month of *May,* because they are not troubled with fears and
cares, but sing sweetly all the day, and sleep securely all the
30   night: and without doubt, honest, innocent, pretty *Maudlin*
does so. I'll bestow Sir *Thomas Overbury's* Milk-maid's wish
upon her, *That she may die in the Spring, and being dead may*
have good store of flowers stuck round about her winding sheet.

The Milk-maid's Mother's Answer.

35   *If all the world and Love were young,*
And truth in every Shepherd's tongue,

These pretty pleasures might me move
To live with thee, and be thy Love.

But time drives flocks from field to fold,
When Rivers rage, and rocks grow cold,
Then Philomel becometh dumb, 5
And age complains of care to come.

The flowers do fade, and wanton fields
To wayward Winter reckoning yields.
A honey tongue, a heart of gall,
Is fancy's spring, but sorrow's fall; 10

Thy gowns, thy shoes, thy beds of roses,
Thy cap, thy kirtle, and thy posies,
Soon break, soon wither, soon forgotten,
In folly ripe, in reason rotten.

Thy Belt of Straw and Ivy-buds, 15
Thy Coral clasps, and Amber-studs,
All these in me no means can move
To come to thee, and be thy Love.

What should we talk of dainties then,
Of better meat than's fit for men? 20
These are but vain: that's only good
Which God hath blessed, and sent for food.

But could Youth last, and love still breed,
Had joys no date, nor age no need;
Then those delights my mind might move 25
To live with thee, and be thy Love.

Mother. Well I have done my Song; but stay honest *Anglers,*
for I will make *Maudlin* to sing you one short Song more.
Maudlin; sing that Song that you sung last night, when young
Corydon the Shepherd played so purely on his *oaten pipe* to you 30
and your Cousin Betty.
Maud. I will Mother.

> *I married a Wife of late,*
> *The more's my unhappy fate:*
> *I married her for love,* 35

As my fancy did me move,
And not for a worldly estate :

But Oh ! the green-sickness
Soon changed her likeness ;
5   *And, all her beauty did fail.*
But 'tis not so,
With those that go,
Through frost and snow,
As all men know,
10   *And, carry the Milking-pail.*

Pisc. Well sung, good Woman, I thank you, I'll give you
another dish of fish one of these days, and then beg another
Song of you. Come Scholar, let *Maudlin* alone : do not you offer
to spoil her voice. Look, yonder comes mine *Hostess*, to call us
15 to supper. How now ? is my Brother *Peter* come ?

Hostess. Yes, and a friend with him, they are both glad to
hear that you are in these parts, and long to see you, and long
to be at supper, for they be very hungry.

CHAP. V.

More Directions how to Fish for, and how to make for the Trout *an* Artificial Minnow, *and* Flies, *with some* Merriment.

Pisc. Well met Brother *Peter*, I heard you and a friend would lodge here tonight, and that hath made me to bring my Friend to lodge here too. My Friend is one that would fain be *a Brother of the Angle*, he hath been an *Angler* but this day, and I have taught him how to catch a *Chub* by dapping with a *Grass-hopper*, and the *Chub* he caught was a lusty one of nineteen inches long. But pray Brother *Peter* who is your companion?

Peter. Brother *Piscator*, my friend is an honest *Country-man*, and his name is *Corydon*, and he is a downright witty companion that met me here purposely to be pleasant and eat a *Trout.* And I have not yet wetted my Line since we met together: but I hope to fit him with a *Trout* for his breakfast, for I'll be early up.

Pisc. Nay Brother, you shall not stay so long: for look you here is a Trout

will fill six reasonable bellies. Come Hostess, dress it presently, and get us what other meat the house will afford, and give us some of your best *Barley-wine*, the good liquor that our honest Fore-fathers did use to drink of; the drink which preserved their health, and made them live so long, and to do so many good deeds.

Peter. O' my word this *Trout* is perfect in season. Come, I thank you, and here is a hearty draught to you, and to all the brothers of the Angle wheresoever they be, and to my young brother's good fortune tomorrow: I will furnish him with a Rod, if you will furnish him with the rest of the Tackling; we will set him up and make him a Fisher.

And I will tell him one thing for his encouragement, that his fortune hath made him happy to be Scholar to such a Master; a Master that knows as much both of the nature and breeding of fish as any man: and can also tell him as well how to catch and cook them, from the *Minnow* to the *Salmon*, as any that I ever met withal.

Pisc. Trust me, brother *Peter*, I find my Scholar to be so suitable to my own humour, which is to be free and pleasant, and civilly merry, that my resolution is to hide nothing that I know from him. Believe me, Scholar, this is my resolution; and so here's to you a hearty draught, and to all that love us, and the honest Art of Angling.

Ven. Trust me, good Master, you shall not sow your seed in barren ground, for I hope to return you an increase answerable to your hopes; but however you shall find me obedient, and thankful, and serviceable to my best ability.

Pisc. 'Tis enough, honest Scholar, come let's to supper. Come my friend *Corydon*, this *Trout* looks lovely, it was twenty two inches when it was taken, and the belly of it looked some part of it as yellow as a Marigold, and part of it as white as a lily, and yet methinks it looks better in this good sauce.

Cor. Indeed honest friend, it looks well, and tastes well, I thank you for it, and so doth my friend *Peter*, or else he is to blame.

Pet. Yes, and so I do, we all thank you, and when we have supped, I will get my friend *Corydon* to sing you a Song for requital.

Cor. I will sing a song, if any body will sing another; else, to be plain with you, *I will sing none*: I am none of those that sing for meat, but for company: I say, *'Tis merry in Hall, when men sing all*.

Pisc. I'll promise you I'll sing a song that was lately made at my request, by Mr *William Basse*, one that hath made the choice songs of the *Hunter in his career*, and of *Tom of Bedlam*, and many others of note; and this that I will sing is in praise of Angling.

Cor. And then mine shall be the praise of a Country man's life: What will the rest sing of?

Pet. I will promise you, I will sing another song in praise of Angling tomorrow night, for we will not part till then, but Fish tomorrow, and sup together, and the next day every man leave Fishing, and fall to his business. 5

Venat. 'Tis a match, and I will provide you a Song or a Catch against then too, which shall give some addition of mirth to the company; for we will be civil and as merry as beggars.

Pisc. 'Tis a match my Masters, let's even say Grace, and turn to the fire, drink the other cup to wet our whistles, and so sing away all sad thoughts. 10

Come on my Masters, who begins? I think it is best to draw cuts, and avoid contention.

Pet. It is a match. Look, the shortest cut falls to *Corydon.* 15

Cor. Well then, I will begin, for I hate contention.

CORYDON'S Song.

Oh the sweet contentment
The country-man doth find!
  high trolollie lollie loe 20
  high trolollie lee,
That quiet contemplation
Possesseth all my mind:
    Then care away,
    And wend along with me. 25

For Courts are full of flattery,
As hath too oft been tried;
  high trolollie lollie loe, &c.
The City full of wantonness,
And both are full of pride: 30
    Then care away, &c.

But oh the honest Country-man
Speaks truly from his heart,
  high trolollie lollie loe, &c.
His pride is in his tillage, 35
His horses, and his cart:
    Then care away, &c.

Our clothing is good sheep skins,
Gray russet for our wives,

high trolollie lollie loe, &c.
'Tis warmth and not gay clothing
That doth prolong our lives:
     Then care away, &c.

5   *The plough man, though he labour hard,*
Yet on the Holy-Day,
     high trolollie lollie loe, &c.
No Emperor so merrily
Does pass his time away:
10   Then care away, &c.

To recompense our tillage,
The Heavens *afford us showers;*
     high trolollie lollie loe, &c.
And for our sweet refreshments
15 *The earth affords us bowers:*
     Then care away, &c.

The Cuckoo *and the* Nightingale
Full merrily do sing,
     high trolollie lollie loe, &c.
20 *And with their pleasant* roundelays
Bid welcome to the Spring.
     Then care away, &c.

This is not half the happiness
The country-man enjoys;
25   *high trolollie lollie loe, &c.*
Though others think they have as much,
Yet he that says so lies:
     Then come away, turn
     Country man with me.
30   *John Chalkhill.*

Pisc. Well sung *Corydon*, this song was sung with mettle; and it was choicely fitted to the occasion; I shall love you for it as long as I know you; I would you were a brother of the Angle, for a companion that is cheerful, and free from swearing
35 and scurrilous discourse, is worth gold. I love such mirth as does not make friends ashamed to look upon one another next morning; nor men (that cannot well bear it) to repent the money they spend when they be warmed with drink: and take this

for a rule, You may pick out such times and such companies, that you may make your selves merrier for a little than a great deal of money; for *'Tis the company and not the charge that makes the feast*: and such a companion you prove, I thank you for it.   5

But I will not compliment you out of the debt that I owe you, and therefore I will begin my Song and wish it may be so well liked.

The Angler's Song.

As inward love breeds outward talk,   10
The Hound *some praise, and some the* Hawk:
Some better pleased with private sport,
Use Tennis, *some a* Mistress *court:*
  But these delights I neither wish,
  Nor envy, while I freely fish.   15

Who Hunts, doth oft in danger ride;
Who Hawks, lures oft both far and wide;
Who uses Games, *shall often prove*
A loser; but who falls in love,
  Is fettered in fond Cupid's *snare:*   20
  My Angle breeds me no such care.

Of Recreation there is none
So free as Fishing is alone;
All other pastimes do no less
Than mind and body both possess: 25
  My hand alone my work can do,
  So I can fish and study too.

I care not, I, to fish in seas,
Fresh rivers best my mind do please,
Whose sweet calm course I contemplate,   30
And seek in life to imitate:
  In civil bounds I fain would keep,
  And for my past offences weep.

And when the timorous Trout *I wait*
To take, and he devours my bait,   35
How poor a thing sometimes I find
Will captivate a greedy mind:

> *And when none bite, I praise the wise,*
> *Whom vain allurements ne'er surprise.*
>
> *But yet though while I fish I fast,*
> *I make good fortune my repast,*
> 5 *And thereunto my friend invite,*
> *In whom I more than that delight :*
> *Who is more welcome to my dish,*
> *Than to my angle was my fish.*
>
> *As well content no prize to take,*
> 10 *As use of taken prize to make :*
> *For so our Lord was pleased when*
> *He fishers made fishers of men :*
> *Where (which is in no other game)*
> *A man may fish and praise his name.*
>
> 15 *The first men that our Saviour dear*
> *Did choose to wait upon him here,*
> *Blest Fishers were ; and fish the last*
> *Food was, that he on earth did taste :*
> *I therefore strive to follow those,*
> 20 *Whom he to follow him hath chose.*

Cor. Well sung brother, you have paid your debt in good coin, we Anglers are all beholding to the good man that made this Song. Come Hostess, give us more Ale, and let's drink to him.

25 And now let's every one go to bed that we may rise early; but first let's pay our reckoning, for I will have nothing to hinder me in the morning, for my purpose is to prevent the Sun-rising.

Pet. A match ; Come *Corydon*, you are to be my Bed-fellow : I know, brother, you and your Scholar will lie together; but 30 where shall we meet tomorrow night ? for my friend *Corydon* and I will go up the water towards *Ware*.

Pisc. And my Scholar and I will go down towards *Waltham*.

Cor. Then let's meet here, for here are fresh sheets that smell of *Lavender*, and I am sure we cannot expect better meat, or 35 better usage in any place.

Pet. 'Tis a match. Good night to every body.

Pisc. And so say I.

Venat. And so say I.

*

Pisc. Good morrow good Hostess, I see my brother *Peter* is still in bed: Come give my Scholar and me a Morning-drink, and a bit of meat to breakfast, and be sure to get a good dish of meat or two against supper, for we shall come home as hungry as Hawks. Come Scholar, let's be going.

Venat. Well now, good Master, as we walk towards the River give me direction, according to your promise, how I shall fish for a *Trout.*

Pisc. My honest Scholar, I will take this very convenient opportunity to do it.

The Trout is usually caught with a worm or a *Minnow,* (which some call a *Pink*) or with a *fly, viz.* either a *natural* or an *artificial fly*: concerning which three I will give you some observations and directions.

And first for Worms: Of these there be very many sorts; some breed only in the earth, as the *Earth-worm*; others of or amongst Plants, as the *Dug-worm*; and others breed either out of excrements, or in the bodies of living creatures, as in the horns of Sheep or Deer; or some of dead flesh, as the *Maggot* or *gentle,* and others.

Now these be most of them particularly good for particular Fishes: but for the *Trout* the *dew-worm*, (which some also call the *Lob-worm*) and the *Brandling* are the chief; and especially the first for a great Trout, and the latter for a less. There be also of *Lob-worms* some called *squirrel-tails*, (a worm that has a red head, a streak down the back and a broad tail) which are noted to be the best, because they are the toughest and most lively, and live longest in the water: for you are to know, that a dead worm is but a dead bait and like to catch nothing, compared to a lively, quick, stirring worm: and for a *Brandling*, he is usually found in an old dunghill, or some very rotten place near to it: but most usually in Cow-dung, or hog's-dung, rather than horse-dung, which is somewhat too hot and dry for that worm. But the best of them are to be found in the bark of the Tanners which they cast up in heaps after they have used it about their leather.

There are also divers other kinds of worms which for colour and shape alter even as the ground out of which they are got: as the *marsh-worm*, the *tag-tail*, the *flag-worm*, the *dock-worm*, the *oak-worm*, the *gilt-tail*, the *twachel* or *lob-worm* (which of all others is the most excellent bait for a *Salmon*) and too many to name, even as many sorts, as some think there be of several herbs or shrubs, or of several kinds of birds in the air; of which I shall say no more, but tell you, that what worms soever you fish with, are the better for being well scoured, that is long kept, before they be used; and in case you have not been so provident, then the way to cleanse and scour them quickly, is to put them all night in water, if they be *Lob-worms*, and then put them into your bag with fennel: but you must not put your Brandlings above an hour in water, and then put them into fennel for sudden use: but if you have time and purpose to keep them long, then they be best preserved in an earthen pot with good store of *Moss*, which is to be fresh every three or four days in Summer, and every week or eight days in Winter: or at least the moss taken from them, and clean washed, and wrung betwixt your hands till it be dry, and then put it to them again. And when your worms, especially the Brandling, begins to be sick, and lose of his bigness, then you may recover him, by putting a little milk or cream (about a spoonful in a day) into them by drops on the moss; and if there be added to the cream an egg beaten and boiled in it, then it will both fatten and preserve them long. And note, that when the *knot*, which is near to the middle of the *brandling* begins to swell, then he is sick, and, if he be not well looked to, is near dying. And for moss, you are to note, that there be divers kinds of it, which I could name to you, but will only tell you, that that which is likest a *Buck's-Horn* is the best, except it be soft white moss, which grows on some heaths, and is hard to be found. And note, that in a very dry time, when you are put to an extremity for worms, Walnut-tree leaves squeezed into water, or salt in water, to make it bitter or salt, and then that water poured on the ground, where you shall see worms are used to rise in the night, will make them to appear above ground presently. And you may take notice some say that *Camphor* put into your bag with your moss and worms, gives them a strong and so tempting a smell, that the fish fare the worse and you the better for it.

And now, I shall show you how to bait your hook with a worm, so as shall prevent you from much trouble, and the loss of many a hook too; when you Fish for a *Trout* with a running-line: that is to say, when you fish for him by hand at the ground, I will direct you in this as plainly as I can, that you may not mistake.

Suppose it be a big Lob-worm, put your hook into him somewhat above the middle, and out again a little below the middle: having so done, draw your worm above the arming of your hook, but note that at the entering of your hook it must not be at the head-end of the worm, but at the tail-end of him, (that the point of your hook may come out toward the head-end) and having drawn him above the arming of your hook, then put the point of your hook into the very head of the worm, till it come near to the place where the point of the hook first came out: and then draw back that part of the worm that was above the shank or arming of your hook, and so fish with it. And if you mean to fish with two worms, then put the second on before you turn back the hook's-head of the first worm; you cannot lose above two or three worms before you attain to what I direct you; and having attained it, you will find it very useful, and thank me for it: For you will run on the ground without tangling.

Now for the *Minnow* or *Pink*, he is not easily found and caught till *March*, or in *April*, for then he appears first in the River, Nature having taught him to shelter and hide himself in the Winter in ditches that be near to the River, and there both to hide and keep himself warm in the mud or in the weeds, which rot not so soon as in a running River, in which place if he were in Winter, the distempered Floods that are usually in that season, would suffer him to take no rest, but carry him head-long to Mills and Weirs to his confusion. And of these *Minnows*, first you are to know, that the biggest size is not the best; and next, that the middle size and the whitest are the best: and then you are to know, that your *Minnow* must be so put on your hook that it must turn round when 'tis drawn against the stream, and that it may turn nimbly, you must put it on a big-sized hook as I shall now direct you, which is thus. Put your hook in at his mouth and out at his gill, then having drawn your hook 2 or 3 inches beyond or through his gill, put it again into his mouth, and the point and beard out at his tail, and then tie the hook and his tail about very neatly with a white thread, which will make it the apter to turn quick in the water: that done, pull back that part of your line which was slack when you did put your hook into the *Minnow* the second time: I say pull that part of your line back so that it shall fasten the head, so that the body of the *Minnow* shall be almost straight on your hook; this done, try how it will turn by drawing it across the

water or against a stream, and if it do not turn nimbly, then
turn the tail a little to the right or left hand, and try again, till it
turn quick; for if not, you are in danger to catch nothing; for
know, that it is impossible that it should turn too quick: And
you are yet to know, that in case you want a *Minnow*, then a
small *Loach* or a *Stickle-back*, or any other small fish that will
turn quick will serve as well: And you are yet to know, that you
may salt them, and by that means keep them ready and fit for
use three or four days, or longer, and that of salt, bay-salt is the
best.

And here let me tell you, what many old Anglers know right
well, that at some times, and in some waters a *Minnow* is not to
be got, and therefore let me tell you, I have (which I will show
to you) an *artificial Minnow*, that will catch a Trout as well as
an *artificial Fly*, and it was made by a handsome Woman that
had a fine hand, and a live *Minnow* lying by her: *the mould or
body of the Minnow was cloth, and wrought upon or over it
thus with a needle: the back of it with very sad French green
silk, and paler green silk towards the belly, shadowed as
perfectly as you can imagine, just as you see a Minnow; the
belly was wrought also with a needle, and it was a part of it
white silk, and another part of it with silver thread; the tail and
fins were of a quill, which was shaven thin, the eyes were of two
little black beads, and the head was so shadowed, and all of it
so curiously wrought, and so exactly dissembled, that it would
beguile any sharp sighted Trout in a swift stream. And this
Minnow I will now show you, (look here it is) and if you like it,
lend it you, to have two or three made by it, for they be easily
carried about an Angler, and be of excellent use; for note, that
a large Trout will come as fiercely at a Minnow, as the highest
mettled Hawk doth seize on a Partridge, or a Grey-hound on a
Hare.* I have been told, that 160 *Minnows* have been found in a
Trout's belly; either the *Trout* had devoured so many; or the
Miller that gave it a friend of mine had forced them down his
throat after he had taken him.

Now for *Flies*, which is the third bait wherewith *Trouts* are
usually taken. You are to know, that there are so many sorts of
Flies as there be of Fruits: I will name you but some of them, as
the *dun-fly*, the *stone-fly*, the *red-fly*, the *moor-fly*, the *tawny-
fly*, the *shell-fly*, the *cloudy*, or *blackish-fly*, the *flag-fly*, the *vine-
fly*: there be of *flies*, *Caterpillars*, and *Canker-flies*, and *Bear-*

flies, and indeed too many either for me to name or for you to remember: and their breeding is so various and wonderful, that I might easily amaze my self, and tire you in a relation of them.

And yet I will exercise your promised patience by saying a little of the *Caterpillar* or the *Palmer-fly* or *worm*, that by them you may guess what a work it were in a Discourse but to run over those very many *flies*, *worms* and little living creatures with which the Sun and Summer adorn and beautify the River banks and Meadows; both for the recreation and contemplation of us Anglers, pleasures which (I think) I my self enjoy more than any other man that is not of my profession.

Pliny holds an opinion, that many have their birth or being from a dew that in the Spring falls upon the leaves of trees; and that some kinds of them are from a dew left upon herbs or flowers; and others from a dew left upon Coleworts or Cabbages: All which kinds of dews being thickened and condensed, are by the Sun's generative heat most of them hatched, and in three days made living creatures; and these of several shapes and colours; some being hard and tough, some smooth and soft; some are horned in their head, some in their tail, some have none: some have hair, some none: some have sixteen feet, some less, and some have none, but (as our *Topsell* hath with great diligence observed)[a] those which have none, move upon the earth or upon broad leaves, their motion being not unlike to the waves of the Sea. Some of them he also observes to be bred of the Eggs of other Caterpillars, and that those in their time turn to be *Butter-flies*: and again, that their Eggs turn the following year to be *Caterpillars*. And some affirm, that every plant has his particular fly or Caterpillar, which it breeds and feeds. I have seen, and may therefore affirm it, a green Caterpillar, or worm, as big as a small Peascod, which had fourteen legs, eight on the belly, four under the neck, and two near the tail. It was found on a hedge of Privet, and was taken thence, and put into a large Box, and a little branch or two of Privet put to it, on which I saw it feed as sharply as a dog gnaws a bone: it lived thus five or six days, and thrived, and changed the colour two or three times, but by some neglect in the keeper of it, it then died and did not turn to a fly: but if it had lived, it had doubtless turned to one of those flies that some call flies of prey, which

[a] *In his history of Serpents.*

those that walk by the Rivers may in Summer, see fasten on smaller flies, and I think make them their food. And 'tis observable, that as there be these *flies of prey* which be very large, so there be others very little, created, I think, only to feed them, and bred out of I know not what; whose life, they say, Nature intended not to exceed an hour, and yet that life is thus made shorter by other flies, or accident.

'Tis endless to tell you what the curious searchers into Nature's productions have observed of these Worms and Flies: But yet I shall tell you what *Aldrovandus*, our *Topsell*, and others say of the *Palmer-worm* or *Caterpillar*; That whereas others content themselves to feed on particular herbs or leaves, (for most think those very leaves that gave them life and shape, give them a particular feeding and nourishment, and that upon them they usually abide) yet he observes, that this is called a *pilgrim* or *palmer-worm*, for his very wandering life and various food; not contenting himself (as others do) with any one certain place for his abode, nor any certain kind of herb or flower for his feeding; but will boldly and disorderly wander up and down, and not endure to be kept to a diet, or fixed to a particular place.

Nay, the very colours of *Caterpillars* are, as one has observed, very elegant and beautiful: I shall (for a taste of the rest) describe one of them, which I will sometime the next month show you feeding on a Willow-tree, and you shall find him punctually to answer this very description: *His lips and mouth somewhat yellow, his eyes black as Jet, his forehead purple, his feet and hinder parts green, his tail two forked and black, the whole body stained with a kind of red spots which run along the neck and shoulder-blade, not unlike the form of Saint Andrew's Cross, or the letter X, made thus cross-wise, and a white line drawn down his back to his tail; all of which add much beauty to his whole body.* And it is to me observable, that at a fixed age this *Caterpillar* gives over to eat, and towards Winter comes to be covered over with a strange shell or crust called an *Aurelia*, and so lives a kind of dead life, without eating all the Winter; and (as others of several kinds turn to be several kinds of flies and vermin the Spring following) so this *Caterpillar* then turns to be a *painted Butter-fly*.[a]

Come, come my Scholar, you see the River stops our morning

---

[a] *View Sir Fra. Bacon exper. 728 & 90. in his Natural History.*

walk, and I will also here stop my discourse, only as we sit down under this *Honey-suckle* hedge, whilst I look a Line to fit the Rod that our brother *Peter* hath lent you, I shall for a little confirmation of what I have said, repeat the observation of *Du Bartas* :[a]

5

> *God not contented to each kind to give,*
> *And to infuse the virtue generative,*
> *By his wise power made many creatures breed*
> *Of lifeless bodies without* Venus' *deed.*

> *So the cold humour breeds the* Salamander,
> *Who (in effect) like to her birth's commander,*
> *With child with hundred winters, with her touch*
> *Quencheth the fire though glowing ne'er so much.*

10

> *So in the fire in burning furnace springs*
> *The Fly* Pyrausta *with the flaming wings;*
> *Without the fire it dies, in it it joys,*
> *Living in that which all things else destroys.*

15

> *So slow* Boötes *underneath him sees*
> *In th'Icy Islands goslings hatched of trees,*
> *Whose fruitful leaves falling into the water,*
> *Are turned ('tis known) to living fowls soon after.*[b]

20

> *So rotten plants of broken ships do change*
> *To Barnacles. O transformation strange!*
> *'Twas first a green tree, then a broken hull,*
> *Lately a mushroom, now a flying Gull.*

25

Venat. O my good Master, this morning-walk has been spent to my great pleasure and wonder: but I pray, when shall I have your direction how to make artificial flies, like to those that the *Trout* loves best? and also how to use them?

Pisc. My honest Scholar, it is now past five of the Clock, we will fish till nine, and then go to breakfast: Go you to yonder *Sycamore-tree*, and hide your Bottle of drink under the hollow root of it; for about that time, and in that place, we will make a brave breakfast with a piece of powdered Beef, and a Radish

30

---

[a] 6. Day of Du Bartas.
[b] View Gerh. Herbal and Camden.

or two that I have in my Fish-bag; we shall, I warrant you, make a good, honest, wholesome, hungry breakfast, and I will then give you direction for the making and using of your flies: and in the mean time there is your Rod and Line, and my advice
5 is, that you fish as you see me do, and let's try which can catch the first Fish.

Venat. I thank you Master, I will observe and practice your direction as far as I am able.

Pisc. Look you Scholar, you see I have hold of a good Fish: I
10 now see it is a Trout; I pray, put that Net under him, and touch not my line, for if you do, then we break all. Well done Scholar, I thank you.

Now for another. Trust me, I have another bite: come Scholar, come lay down your Rod, and help me to land this as
15 you did the other. So, now we shall be sure to have a good dish of Fish for supper.

Venat. I am glad of that; but I have no fortune: sure, Master, yours is a better Rod, and better tackling.

Pisc. Nay, then take mine, and I will fish with yours. Look
20 you, Scholar, I have another; come, do as you did before. And now I have a bite at another: Oh me! he has broke all; there's half a line and a good hook lost.

Venat. Aye and a good *Trout* too.

Pisc. Nay, the *Trout* is not lost, for pray take notice no man
25 can lose what he never had.

Venat. Master, I can neither catch with the first nor second Angle: I have no fortune.

Pisc. Look you, Scholar, I have yet another: and now having caught three brace of Trouts, I will tell you a short Tale as we
30 walk towards our breakfast: *A Scholar (a Preacher I should say) that was to preach to procure the approbation of a Parish, that he might be their Lecturer, had got from his Fellow-pupil the copy of a Sermon that was first preached with great commendation by him that composed it; and though the
35 borrower of it preached it word for word, as it was at first, yet it was utterly disliked as it was preached by the second to his Congregation: which the sermon-borrower complained of to the lender of it, and was thus answered; I lent you indeed my* Fiddle, *but not my* Fiddlestick; *for you are to know, that every
40 one cannot make music with my words, which are fitted for my own mouth.* And so, my Scholar, you are to know, that as the

ill pronunciation or ill accenting of words in a Sermon spoils it, so the ill carriage of your line, or not fishing even to a foot in a right place, makes you lose your labour: and you are to know, that though you have my *Fiddle*, that is, my very Rod and Tacklings with which you see I catch Fish; yet you have not my *Fiddle-stick*, that is, you yet have not skill to know how to carry your hand and line, nor how to guide it to a right place: and this must be taught you (for you are to remember I told you, Angling is an Art) either by practice, or a long observation, or both. But take this for a rule, when you fish for a Trout with a Worm, let your line have so much, and not more Lead than will fit the stream in which you fish; that is to say; more in a great troublesome stream than in a smaller that is quieter; as near as may be, so much as will sink the bait to the bottom, and keep it still in motion, and not more.

But now let's say Grace and fall to breakfast: what say you, Scholar, to the providence of an old Angler? does not this meat taste well? and was not this place well chosen to eat it? for this Sycamore-tree will shade us from the Sun's heat.

Venat. All excellent good, and my stomach excellent good too. And I now remember and find that true which devout *Lessius* says, *That poor men, and those that fast often, have much more pleasure in eating than rich men and gluttons, that always feed before their stomachs are empty of their last meat, and call for more: for by that means they rob themselves of that pleasure that hunger brings to poor men*. And I do seriously approve of that saying of yours, *That you had rather be a civil, well governed, well grounded, temperate, poor Angler, than a drunken Lord*. But I hope there is none such; however I am certain of this, that I have been at many very costly dinners that have not afforded me half the content that this has done, for which I thank God and you.

And now good Master, proceed to your promised direction for making and ordering my Artificial fly.

Pisc. My honest Scholar, I will do it, for it is a debt due unto you by my promise: and because you shall not think your self more engaged to me than indeed you really are, I will freely give you such directions as were lately given to me by an ingenuous brother of the Angle, an honest man, and a most excellent *Fly-fisher*.

You are to note, that there are twelve kinds of Artificial made

Flies to Angle with upon the top of the water (note by the way, that the fittest season of using these is in a blustering windy day, when the waters are so troubled that the natural fly cannot be seen, or rest upon them). The first is the *dun-fly* in *March*, the body is made of *dun wool*, the wings of the Partridge's feathers. The second is another *dun-Fly*, the body of *Black wool*, and the wings made of the black Drake's feathers, and of the feathers under his tail. The third is the *stone-fly* in *April*, the body is made of *black wool* made yellow under the wings, and under the tail, and so made with wings of the Drake. The fourth is the *ruddy Fly* in the beginning of *May*, the body made of *red wool* wrapped about with black silk, and the feathers are the wings of the Drake, with the feathers of a red Capon also, which hang dangling on his sides next to the tail. The fifth is the *yellow* or *greenish-fly* (in *May* likewise) the body made of *yellow wool*, and the wings made of the red cock's hackle or tail. The sixth is, the *black Fly* in *May* also, the body made of *black wool* and lapped about with the harl of a Peacock's tail; the wings are made of the wings of a brown Capon with his blue feathers in his head. The seventh is the sad *yellow-fly* in *June*, the body is made of *black wool*, with a yellow list on either side, and the wings taken off the wings of a Buzzard, bound with black braked hemp. The eighth is the *moorish fly* made with the body of duskish Wool, and the wings made of the blackish mail of the Drake. The ninth is the *tawny-fly*, good until the middle of *June*; the body made of *tawny-wool*, the wings made contrary one against the other, made of the whitish mail of the wild Drake. The tenth is the *Wasp-fly* in *July*, the body made of *black wool*, lapped about with yellow silk, the wings made of the feathers of the Drake, or of the Buzzard. The Eleventh is the *shell-fly*, good in mid *July*, the body made of greenish wool, lapped about with the harl of a Peacock's tail; and the wings made of the wings of the Buzzard. The twelfth is the dark *Drake-fly*, good in *August*, the body made with *black Wool*, lapped about with black silk: his wings are made with the mail of the black Drake, with a black head. Thus have you a Jury of flies likely to betray and condemn all the Trouts in the River.

I shall next give you some other Directions for Fly-fishing, such as are given by Mr *Thomas Barker*, a Gentleman that hath spent much time in Fishing: but I shall do it with a little variation.

First, let your Rod be light, and very gentle; I take the best to be of two pieces, and let not your Line exceed (especially for three or four links next to the hook) I say, not exceed three or four hairs at the most, though you may Fish a little stronger above in the upper part of your Line: but if you can attain to 5 Angle with one hair, you shall have more rises and catch more Fish. Now you must be sure not to cumber your self with too long a Line, as most do: and before you begin to Angle, cast to have the wind on your back, and the Sun (if it shines) to be before you, and to fish down the stream; and carry the point or 10 top of your Rod downward; by which means the shadow of your self, and Rod too will be the least offensive to the Fish, for the sight of any shade amazes the fish, and spoils your sport, of which you must take a great care.

In the middle of *March* (till which time a man should not in 15 honesty catch a Trout) or in *April*, if the weather be dark, or a little windy or cloudy, the best fishing is with the *Palmer-worm*, of which I last spoke to you, but of these there be divers kinds, or at least of divers colours; these and the *May-fly* are the ground of all Fly-angling, which are to be thus made. 20

First, you must arm your hook with the line in the inside of it, then take your Scissors, and cut so much of a brown Mallard's feather as in your own reason will make the wings of it, you having withal regard to the bigness or littleness of your hook, then lay the outmost part of your feather next to your hook, 25 then the point of your feather next the shank of your hook; and having so done, whip it three or four times about the hook with the same Silk, with which your hook was armed, and having made the Silk fast, take the hackle of a *Cock* or *Capon's* neck, or a *Plover's* top, which is usually better: take off the one side 30 of the feather, and then take the hackle, Silk, or Crewel, Gold or Silver thread, make these fast at the bent of the hook, that is to say, below your arming; then you must take the hackle, the Silver or Gold thread, and work it up to the wings, shifting or still removing your fingers as you turn the Silk about the hook: 35 and still looking at every stop or turn, that your Gold, or what materials soever you make your *Fly* of, do lie right and neatly; and if you find they do so, then when you have made the head, make all fast, and then work your hackle up to the head, and make that fast: and then with a needle or pin divide the wing 40 into two, and then with the arming Silk whip it about cross-

ways betwixt the wings; and then with your thumb you must turn the point of the feather towards the bent of the hook, and then work three or four times about the shank of the hook, and then view the proportion, and if all be neat and to your liking
5 fasten.

I confess, no direction can be given to make a man of a dull capacity able to make a Fly well: and yet I know, this with a little practice will help an ingenuous Angler in a good degree: but to see a Fly made by an Artist in that kind, is the best
10 teaching to make it, and then an ingenuous Angler may walk by the River and mark what flies fall on the water that day, and catch one of them, if he see the *Trouts* leap at a fly of that kind: and then having always hooks ready hung with him, and having a bag also always with him, with Bear's hair, or the hair of a
15 brown or sad-coloured Heifer, hackles of a Cock or Capon, several coloured Silk and Crewel to make the body of the fly, the feathers of a Drake's head, black or brown Sheep's wool, or Hog's wool, or hair, thread of Gold and of Silver: Silk of several colours (especially sad coloured to make the fly's head): and
20 there be also other coloured feathers both of little birds and of peckled fowl. I say, having those with him in a bag, and trying to make a fly, though he miss at first, yet shall he at last hit it better, even to such a perfection, as none can well teach him; and if he hit to make his Fly right, and have the luck to hit also
25 where there is store of *Trouts*, a dark day, and a right wind, he will catch such store of them, as will encourage him to grow more and more in love with the Art of *Fly-making*.

Venat. But my loving master, if any wind will not serve, then I wish I were in *Lapland*, to buy a good wind of one of the
30 honest Witches, that sell so many winds there, and so cheap.

Pisc. Marry Scholar, but I would not be there, nor indeed from under this tree: for look how it begins to rain, and by the clouds (if I mistake not) we shall presently have a smoking shower, and therefore sit close, this *Sycamore-tree* will shelter
35 us: and I will tell you, as they shall come into my mind, more observations of fly-fishing for a Trout.

But first for the wind, you are to take notice, that of the winds the *South wind* is said to be best. One observes, That

—*When the wind is South,*
40   *It blows your bait into a fish's mouth.*

Next to that, the *West* wind is believed to be the best: and having told you that the *East* wind is the worst, I need not tell you which wind is the best in the third degree: And yet (as *Solomon* observes) that *He that considers the wind shall never sow*: so he that busies his head too much about them, (if the weather be not made extreme cold by an East wind) shall be a little superstitious: For as it is observed by some, That there is no good Horse of a bad colour; so I have observed that if it be a cloudy day, and not extreme cold, let the Wind sit in what corner it will, and do its worst I heed it not. And yet take this for a rule, that I would willingly fish standing on the Lee-shore: and you are to take notice, that the fish lies or swims nearer the bottom, and in deeper water in Winter than in Summer; and also nearer the bottom in any cold day, and then gets nearest the Lee-side of the water.

But I promised to tell you more of the Fly-fishing for a *Trout*, which I may have time enough to do, for you see it rains *May-butter*: First for a *May-fly*, you may make his body with greenish coloured Crewel, or Willowish colour; darkening it in most places with waxed Silk, or ribbed with black hair, or some of them ribbed with silver thread; and such Wings for the colour as you see the fly to have at that season; nay, at that very day on the water. Or you may make the Oak-fly with an Orange-tawny and black ground, and the brown of a Mallard's feather for the Wings; and you are to know, that these two are most excellent flies, that is, the *May-fly* and the *Oak-Fly*. And let me again tell you, that you keep as far from the water as you can possibly, whether you fish with a fly or worm, and fish down the stream; and when you fish with a fly, if it be possible, let no part of your line touch the water, but your fly only; and be still moving your fly upon the water, or casting it into the water, you your self being also always moving down the stream. Mr *Barker* commends several sorts of the *Palmer* flies, not only those ribbed with silver and gold, but others that have their bodies all made of black, or some with red, and a red hackle; you may also make the *Hawthorn-fly*, which is all black, and not big, but very small, the smaller the better; or the *Oak-Fly*, the body of which is Orange-colour and black Crewel, with a brown Wing; or a fly made with a *Peacock's* feather, is excellent in a bright day: You must be sure you want not in your *Magazine-bag* the *Peacock's* feather, and grounds of such wool and Crewel as will make the Grasshopper; and note that usually the smallest flies are the

best; and note also, that the light fly does usually make most sport in a dark day, and the darkest and least fly in a bright or clear day; and lastly note, that you are to repair upon any occasion to your *Magazine-bag*, and upon any occasion vary and
5 make them lighter or sadder according to your fancy or the day.

And now I shall tell you, that the fishing with a natural fly is excellent, and affords much pleasure; they may be found thus, the *May-fly* usually in and about that month near to the River side, especially against rain; the *Oak-Fly* on the butt or body of
10 an *Oak* or *Ash* from the beginning of *May* to the end of *August*; it is a brownish fly, and easy to be so found, and stands usually with his head downward, that is to say, towards the root of the tree; the small black fly, or Hawthorn fly, is to be had on any Hawthorn bush after the leaves be come forth: with these and a
15 short Line (as I showed to Angle for a *Chub*) you may dap or dop, and also with a *Grasshopper* behind a tree, or in any deep hole, still making it to move on the top of the water, as if it were alive, and still keeping your self out of sight; you shall certainly have sport if there be *Trouts*; yea, in a hot day, but especially in
20 the evening of a hot day you will have sport.

And now, Scholar, my direction for fly-fishing is ended with this shower, for it has done raining; and now look about you, and see how pleasantly that Meadow looks; nay, and the Earth smells as sweetly too. Come, let me tell you what holy Mr
25 *Herbert* says of such days and flowers as these, and then we will thank God that we enjoy them, and walk to the River and sit down quietly, and try to catch the other brace of *Trouts*.

> *Sweet day, so cool, so calm, so bright,*
> *The bridal of the earth and sky,*
30 > *Sweet dews shall weep thy fall tonight,*
> > *for thou must die.*

> *Sweet Rose, whose hue angry and brave*
> *Bids the rash gazer wipe his eye,*
> *Thy root is ever in its grave,*
35 > > *and thou must die.*

> *Sweet Spring, full of sweet days and roses,*
> *A box where sweets compacted lie;*
> *My Music shows you have your closes,*
> > *and all must die.*

> *Only a sweet and virtuous soul,*
> *Like seasoned Timber never gives,*
> *But when the whole world turns to coal,*
> > *then chiefly lives.*

Venat. I thank you, good Master, for your good direction for 5
Fly-fishing, and for the sweet enjoyment of the pleasant day,
which is so far spent without offence to God or man: and I
thank you for the sweet close of your discourse with Mr
Herbert's Verses, who I have heard loved Angling: and I do the
rather believe it, because he had a spirit suitable to Anglers, and 10
to those primitive Christians, that you love, and have so much
commended.
Pisc. Well my loving Scholar, and I am pleased, to know that
you are so well pleased with my direction and discourse.

And since you like these Verses of Mr *Herbert's* so well, let 15
me tell you what a reverend and learned Divine that professes
to imitate him (and has indeed done so most excellently) hath
writ of our *Book* of *Common Prayer*, which I know you will
like the better, because he is a friend of mine, and I am sure no
enemy to Angling.   20

> *What? prayer by th'book? and common? Yes, why not?*
> > *The Spirit of grace,*
> > *And supplication,*
> > *Is not left free alone*
> > *For time and place,*   25
> *But manner too: to read or speak by rote,*
> > *Is all alike to him, that prays,*
> > *In's heart, what with his mouth he says.*
>
> *They that in private by themselves alone*
> > *Do pray, may take*   30
> > *What liberty they please,*
> > *In choosing of the ways*
> > *Wherein to make*
> *Their souls most intimate affections known*
> > *To him that sees in secret, when*   35
> > *Th'are most conceal'd from other men.*
>
> *But he, that unto others leads the way*
> > *In public prayer,*
> > *Should do it so*
> > *As all that hear may know*   40

> They need not fear
> To *tune their hearts unto his tongue, and say,*
> Amen; *nor doubt they were betrayed*
> To blaspheme, *when they meant to have* prayed.

5
> *Devotion will add Life unto the Letter,*
> *And why should not*
> *That which Authority*
> *Prescribes, esteemed be*
> *Advantage got?*
10
> *If th'prayer be good, the commoner the better,*
> *Prayer in the Church's words, as well*
> *As sense, of all prayers bears the bell.*

                                        Ch. Harvie.

And now, Scholar, I think it will be time to repair to our
15 Angle-rods, which we left in the water, to fish for themselves,
and you shall choose which shall be yours; and it is an even lay,
one of them catches.

And let me tell you, this kind of fishing with a dead rod, and
laying night-hooks, are like putting money to Use, for they both
20 work for the Owners, when they do nothing but sleep, or eat,
or rejoice; as you know we have done this last hour, and sat as
quietly and as free from cares under this *Sycamore*, as *Virgil's*
Tityrus and his *Meliboeus* did under their broad *Beech-tree*: No
life, my honest Scholar, no life so happy and so pleasant, as the
25 life of a well governed *Angler*; for when the *Lawyer* is swallowed up with business, and the *States-man* is preventing or
contriving plots, then we sit on *Cowslip-banks*, hear the birds
sing, and possess our selves in as much quietness as these silent
silver streams, which we now see glide so quietly by us. Indeed
30 my good Scholar, we may say of *Angling*, as Dr *Butler* said of
Strawberries; Doubtless God could have made a better berry,
but doubtless God never did: And so (if I might be Judge) *God*
never did make a more calm, quiet, innocent recreation than
Angling.
35 I'll tell you Scholar, when I sat last on this *Primrose-bank*,
and looked down these Meadows; I thought of them as *Charles*
the Emperor did of the City of *Florence: That they were too*
pleasant to be looked on, but only on Holy-days: as I then sat
on this very grass, I turned my present thoughts into verse:
40 'Twas a wish which I'll repeat to you.

The Angler's wish.

I in these flowery Meads would be :
These Crystal streams should solace me ;
To whose harmonious bubbling noise,
I with my Angle would rejoice 5
Sit here and see the Turtle-dove,
Court his chaste Mate to acts of love,
Or on that bank, feel the west wind
Breathe health and plenty, please my mind
To see sweet dew-drops kiss these flowers, 10
And then, washed off by April-*showers :*
Here hear my Kenna sing* a song,
There see a Black-bird feed her young,
Or a Laverock build her nest ;
Here, give my weary spirits rest, 15
And raise my low pitched thoughts above
Earth, or what poor mortals love :
      Thus free from Law-suits, *and the noise*
      Of Princes' Courts I would rejoice.

Or, with my Bryan, and a book, 20
Loiter long days near Shawford-brook ;
There sit by him, and eat my meat,
There see the Sun both rise and set :
There bid good morning to next day,
There meditate my time away : 25
      And angle on, and beg to have
      A quiet passage to a welcome grave.

When I had ended this composure, I left this place, and saw a
Brother of the Angle sit under that *honey-suckle-hedge* (one that
will prove worth your acquaintance) I sat down by him, and 30
presently we met with an accidental piece of merriment, which I
will relate to you ; for it rains still.

On the other side of this very hedge sat a gang of *Gipsies*, and
near to them sat a gang of *Beggars* : the *Gipsies* were then to
divide all the money that had been got that week, either by 35
stealing linen or poultry, or by Fortune-telling, or Legerdemain,
or indeed by any other sleights and secrets belonging to their
mysterious Government. And the sum that was got that week
proved to be but twenty and some odd shillings. The odd money

---

* Like Hermit poor.

was agreed to be distributed amongst the poor of their own
Corporation; and for the remaining twenty shillings, that was
to be divided unto four Gentlemen *Gipsies*, according to their
several degrees in their Commonwealth.

5   And the first or chiefest *Gipsy*, was by consent to have a third
part of the twenty shillings; which all men know is 6s. 8d.

The second was to have a fourth part of the 20s. which all
men know to be 5s.

The third was to have a fifth part of the 20s. which all men
10 know to be 4s.

The fourth and last *Gipsy*, was to have a sixth part of the 20s.
which all men know to be 3s. 4d.

<pre>
            As for example,
            3 times 6s. 8d. is   − − − − − − − 20s.
15   And so is 4 times 5s.   − − − − − − − 20s.
            And so is 5 times 4s.   − − − − − − − 20s.
            And so is 6 times 3s. 4d. − − − − − − − 20s.
</pre>

And yet he that divided the money was so very a *Gipsy*, that
though he gave to every one these said sums, yet he kept one
20 shilling of it for himself.

<pre>
            As for Example,   s.   d.
                                     6   8
                                     5   0
                                     4   0
25   3   4
                        make but   19   0
</pre>

But now you shall know, that when the four *Gipsies* saw that
he had got one shilling by dividing the money, though not one
of them knew any reason to demand more, yet like Lords and
30 Courtiers every *Gipsy* envied him that was the gainer, and
wrangled with him, and every one said the *remaining shilling
belonged to him*: and so they fell to so high a contest about it,
as none that knows the faithfulness of one *Gipsy* to another,
will easily believe; only we that have lived these last twenty
35 years, are certain that money has been able to do much mischief.
However the *Gipsies* were too wise to go to Law, and did
therefore choose their choice friends *Rook* and *Shark*, and our

late English *Gusman* to be their Arbitrators and Umpires; and so they left this *Honey-suckle-hedge*, and went to *tell fortunes*, and *cheat*, and get more money and lodging in the next Village.

When these were gone we heard as high a contention amongst the *beggars, Whether it was easiest to rip a Cloak, or to unrip a Cloak?* One *beggar* affirmed it was all one. But that was denied by asking her, *If doing and undoing were all one?* then another said, *'Twas easiest to unrip a Cloak*, for that was to let it alone. But she was answered, by asking her, how she unripped it, if she let it alone? And she confessed her self mistaken. These and twenty such like questions were proposed, and answered with as much beggarly Logic and earnestness, as was ever heard to proceed from the mouth of the most pertinacious Schismatic; and sometimes all the Beggars (whose number was neither more nor less than the Poets' nine Muses) talked all together about this ripping and unripping, and so loud that not one heard what the other said; but at last one beggar craved audience, and told them, that old Father *Clause*, whom *Ben Jonson* in his Beggars-bush created King of their Corporation, was that night to lodge at an Ale-house (called *Catch-her-by-the-way*) not far from *Waltham-Cross*, and in the high-road towards *London*; and he therefore desired them to spend no more time about that and such like questions, but refer all to Father *Clause* at night, for he was an upright Judge, and in the mean time draw cuts what Song should be next sung, and who should sing it; They all agreed to the motion, and the lot fell to her that was the youngest, and veriest Virgin of the Company, and she sung *Frank Davison's* Song, which he made forty years ago, and all the others of the company joined to sing the burden with her: the Ditty was this, but first the burden.

> *Bright shines the Sun, play beggars, play,*
> *Here's scraps enough to serve today.*

> *What noise of viols is so sweet*
> *As when our merry clappers ring?*
> *What mirth doth want when beggars meet?*
> *A beggar's life is for a King:*
>   *Eat, drink and play, sleep when we list,*
>   *Go where we will so stocks be missed.*
>   *Bright shines the Sun, play beggars play,*
>   *Here's scraps enough to serve today.*

The world is ours and ours alone,
For we alone have world at will;
We purchase not, all is our own,
Both fields and streets we beggars fill:
5   *Play beggars play, play beggars play,*
Here's scraps enough to serve today.

A hundred herds of black and white
Upon our Gowns securely feed
And yet if any dare us bite,
10   *He dies therefore as sure as Creed:*
Thus beggars Lord it as they please,
And only beggars live at ease:
Bright shines the sun, play beggars play,
Here's scraps enough to serve today.

15   *Venat.* I thank you good Master, for this piece of merriment, and this Song, which was well humoured by the Maker, and well remembered by you.

Pisc. But I pray forget not the Catch which you promised to make against night, for our Country-man, honest *Corydon*, will
20 expect your Catch and my Song, which I must be forced to patch up, for it is so long since I learnt it, that I have forgot a part of it. But come, now it hath done raining, let's stretch our legs a little in a gentle walk to the River, and try what interest our Angles will pay us for lending them so long to be used by the *Trouts*, lent
25 them indeed, like Usurers, for our profit and their destruction.

Venat. Oh me, look you Master, a fish a fish, oh 'las Master, I have lost her!

Pisc. Aye marry Sir, that was a good fish indeed: if I had had the luck to have taken up that Rod, then 'tis twenty to one, he
30 should not have broke my line by running to the rod's end as you suffered him: I would have held him within the bent of my Rod (unless he had been fellow to the great *Trout* that is near an ell long, which was of such a length and depth, that he had his picture drawn, and now is to be seen at mine Host *Rickaby's*
35 at the *George* in *Ware*), and it may be, by giving that very great *Trout* the Rod, that is, by casting it to him into the water, I might have caught him at the long run, for so I use always to do when I meet with an overgrown fish, and you will learn to do so too hereafter: for I tell you, Scholar, fishing is an Art, or at
40 least, it is an Art to catch fish.

Venat. But Master, I have heard that the great *Trout* you speak of is a *Salmon*.

Pisc. Trust me Scholar, I know not what to say to it. There are many Country people that believe *Hares* change Sexes every year: And there be very many learned men think so too, for in their dissecting them they find many reasons to incline them to that belief. And to make the wonder seem yet less that Hares change Sexes, note that Doctor *Mer. Casaubon* affirms in his book of credible and incredible things, that *Gasper Peucerus* a learned Physician, tells us of a people that once a year turn wolves, partly in shape, and partly in conditions. And so whether this were a *Salmon* when he came into the fresh water, and his not returning into the Sea hath altered him to another colour or kind, I am not able to say; but I am certain he hath all the signs of being a *Trout* both for his *shape*, *colour*, and *spots*, and yet many think he is not.

Venat. But Master, will this *Trout* which I had hold of die? for it is like he hath the hook in his belly.

Pisc. I will tell you Scholar, that unless the hook be fast in his very Gorge, 'tis more than probable he will live, and a little time with the help of the water, will rust the hook, and it will in time wear away: as the gravel doth in the horse hoof, which only leaves a false quarter.

And now Scholar, let's go to my Rod. Look you Scholar, I have a fish too, but it proves a logger-headed *Chub*, and this is not much amiss, for this will pleasure some poor body, as we go to our lodging to meet our Brother *Peter* and honest *Corydon*. Come, now bait your hook again, and lay it into the water, for it rains again; and we will even retire to the *Sycamore tree*, and there I will give you more directions concerning Fishing: For I would fain make you an Artist.

Venat. Yes, good Master, I pray let it be so.

Pisc. Well Scholar, now we are sat down and are at ease, I shall tell you a little more of *Trout* fishing, before I speak of the *Salmon* (which I purpose shall be next), and then of the *Pike* or *Luce.* You are to know, there is night as well as day-fishing for a *Trout*, and that in the night the best *Trouts* come out of their holes: and the manner of taking them, is on the top of the water with a great *Lob* or *Garden-worm*, or rather two, which you are to fish with in a place where the waters run somewhat quietly (for in a stream the bait will not be so well discerned). I

say in a *quiet* or dead place near to some swift, there draw your
bait over the top of the water to and fro, and if there be a good
Trout in the hole, he will take it, especially if the night be dark:
for then he is bold and lies near the top of the water, watching
5   the motion of any *Frog* or *Water-Rat* or *Mouse* that swims
betwixt him and the sky; these he hunts after, if he sees the
water but wrinkle, or move in one of these dead holes, where
these great old *Trouts* usually lie near to their holds; for you
are to note, that the great old *Trout* is both subtle and fearful,
10 and lies close all day, and does not usually stir out of his hold,
but lies in it as close in the day, as the *timorous Hare* does in
her form: for the chief feeding of either is seldom in the day,
but usually in the night, and then the great *Trout* feeds very
boldly.
15   And you must fish for him with a strong Line, and not a little
hook, and let him have time to gorge your hook, for he does not
usually forsake it, as he oft will in the day-fishing: and if the
night be not dark, then Fish so with an *Artificial fly* of a light-
colour, and at the snap: nay, he will sometimes rise at a dead
20 *Mouse*, or a piece of cloth, or any thing, that seems to swim
across the water, or to be in motion: this is a choice way, but I
have not oft used it, because it is void of the pleasures, that such
days as these, that we two now enjoy, afford an Angler.
    And you are to know, that in *Hampshire*, which I think
25 exceeds all *England* for swift, shallow, clear, pleasant Brooks,
and store of *Trouts*, they use to catch *Trouts* in the night, by the
light of a Torch or straw, which when they have discovered,
they strike with a *Trout-spear* or other ways. This kind of way
they catch very many, but I would not believe it till I was an
30 eye-witness of it, nor do I like it now I have seen it.
    Venat. But Master, do not *Trouts* see us in the night?
    Pisc. Yes, and hear, and smell too, both then and in the day-
time, for *Gesner* observes, the *Otter* smells a Fish forty furlongs
off him in the water: and that it may be true, seems to be
35 affirmed by Sir *Francis Bacon* (in the eighth Century of his
Natural History) who there proves, that waters may be the
Medium of sounds, by demonstrating it thus, *That if you knock*
two stones together very deep under the water, those that stand
on a bank near to that place may hear the noise without any
40 *diminution of it by the water*. He also offers the like experiment
concerning the letting an *Anchor* fall by a very long cable or

rope on a rock, or the sand within the Sea: and this being so
well observed and demonstrated, as it is by that learned man,
has made me to believe that *Eels* unbed themselves, and stir at
the noise of Thunder, and not only, as some think, by the
motion or stirring of the earth which is occasioned by that   5
Thunder.

And this reason of Sir *Francis Bacon* (*Exper.* 792.) has made
me crave pardon of one that I laughed at for affirming, that he
knew *Carps* come to a certain place in a Pond, to be fed at the
ringing of a Bell, or the beating of a Drum: and however, it   10
shall be a rule for me to make as little noise as I can when I am
fishing, until Sir *Francis Bacon* be confuted, which I shall give
any man leave to do.

And, lest you may think him singular in this opinion, I will
tell you, this seems to be believed by our learned Doctor   15
Hakewill, who (in his *Apology of Gods Power and Providence*,
f. 360) quotes *Pliny* to report, that one of the Emperors had
particular Fish-ponds, and in them several Fish, that appeared
and came when they were called by their particular names: and
St *James* tells us (*chap.* 1. *and* 7.) that all things in the Sea have   20
been tamed by Mankind. And *Pliny* tells us (*lib.* 9. 35.) that
Antonia the Wife of *Drusus* had a *Lamprey*, at whose gills she
hung Jewels or Ear-rings; and that others have been so tender-
hearted, as to shed tears at the death of Fishes, which they have
kept and loved. And these Obervations, which will to most   25
hearers seem wonderful, seem to have a further confirmation
from *Martial* (*lib.* 4. *epig.* 30.) who writes thus:

>   *Piscator fuge ne nocens, &c.*
> Angler, *would'st thou be guiltless? then forbear,*
> *For these are* sacred fishes *that swim here;*   30
> *Who know their Sovereign, and will lick his hand;*
> *Than which none's greater in the world's command:*
> *Nay more, th'have names, & when they called are,*
> *Do to their several Owner's Call repair.*

All the further use that I shall make of this, shall be, to advise   35
Anglers to be patient, and *forbear swearing, lest they be heard
and catch no Fish.*

And so I shall proceed next to tell you, it is certain, that
certain fields near *Leominster*, a Town in *Hereford-shire*, are

observed to make the sheep that graze upon them more fat than the next, and also to bear finer wool; that is to say, that, that year in which they feed in such a particular pasture, they shall yield finer wool than they did that year before they came to feed in it, and coarser again if they shall return to their former pasture; and again return to a finer wool being fed in the fine-wool-ground. Which I tell you, that you may the better believe that I am certain, if I catch a *Trout* in one Meadow, he shall be *white* and *faint*, and very like to be *lousy*; and as certainly, if I catch a *Trout* in the next Meadow, he shall be *strong*, and *red*, and *lusty*, and much better meat: Trust me, Scholar, I have caught many a *Trout* in a particular Meadow, that the very shape and the enamelled colour of him hath been such, as hath joyed me to look on him; and I have then with much pleasure concluded with *Solomon, Everything is beautiful in his season.*

I should by promise speak next of the *Salmon*, but I will by your favour say a little of the *Umber* or *Grayling*; which is so like a *Trout* for his shape and feeding, that I desire I may exercise your patience with a short discourse of him, and then the next shall be of the *Salmon.*

Observations of the Umber or Grayling
and directions how to fish for them.

Pisc. The *Umber* and *Grayling* are thought by some to differ as
the *Herring* and *Pilchard* do. But though they may do so in
other Nations, I think those in *England* differ nothing but in
their names. *Aldrovandus* says, they be of a *Trout* kind: and
Gesner says, that in his Country (which is *Switzerland*) he is
accounted the choicest of all Fish. And in *Italy*, he is in the
month of *May* so highly valued, that he is sold then at a much
higher rate than any other Fish. The *French* (which call the
Chub Un Vilain) call the *Umber* of the Lake *Leman, Un Omble
Chevalier*; and they value the *Umber* or Grayling so highly, that
they say he feeds on Gold, and say that many have been caught
out of their famous River of *Loire*, out of whose bellies grains
of Gold have been often taken. And some think that he feeds on
Water-thyme, and smells of it at his first taking out of the
water; and they may think so with as good reason as we do,
that our Smelts smell like Violets at their being first caught;
which I think is a truth. *Aldrovandus* says, the *Salmon*, the
Grayling, and *Trout*, and all Fish that live in clear and sharp
streams, are made by their mother *Nature* of such exact shape
and pleasant colours, purposely to invite us to a joy and
contentedness in feasting with her. Whether this is a truth or
not, is not my purpose to dispute; but 'tis certain, all that write
of the *Umber* declare him to be very medicinable. And *Gesner*
says, that the fat of an *Umber* or *Grayling* being set with a little
Honey a day or two in the Sun in a little glass, is very excellent
against redness, or swarthiness, or any thing that breeds in the
eyes. *Salvian* takes him to be called *Umber* from his swift
swimming or gliding out of sight, more like a shadow or a Ghost
than a fish. Much more might be said both of his smell and
taste, but I shall only tell you, that St *Ambrose* the glorious
Bishop of *Milan* (who lived when the Church kept Fasting-days)
calls him the *flower-fish*, or flower of Fishes, and that he was so
far in love with him, that he would not let him pass without the

honour of a long Discourse; but I must; and pass on to tell you how to take this dainty fish.

First, Note, That he grows not to the bigness of a Trout; for the biggest of them do not usually exceed eighteen inches, he lives in such Rivers as the Trout does, and is usually taken with the same baits as the Trout is, and after the same manner, for he will bite both at the *Minnow*, or *Worm*, or *Fly*, (though he bites not often at the Minnow) and is very gamesome at the *Fly*, and much simpler, and therefore bolder than a *Trout*, for he will rise twenty times at a fly, if you miss him, and yet rise again. He has been taken with a fly made of the red feathers of a *Parakeet*, a strange outlandish bird, and he will rise at a fly not unlike a gnat or a small moth, or indeed, at most flies that are not too big. He is a Fish that lurks close all winter, but is very pleasant and jolly after mid-*April*, and in *May*, and in the hot months: he is of a very fine shape, his flesh is white, his teeth, those little ones that he has, are in his throat, yet he has so tender a mouth, that he is oftener lost after an Angler has hooked him, than any other Fish. Though there be many of these Fishes in the delicate River *Dove*, and in *Trent*, and some other smaller Rivers, as that which runs by *Salisbury*, yet he is not so general a Fish as the *Trout*, nor to me so good to eat or to angle for. And so I shall take my leave of him, and now come to some Observations of the *Salmon*, and how to catch him.

CHAP. VII.

Observations of the Salmon, with directions how to fish for him.

Pisc. The *Salmon* is accounted the King of fresh-water-fish, and is ever bred in Rivers relating to the Sea, yet so high or so far from it as admits of no tincture of salt, or brackishness; He is said to breed or cast his spawn in most Rivers in the month of *August*: some say, that then they dig a hole or grave in a safe place in the gravel, and there place their eggs or spawn (after the Milter has done his natural Office) and then hide it most cunningly, and cover it over with gravel and stones; and then leave it to their Creator's protection, who by a gentle heat which he infuses into that cold element makes it brood and beget life in the spawn, and to become *Samlets* early in the spring next following.

The *Salmons* having spent their appointed time, and done this Natural Duty in the fresh waters; they then haste to the Sea before Winter, both the Milter and Spawner; but, if they be stopped by *Flood-gates* or *Weirs*, or lost in the fresh waters; then, those so left behind, by degrees grow *sick*, and *lean*, and *unseasonable*, and *kipper*; that is to say, have bony gristles grow out of their lower chaps (not unlike a Hawk's beak) which hinders their feeding, and in time such Fish so left behind, pine away and die. 'Tis observed, that he may live thus one year from the Sea; but he then grows insipid, and tasteless, and loses both his blood and strength, and pines and dies the second year. And 'tis noted, that those little *Salmons* called *Skeggers*, which abound in many Rivers relating to the *Sea*, are bred by such sick *Salmons*, that might not go to the Sea, and that though they abound, yet they never thrive to any considerable bigness.

But if the old *Salmon* gets to the Sea, then that gristle which shows him to be *kipper* wears away, or is cast off (as the *Eagle* is said to cast his bill) and he recovers his strength, and comes next Summer to the same River (if it be possible) to enjoy the former pleasures that there possessed him; for (as one has wittily observed) he has (like some persons of Honour and

Riches, which have both their Winter and Summer houses) the fresh Rivers for Summer, and the salt water for Winter to spend his life in; which is not (as Sir *Francis Bacon* hath observed in his *History of Life and Death*) above ten years: And it is to be
5   observed, that though the *Salmon* does grow big in the Sea, yet he grows not fat but in fresh Rivers; and it is observed, that the farther they get from the Sea, they be both the fatter and better.

Next, I shall tell you, that though they make very hard shift to get out of the fresh Rivers into the Sea: yet they will make
10 harder shift to get out of the salt into the fresh Rivers, to spawn, or possess the pleasures that they have formerly found in them: to which end, they will force themselves through *Flood-gates*, or over *Weirs*, or *hedges*, or *stops* in the water, even to a height beyond common belief. *Gesner* speaks of such places, as are
15 known to be above eight foot high above water. And our *Camden* mentions (in his *Britannia*) the like wonder to be in *Pembroke-shire*, where the River *Teifi* falls into the Sea, and that the fall is so down-right, and so high, that the people stand and wonder at the strength and sleight by which they see the
20 *Salmon* use to get out of the Sea into the said River; and the manner and height of the place is so notable, that it is known far by the name of the *Salmon-leap*; concerning which, take this also out of *Michael Drayton*, my honest old friend. As he tells it you in his *PolyOlbion*.

25   And when the *Salmon* seeks a fresher stream to find,
                (Which hither from the Sea, comes yearly by his kind)
                As he towards season grows, and stems the watery tract
                Where Teifi falling down, makes an high cataract,
                Forced by the rising rocks that there her course oppose
30   As though within her bounds they meant her to inclose;
                Here, when the labouring fish does at the foot arrive,
                And finds that by his strength he does but vainly strive,
                His tail takes in his mouth, and bending like a bow
                That's to full compass drawn, aloft himself doth throw,
35   Then springing at his height, as doth a little wand,
                That bended end to end, and started from man's hand
                Far off it self doth cast; so, does the *Salmon* vault,
                And if at first he fails, his second Somersault,
                He instantly essays, and from his nimble ring,
40   Still jerking, never leaves until himself he fling
                Above the opposing stream.—

This *Michael Drayton* tells you of this leap or *Somersault* of the *Salmon*.

And next I shall tell you, that it is observed by *Gesner* and others, that there is no better *Salmon* than in England: and that though some of our Northern Countries have as fat and as large as the River *Thames*, yet none are of so excellent a taste.

And as I have told you that Sir *Francis Bacon* observes, the age of a *Salmon* exceeds not ten years, so let me next tell you, that his growth is very sudden: it is said, that after he is got into the Sea, he becomes from a *Samlet*, not so big as a Gudgeon, to be a *Salmon*, in as short a time as a Gosling becomes to be a Goose. Much of this has been observed by tying a *Ribbon* or some known *tape* or *thread*, in the tail of some young *Salmons*, which have been taken in Weirs as they have swimmed toward the salt water, and then by taking a part of them again with the known mark at the same place at their return from the Sea, which is usually about six months after; and the like experiment hath been tried upon young *Swallows*, who have after six months' absence, been observed to return to the same chimney, there to make their nests and habitations for the Summer following: which has inclined many to think, that every *Salmon* usually returns to the same River in which it was bred, as young *Pigeons* taken out of the same *Dove-cote*, have also been observed to do.

And you are yet to observe further, that the He *Salmon* is usually bigger than the Spawner, and that he is more kipper, and less able to endure a winter in the fresh water, than the She is, yet she is at that time of looking less kipper and better, as watery, and as bad meat.

And yet you are to observe, that as there is no general rule without an exception, so there are some few Rivers in this Nation, that have *Trouts* and *Salmons* in season in winter, as 'tis certain there be in the River *Wye* in *Monmouth-shire*, where they be in season (as *Camden* observes) from *September* till *April*. But, my Scholar, the observation of this and many other things, I must in manners omit, because they will prove too large for our narrow compass of time, and therefore I shall next fall upon my direction *how to fish for this Salmon*.

And for that, first, you shall observe, that usually he stays not long in a place (as *Trouts* will) but (as I said) covets still to go nearer the Spring head; and that he does not (as the *Trout* and

many other fish) lie near the water side or bank or roots of trees, but swims in the deep and broad parts of the water, and usually in the middle, and near the ground; and that there you are to fish for him, and that it is to be caught as the *Trout* is, with a
5   *Worm*, a *Minnow*, (which some call a *Pink*) or with a *Fly*.

And you are to observe, that he is very seldom observed to bite at a *Minnow*, (yet sometimes he will) and not usually at a *fly*, but more usually at a *Worm*, and then most usually at a *Lob* or *Garden-worm*, which should be well scoured that is to say,
10 kept seven or eight days in Moss before you fish with them: and if you double your time of eight into sixteen, twenty or more days, it is still the better, for the worms will still be clearer, tougher, and more lively, and continue so longer upon your hook, and they may be kept longer by keeping them cool and in
15 fresh Moss, and some advise to put Camphor into it.

Note also, that many use to fish for a *Salmon* with a ring of wire on the top of their Rod, through which the Line may run to as great a length as is needful when he is hooked. And to that end, some use a wheel about the middle of their Rod, or near
20 their hand, which is to be observed better by seeing one of them, than by a large demonstration of words.

And now I shall tell you, that which may be called a secret: I have been a-fishing with old *Oliver Henley*, (now with God) a noted Fisher, both for *Trout* and *Salmon*, and have observed,
25 that he would usually take three or four worms out of his bag, and put them into a little box in his pocket, where he would usually let them continue half an hour or more, before he would bait his hook with them; I have asked him his reason, and he has replied, *He did but pick the best out to be in readiness*
30 *against he baited his hook the next time*: But he has been observed both by others, and my self, to catch more fish than I or any other body, that has ever gone a-fishing with him could do; and especially *Salmons*; and I have been told lately by one of his most intimate and secret friends, that the box in which he
35 put those worms, was anointed with a drop, or two or three, of the Oil of *Ivy berries*, made by expression or infusion; and told that by the worms remaining in that box an hour, or a like time, they had incorporated a kind of smell that was irresistibly attractive, enough to force any Fish within the smell of them, to
40 bite. This I heard not long since from a friend, but have not tried it; yet I grant it probable, and refer my Reader to Sir

Francis Bacon's Natural History, where he proves fishes may hear and doubtless can more probably smell : and I am certain *Gesner* says, the *Otter* can smell in the water, and I know not but that Fish may do so too : 'tis left for a lover of Angling, or any that desires to improve that Art, to try this conclusion.

I shall also impart two other Experiments (but not tried by myself) which I will deliver in the same words that they were given me by an excellent Angler and a very friend, in writing ; he told me the latter was too good to be told, but in a learned language, lest it should be made common.

Take the stinking oil, drawn out of Polypody *of the Oak by a retort, mixed with* Turpentine, *and* Hive-honey, *and anoint your bait therewith, and it will doubtless draw the fish to it.*

The other is this : *Vulnera hederæ grandissimæ inflicta sudant Balsamum* oleo gelato, albicantique persimile, odoris vero longe suavissimi.

'Tis supremely sweet to any fish, and yet *Asafœtida* may do the like.

But in these things I have no great faith, yet grant it probable, and have had from some chemical men (namely, from Sir *George Hastings* and others) an affirmation of them to be very advantageous : but no more of these, especially not in this place.

I might here, before I take my leave of the *Salmon*, tell you, that there is more than one sort of them, as namely, a *Tecon*, and another called in some places a *Samlet*, or by some, a *Skegger* : but these (and others which I forbear to name) may be Fish of another kind, (and differ, as we know a *Herring* and a *Pilchard* do), which I think are as different, as the Rivers in which they breed, and must by me be left to the disquisitions of men of more leisure, and of greater abilities, than I profess my self to have.

And lastly, I am to borrow so much of your promised patience, as to tell you that the *Trout* or *Salmon* being in season, have at their first taking out of the water (which continues during life) their bodies adorned, the one with such red spots, and the other with such black or blackish spots, as give them such an addition of natural beauty, as I think, was never given to any woman by the Artificial Paint or Patches in which they so much pride themselves in this Age. And so I shall leave them both and proceed to some Observations of the *Pike*.

CHAP. VIII.

Observations of the Luce *or* Pike, *with directions how to fish for him.*

Pisc. The mighty *Luce* or *Pike* is taken to be the Tyrant (as the *Salmon* is the King) of the fresh waters. 'Tis not to be doubted, but that they are bred, some by generation, and some not: as namely, of a Weed called *Pickerel-weed*, unless learned *Gesner* be much mistaken, for he says, this weed and other glutinous matter, with the help of the Sun's heat in some particular Months, and some Ponds apted for it by nature, do become *Pikes*. But doubtless divers *Pikes* are bred after this manner, or are brought into some Ponds some such other ways as is past man's finding out, of which we have daily testimonies.

Sir *Francis Bacon* in his History of Life and Death, observes the *Pike* to be the longest lived of any fresh-water-fish, and yet he computes it to be not usually above forty years; and others think it to be not above ten years; and yet *Gesner* mentions a *Pike* taken in *Swedeland* in the Year 1449 with a Ring about his neck, declaring he was put into that Pond by *Frederick* the second, more than two hundred years before he was last taken, as by the Inscription in that Ring (being Greek) was interpreted by the then Bishop of *Worms*. But of this no more, but that it is observed, that the old or very great Pikes have in them more of state than goodness; the smaller or middle sized Pikes being by the most and choicest Palates observed to be the best meat; and contrary, the Eel is observed to be the better for age and bigness.

All Pikes that live long prove chargeable to their Keepers, because their life is maintained by the death of so many other Fish, even those of their own kind, which has made him by some Writers to be called the *Tyrant* of the Rivers, or the *Fresh-water-wolf*, by reason of his bold, greedy devouring disposition; which is so keen, as *Gesner* relates, a man going to a Pond (where it seems a *Pike* had devoured all the fish) to water his Mule, had a *Pike* bite his Mule by the lips; to which the *Pike* hung so fast, that the Mule drew him out of the water, and by that accident

the owner of the Mule angled out the *Pike*. And the same *Gesner*
observes, that a maid in *Poland* had a *Pike* bite her by the foot
as she was washing clothes in a Pond. And I have heard the like
of a woman in *Kenilworth* Pond, not far from *Coventry*. But I
5 have been assured by my friend Mr *Seagrave*, (of whom I spake
to you formerly), that keeps tame *Otters*, that he hath known a
Pike in extreme hunger fight with one of his Otters for a Carp
that the Otter had caught and was then bringing out of the
water. I have told you who relates these things, and tell you they
10 are persons of credit, and shall conclude this observation, by
telling you what a wise man has observed, *It is a hard thing to
persuade the belly, because it has no ears*.

But if these relations be disbelieved, it is too evident to be
doubted, that a *Pike* will devour a Fish of his own kind, that
15 shall be bigger than his belly or throat will receive, and swallow
a part of him, and let the other part remain in his mouth till the
swallowed part be digested, and then swallow that other part
that was in his mouth, and so put it over by degrees; which is
not unlike the Ox and some other beasts, taking their meat not
20 out of their mouth immediately into their belly, but first into
some place betwixt, and then chew it, or digest it by degrees
after, which is called *Chewing the Cud*. And doubtless *Pikes*
will bite when they are not hungry, but as some think even for
very anger, when a tempting bait comes near to them.

25 And it is observed, that the *Pike* will eat venomous things (as
some kind of *Frogs* are) and yet live without being harmed by
them: for, as some say, he has in him a natural Balsam or
Antidote against all poison: and he has a strange heat, that
though it appear to us to be cold, can yet digest or put over, any
30 Fish-flesh by degrees without being sick. And others observe,
that he never eats the venomous *Frog*, till he have first killed
her, and then (as *Ducks* are observed to do to *Frogs* in spawning
time, at which time some *Frogs* are observed to be venomous)
so thoroughly washed her, by tumbling her up and down in the
35 water, that he may devour her without danger. And *Gesner*
affirms, that a *Polonian* Gentleman did faithfully assure him, he
had seen two young Geese at one time in the belly of a *Pike*.
And doubtless a *Pike* in his height of hunger will bite at and
devour a dog that swims in a Pond, and there have been
40 examples of it, or the like; for as I told you, *The belly has no
ears when hunger comes upon it*.

The *Pike* is also observed to be a solitary, melancholy and a bold Fish : Melancholy, because he always swims or rests himself alone, and never swims in shoals or with company, as *Roach* and *Dace*, and most other Fish do : And bold, because he fears not a shadow, or to see or be seen of any body, as the *Trout* and *Chub*, and all other Fish do.

And it is observed by *Gesner*, that the Jaw-bones, and Hearts, and Galls of *Pikes* are very medicinable for several diseases, or to stop blood, to abate Fevers, to cure Agues, to oppose or expel the infection of the Plague, and to be many ways medicinable and useful for the good of Mankind ; but he observes, that the biting of a *Pike* is venomous and hard to be cured.

And it is observed, that the *Pike* is a fish that breeds but once a year, and that other fish (as namely *Loaches*) do breed oftener : as we are certain tame Pigeons do almost every month, and yet the *Hawk* (a Bird of Prey, as the *Pike* is of Fish) breeds but once in twelve months : and you are to note, that his time of breeding or spawning is usually about the end of *February*, (or somewhat later, in *March*, as the weather proves colder or warmer) and to note, that his manner of breeding is thus, a He and a She *Pike* will usually go together out of a River into some ditch or creek, and that there the Spawner casts her eggs, and the Milter hovers over her all that time that she is casting her spawn, but touches her not.

I might say more of this, but it might be thought curiosity or worse, and shall therefore forbear it, and take up so much of your attention, as to tell you, that the best of *Pikes* are noted to be in *Rivers*, next those in great *Ponds*, or *Meres*, and the worst in small Ponds.

But before I proceed further, I am to tell you that there is a great antipathy betwixt the *Pike* and some *Frogs* ; and this may appear to the reader of *Dubravius* (a Bishop in *Bohemia*) who in his Book of Fish and Fish-ponds, relates what, he says, he saw with his own eyes, and could not forbear to tell the Reader. Which was :

As he and the Bishop Thurzo *were walking by a large Pond in* Bohemia, *they saw a Frog, when the Pike lay very sleepily and quiet by the shore side, leap upon his head, and the Frog having expressed malice or anger by his swollen cheeks and staring eyes, did stretch out his legs and embraced the* Pike's *head, and presently reached them to his eyes, tearing with them*

and his teeth those tender parts; the Pike *moved with anguish, moves up and down the water, and rubs himself against weeds, and whatever he thought might quit him of his enemy; but all in vain, for the frog did continue to ride triumphantly,*
5   *and to bite and torment the* Pike, *till his strength failed, and then the frog sunk with the* Pike *to the bottom of the water; then presently the frog appeared again at the top and croaked, and seemed to rejoice like a* Conqueror, *after which he presently retired to his secret hole. The Bishop, that had beheld the battle,*
10 *called his fisherman to fetch his nets, and by all means to get the* Pike, *that they might declare what had happened : and the* Pike *was drawn forth, and both his eyes eaten out, at which when they began to wonder, the Fisherman wished them to forbear, and assured them he was certain that* Pikes *were often so*
15 *served.*

I told this (which is to be read in the sixth Chapter of the Book of *Dubravius*) unto a friend, who replied, *It was as improbable as to have the mouse scratch out the cat's eyes.* But he did not consider, that there be fishing Frogs (which the
20 *Dalmatians* call the Water-Devil) of which I might tell you as wonderful a story, but I shall tell you, that 'tis not to be doubted, but that there be some Frogs so fearful of the Water-snake, that, when they swim in a place in which they fear to meet with him, they then get a reed across into their mouths, which if they two
25 meet by accident, secures the frog from the strength and malice of the *Snake*, and note, that the frog usually swims the fastest of the two.

And let me tell you, that as there be *Water-* and *Land-frogs*, so there be *Land-* and *Water-snakes*. Concerning which take
30 this observation, that the Land-snake breeds, and hatches her eggs, which become young Snakes, in some old dunghill, or a like hot place; but the Water-snake, which is not venomous (and as I have been assured by a great observer of such secrets) does not hatch but breed her young alive, which she does not
35 then forsake, but bides with them, and in case of danger will take them all into her mouth and swim away from any apprehended danger, and then let them out again when she thinks all danger to be past; These be accidents that we Anglers sometimes see and often talk of.

40 But whither am I going? I had almost lost my self by remembering the Discourse of *Dubravius*. I will therefore stop

here, and tell you according to my promise how to catch this *Pike*.

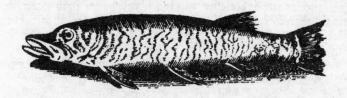

His feeding is usually of *fish* or *frogs*, and sometimes a weed of his own called *Pickerel-weed*. Of which I told you some think some *Pikes* are bred; for they have observed, that where none 5 have been put into Ponds, yet they have there found many: and that there has been plenty of that weed in those Ponds, and that that weed both breeds and feeds them; but whether those *Pikes* so bred will ever breed by generation as the others do, I shall leave to the disquisitions of men of more curiosity and leisure 10 than I profess my self to have; and shall proceed to tell you that you may fish for a *Pike*, either with a *ledger* or a *walking-bait*; and you are to note, that I call that a Ledger bait, which is fixed, or made to rest in one certain place when you shall be absent from it: and I call that a walking bait, which you take with you, 15 and have ever in motion. Concerning which two, I shall give you this direction; That your ledger bait is best to be a living bait, though a dead one may catch, whether it be a fish or a frog; and that you may make them live the longer, you may or indeed you must take this course. 20

First, for your live bait of fish, a *Roach* or *Dace* is (I think) best and most tempting, and a *Perch* is the longest lived on a hook, and having cut off his fin on his back, which may be done without hurting him, you must take your knife (which cannot be too sharp) and betwixt the head and the fin on the back, cut 25 or make an incision, or such a scar, as you may put the arming wire of your hook into it, with as little bruising or hurting the fish as art and diligence will enable you to do; and so carrying your arming wire along his back, unto, or near the tail of your Fish, betwixt the skin and the body of it, draw out that wire or 30 arming of your hook at another scar near to his tail: then tie him about it with thread, but no harder than of necessity to

prevent hurting the fish ; and the better to avoid hurting the fish, some have a kind of probe to open the way, for the more easy entrance and passage of your wire or arming : but as for these, time, and a little experience will teach you better than I can by
5   words ; therefore I will for the present say no more of this, but come next to give you some directions, how to bait your hook with a frog.

Ven. But, good Master, did you not say even now, that some *Frogs* were venomous, and is it not dangerous to touch them ?
10   *Pisc.* Yes, but I will give you some Rules or Cautions concerning them : And first, you are to note, that there are two kinds of *Frogs* ; that is to say (if I may so express my self) a *flesh-* and a *fish-frog* : by *flesh-frogs*, I mean *frogs* that breed and live on the land ; and of these there be several sorts also and
15   of several colours, some being peckled, some greenish, some blackish, or brown : the green *Frog*, which is a small one, is by *Topsell* taken to be venomous ; and so is the *paddock* or *Frog-paddock* which usually keeps or breeds on the land, and is very large and bony, and big, especially the She frog of that kind ; yet
20   these will sometimes come into the water, but it is not often ; and the land-frogs are some of them observed by him, to breed by laying eggs : and others to breed of the slime and dust of the earth, and that in winter they turn to slime again, and that the next Summer that very slime returns to be a living creature ; this
25   is the opinion of *Pliny* : and *Cardanus* undertakes to give a reason for the raining of Frogs : but if it were in my power, it should rain none but water-Frogs, for those, I think are not venomous, especially the right water-Frog, which about *February* or *March* breeds in ditches by slime, and blackish eggs in
30   that slime : about which time of breeding the He and She Frogs are observed to use divers *Somersaults* and to croak and make a noise, which the land-frog, or Paddock frog never does. Now of these water-frogs, if you intend to fish with a frog for a Pike, you are to choose the yellowest that you can get, for that the
35   Pike ever likes best. And thus use your frog, that he may continue long alive.

Put your hook into his mouth, which you may easily do from the middle of *April* till *August*, and then the frog's mouth grows up, and he continues so for at least six months without eating,

* In his 16ᵗʰ Book, *De subtil. ex.*

but is sustained, none but he whose name is Wonderful, knows how; I say, put your hook, I mean the arming-wire through his mouth, and out at his gills, and then with a fine needle and silk sew the upper part of his leg with only one stitch to the arming-wire of your hook, or tie the frog's leg above the upper joint to   5
the armed-wire; and in so doing, use him as though you loved him, that is, harm him as little as you may possibly, that he may live the longer.

And now, having given you this direction for the baiting your ledger hook with a live Fish or frog, my next must be to tell you,   10
how your hook thus baited must or may be used: and it is thus. Having fastened your hook to a line (which if it be not fourteen yards long, should not be less than twelve), you are to fasten that line to any bough near to a hole where a Pike is, or is likely to lie, or to have a haunt; and then wind your line on any   15
forked stick, all your line except half a yard of it or rather more; and split that forked stick with such a nick or notch at one end of it, as may keep the line from any more of it ravelling from about the stick, than so much of it as you intend; and choose your forked stick to be of that bigness as may keep the Fish or   20
frog from pulling the forked stick under the water till the Pike bites; and then the Pike having pulled the line forth of the cleft or nick of that stick in which it was gently fastened, he will have line enough to go to his hold and pouch the bait: and if you would have this ledger bait to keep at a fixed place, undisturbed   25
by wind or other accidents which may drive it to the shore side, (for you are to note, that it is likeliest to catch a Pike in the midst of the water) then hang a small Plummet of lead, a stone, or piece of tile, or a turf in a string, and cast it into the water, with the forked stick, to hang upon the ground to be a kind of   30
Anchor to keep the forked stick from moving out of your intended place till the Pike come. This I take to be a very good way, to use so many ledger baits as you intend to make trial of.

Or if you bait your hooks thus with live Fish or Frogs, and in a windy day, fasten them thus to a bough or bundle of straw,   35
and by the help of that wind can get them to move across a *Pond* or *mere*, you are like to stand still on the shore and see sport presently if there be any store of *Pikes*; or these live baits may make sport, being tied about the body or wings of a *Goose* or *Duck*, and she chased over a *Pond*: and the like may be done   40
with turning three or four live baits thus fastened to bladders,

or boughs, or bottles of hay or flags, to swim down a River,
whilst you walk quietly along on the shore, and are still in
expectation of sport. The rest must be taught you by practice,
for time will not allow me to say more of this kind of fishing
5 with live baits.

And for your dead bait for a *Pike*, for that you may be taught
by one day's going a-fishing with me, or any other body that
fishes for him, for the baiting your hook with a dead *Gudgeon*
or a *Roach*, and moving it up and down the water, is too easy a
10 thing to take up any time to direct you to do it; and yet, because
I cut you short in that, I will commute for it, by telling you that
that was told me for a secret: it is this:

Dissolve Gum *of* Ivy *in* Oil *of* Spike, *and therewith anoint
your dead bait for a* Pike; *and then cast it into a likely place,*
15 *and when it has lain a short time at the bottom, draw it towards
the top of the water and so up the stream; and it is more than
likely that you have a* Pike *follow with more than common
eagerness.*

And some affirm, that any bait anointed with the marrow of
20 the Thigh-bone of an *Heron* is a great temptation to any Fish.

These have not been tried by me, but told me by a friend of
note, that pretended to do me a courtesy, but if this direction to
catch a *Pike* thus, do you no good, yet I am certain this direction
how to roast him when he is caught, is choicely good, for I have
25 tried it; and it is somewhat the better for not being common;
but with my direction you must take this Caution, that your
Pike must not be a small one, that is, it must be more than half
a Yard, and should be bigger.

First open your Pike *at the gills, and if need be, cut also a*
30 *little slit towards the belly; out of these take his guts, and keep
his liver, which you are to shred very small with* Thyme, Sweet-
marjoram, *and a little* Winter-savory; *to these put some pickled*
Oysters, *and some* Anchovies, *two or three, both these last
whole (for the* Anchovies *will melt, and the* Oysters *should not);*
35 *to these you must add also a pound of sweet butter, which you
are to mix with the herbs that are shred, and let them all be well
salted (if the* Pike *be more than a yard long, then you may put
into these herbs more than a pound, or if he be less, then less
Butter will suffice): these being thus mixed with a blade or two*
40 *of* Mace, *must be put into the* Pike's *belly, and then his belly so
sewed up, as to keep all the Butter in his belly if it be possible,*

if not, then as much of it as you possibly can, but take not off
the scales; then you are to thrust the spit through his mouth out
at his tail, and then take four, or five, or six split sticks, or very
thin lathes, and a convenient quantity of Tape or Filleting, these
lathes are to be tied round about the Pike's *body from his head* 5
to his tail, and the Tape tied somewhat thick to prevent his
breaking or falling off from the spit; let him be roasted very
leisurely, and often basted with Claret wine, and Anchovies, and
Butter mixed together, and also with what moisture falls from
him into the pan: when you have roasted him sufficiently you 10
are to hold under him (when you unwind or cut the Tape that
ties him) such a dish as you purpose to eat him out of; and let
him fall into it with the sauce that is roasted in his belly, and by
this means the Pike *will be kept unbroken and complete: then,*
to the sauce which was within, and also that sauce in the pan, 15
you are to add a fit quantity of the best Butter, and to squeeze
the juice of three or four Oranges: lastly, you may either put
into the Pike *with the* Oysters, *two cloves of Garlic, and take it*
whole out, when the Pike *is cut off the spit, or to give the sauce*
a haut goût, *let the dish (into which you let the* Pike *fall) be* 20
rubbed with it: the using or not using of this Garlic is left to
your discretion.

M.B.

This dish of meat is too good for any but Anglers or very
honest men; and I trust, you will prove both, and therefore I 25
have trusted you with this secret.

Let me next tell you, that *Gesner* tells us there are no Pikes in
Spain, and that the largest are in the Lake *Trasimene* in *Italy*;
and the next, if not equal to them, are the Pikes of *England*, and
that in *England*, *Lincoln*shire boasteth to have the biggest. Just 30
so doth *Sussex* boast of four sorts of fish; namely an *Arundel*
Mullet, a *Chichester Lobster*, a *Selsey Cockle*, and an *Amberley*
Trout.

But I will take up no more of your time with this relation, but
proceed to give you some observations of the *Carp*, and how to 35
angle for him, and to dress him, but not till he is caught.

Observations of the Carp, *with Directions how to fish for him.*

Pisc. The *Carp* is the Queen of Rivers: a stately, a good, and a
very subtle fish, that was not at first bred, nor hath been long in
England, but is now naturalized. It is said, they were brought
hither by one Mr *Mascall* a Gentleman, that then lived at
Plumstead in Sussex, a County that abounds more with this fish
than any in this Nation.

You may remember that I told you, *Gesner* says, there are no
Pikes in *Spain*; and doubtless, there was a time, about a hundred
or a few more years ago, when there were no *Carps* in *England*,
as may seem to be affirmed by Sir *Richard Baker*, in whose
Chronicle you may find these Verses:

> *Hops and Turkeys, Carps and Beer*
> *Came into* England *all in a year.*

And doubtless as of Sea-fish the *Herring* dies soonest out of
the water, and of fresh-water-fish the *Trout*, so (except the *Eel*)
the *Carp* endures most hardness, and lives longest out of his
own proper Element. And therefore the report of the Carp's
being brought out of a foreign Country into this Nation is the
more probable.

Carps and Loaches are observed to Breed several months in
one year, which Pikes and most other fish do not. And this is
partly proved by tame and wild *Rabbits*, as also by some *Ducks*,
which will lay eggs nine of the twelve months, and yet there be
other *Ducks* that lay not longer than about one month. And it
is the rather to be believed, because you shall scarce or never
take a *Male-Carp* without a *Milt*, or a *Female* without a *Roe* or
spawn, and for the most part very much; and especially all the
Summer season; and it is observed, that they breed more
naturally in ponds than in running waters, (if they breed there
at all); and those that live in Rivers are taken by men of the best
palates to be much the better meat.

And it is observed, that in some ponds *Carps* will not breed, especially in cold ponds; but where they will breed, they breed innumerably; *Aristotle* and *Pliny* say, six times in a year, if there be no *Pikes* nor *Perch* to devour their Spawn, when it is cast
5 upon grass, or flags or weeds, where it lies ten or twelve days before it be enlivened.

The *Carp*, if he have water-room and good feed, will grow to a very great bigness and length: I have heard, to be much above a yard long. 'Tis said, (by *Jovius*, who hath writ of Fishes) that
10 in the Lake *Como* in *Italy*, *Carps* have thriven to be more than fifty pound weight, which is the more probable, for as the *Bear* is conceived and born suddenly; and being born is but short-lived: So on the contrary, the *Elephant* is said to be two years in his dam's belly (some think he is ten years in it) and being
15 born grows in bigness twenty years; and 'tis observed too that he lives to the Age of a hundred years. And 'tis also observed that the *Crocodile* is very long-lived, and more than that, that all that long life he thrives in bigness, and so I think some *Carps* do, especially in some places; though I never saw one above 23.
20 inches, which was a great and a goodly Fish: But have been assured there are of a far greater size, and in *England* too.

Now, as the increase of *Carps* is wonderful for their number; so there is not a reason found out, I think by any, why they should breed in some Ponds, and not in others of the same
25 nature, for soil and all other circumstances: and as their breeding, so are their decays also very mysterious: I have both read it, and been told by a Gentleman of tried honesty, that he has known sixty or more large *Carps* put into several ponds near to a house, where by reason of the stakes in the ponds, and
30 the Owner's constant being near to them, it was impossible they should be stole away from him: and that when he has after three or four years emptied the pond, and expected an increase from them by breeding young ones (for that they might do so, he had, as the rule is, put in three Milters for one Spawner) he
35 has, I say, after three or four years, found neither a young nor old *Carp* remaining. And the like I have known of one that has almost watched the pond, and at a like distance of time, at the fishing of a pond, found of seventy or eighty large *Carps* not above five or six: and that he had forborne longer to fish the
40 said pond, but that he saw in a hot day in Summer, a large *Carp* swim near the top of the water with a Frog upon his head, and

that he upon that occasion caused his pond to be let dry : and I
say, of seventy or eighty *Carps*, only found five or six in the said
pond, and those very sick and lean, and with every one a Frog
sticking so fast on the head of the said *Carps*, that the *Frog*
would not be got off without extreme force or killing : and the   5
Gentleman that did affirm this to me, told me he saw it, and did
declare his belief to be, (and I also believe the same) that he
thought the other *Carps* that were so strangely lost, were so
killed by frogs, and then devoured.

And a person of honour now living in *Worcestershire** assured   10
me he had seen a necklace or collar of Tadpoles hang like a chain
or necklace of beads about a *Pike's* neck, and to kill him ; whether
it were for meat or malice, must be to me a question.

But I am fallen into this Discourse by accident, of which I
might say more, but it has proved longer than I intended, and   15
possibly may not to you be considerable ; I shall therefore give
you three or four more short observations of the *Carp*, and then
fall upon some directions how you shall fish for him.

The age of Carps is by Sir *Francis Bacon* (in his History of
Life and Death) observed to be but ten years ; yet others think   20
they live longer. *Gesner* says a *Carp* has been known to live in
the *Palatinate* above a hundred years : But most conclude, that
(contrary to the *Pike* or *Luce*) all *Carps* are the better for age
and bigness ; the tongues of *Carps* are noted to be choice and
costly meat, especially to them that buy them : but *Gesner* says,   25
Carps have no tongue like other Fish, but a piece of flesh-like-
Fish in their mouth like to a tongue, and should be called a
palate : But it is certain it is choicely good, and that the *Carp* is
to be reckoned amongst those leather-mouthed fish, which I told
you have their teeth in their throat, and for that reason he is   30
very seldom lost by breaking his hold, if your hook be once
stuck into his chaps.

I told you that Sir *Francis Bacon* thinks that the *Carp* lives
but ten years, but *Janus Dubravius* has writ a Book of Fish and
Fish-ponds, in which he says, That *Carps* begin to Spawn at the   35
age of three years, and continue to do so till thirty : he says also,
That in the time of their breeding, which is in Summer, when
the Sun hath warmed both the earth and water, and so apted
them also for generation ; that then three or four Male-*Carps*

* *Mr. Fr. Ru.*

will follow a Female; and that then she putting on a seeming
coyness, they force her through weeds and flags, where she lets
fall her Eggs or Spawn, which sticks fast to the weeds; and then
they let fall their Milt upon it, and so it becomes in a short time
5 to be a living Fish; and as I told you, it is thought the *Carp* does
this several months in the year, and most believe that most fish
breed after this manner, except the Eel: and it has been
observed, that when the Spawner has weakened her self by
doing that natural office, that two or three Milters have helped
10 her from off the weeds, by bearing her up on both sides, and
guarding her into the deep. And you may note, that though this
may seem a curiosity not worth observing, yet others have
judged it worth their time and costs, to make *Glass-hives*, and
order them in such a manner as to see how *Bees* have bred and
15 made their *Honey-combs*, and how they have obeyed their King,
and governed their Common-wealth. But it is thought that all
Carps are not bred by generation, but that some breed other
ways, as some *Pikes* do.

   The Physicians make the *galls* and *stones* in the heads of
20 *Carps* to be very medicinable; but 'tis not to be doubted but
that in *Italy* they make great profit of the Spawn of *Carps*, by
selling it to the *Jews*, who make it into red *Caviare*, the *Jews* not
being by their Law admitted to eat of *Caviare* made of the
Sturgeon, that being a Fish that wants scales, and (as may
25 appear in *Levit.* 11.) by them reputed to be unclean.

   Much more might be said out of him, and out of *Aristotle*,
which *Dubravius* often quotes in his Discourse of Fishes; but it
might rather perplex than satisfy you, and therefore I shall
rather choose to direct you how to catch, than spend more time
30 in discoursing either of the nature or the breeding of this *CARP*,

or of any more circumstances concerning him; but yet I shall remember you of what I told you before, that he is a very subtle Fish, and hard to be caught.

And my first direction is, that if you will Fish for a *Carp*, you must put on a very large measure of *patience*; especially to fish for a *River Carp*: I have known a very good Fisher angle diligently four or six hours in a day, for three or four days together for a *River Carp*, and not have a bite: and you are to note, that in some ponds it is as hard to catch a Carp as in a River; that is to say, where they have store of feed, and the water is of a clayish colour: But you are to remember, that I have told you there is no rule without an exception, and therefore being possessed with that hope and patience which I wish to all Fishers, especially to the *Carp-Angler*, I shall tell you with what bait to fish for him. But first you are to know, that it must be either early or late; and let me tell you, that in hot weather (for he will seldom bite in cold) you cannot be too early or too late at it. And some have been so curious as to say, the 10. of *April* is a fatal day for Carps.

The Carp bites either at worms or at paste; and of worms I think the bluish Marsh or Meadow worm is best; but possibly another worm not too big may do as well, and so may a green Gentle: And as for pastes, there are almost as many sorts as there are Medicines for the Toothache, but doubtless sweet pastes are best; I mean, pastes made with honey or with sugar: which, that you may the better beguile this crafty Fish, should be thrown into the Pond or place in which you fish for him some hours or longer before you undertake your trial of skill with the Angle-rod: and doubtless if it be thrown into the water a day or two before, at several times and in small pellets, you are the likelier when you fish for the Carp to obtain your desired sport; or in a large Pond to draw them to any certain place, that they may the better and with more hope be fished for, you are to throw into it in some certain place, either Grains or Blood mixed with Cow dung, or with Bran; or any Garbage, as Chicken's guts or the like, and then some of your small sweet pellets with which you purpose to angle: and these small pellets being a few of them also thrown in as you are Angling will be the better.

And your paste must be thus made: Take the flesh of a Rabbit or Cat cut small, and Bean-flour, and if that may not be easily got, get other flour, and then mix these together, and put to them either Sugar, or Honey, which I think better, and then beat these together in a Mortar, or sometimes work them in your hands, (your hands being very clean) and then make it into a Ball, or two, or three, as you like best for your use; but you must work or pound it so long in the Mortar, as to make it so tough as to hang upon your hook without washing from it, yet not too hard; or that you may the better keep it on your hook, you may knead with your paste a little (and not much) white or yellowish wool.

And if you would have this paste keep all the year for any other Fish, then mix with it *Virgin wax* and *clarified honey*, and work them together with your hands before the Fire, then make these into balls, and they will keep all the year.

And if you fish for a Carp with Gentles, then put upon your hook a small piece of Scarlet about this bigness ▪ , it being soaked in, or anointed with *Oil of Peter*, called by some *Oil of the Rock*; and if your Gentles be put two or three days before into a box or horn anointed with honey, and so put upon your hook as to preserve them to be living, you are as like to kill this crafty fish this way as any other. But still as you are fishing chew a little white or brown bread in your mouth, and cast it into the pond about the place where your Float swims. Other baits there be, but these with diligence, and patient watchfulness, will do it better than any that I have ever practised, or heard of: And yet I shall tell you, that the crumbs of white bread and honey made into a paste is a good bait for a *Carp*, and you know it is more easily made. And having said thus much of the *Carp*, my next discourse shall be of the *Bream*, which shall not prove so tedious, and therefore I desire the continuance of your attention.

But first I will tell you how to make this *Carp* that is so curious to be caught, so curious a dish of meat, as shall make him worth all your labour and patience; and though it is not without some trouble and charges, yet it will recompense both.

Take a Carp *(alive if possible) scour him, and rub him clean with water and salt, but scale him not, then open him, and put him with his blood and his liver (which you must save when you open him) into a small pot or kettle; then take sweet Marjoram, Thyme and Parsley, of each half a handful, a sprig of Rosemary, and another of Savory, bind them into two or three small bundles, and put them to your Carp, with four or five whole Onions, twenty pickled Oysters, and three Anchovies. Then*

*pour upon your Carp as much Claret wine as will only cover
him; and season your Claret well with salt, Cloves and Mace,
and the rinds of Oranges and Lemons, that done, cover your
pot and set it on a quick-fire, till it be sufficiently boiled; then
take out the Carp and lay it with the broth into the dish, and
pour upon it a quarter of a pound of the best fresh butter melted
and beaten, with half a dozen spoonfuls of the broth, the yolks
of two or three eggs, and some of the herbs shred; garnish your
dish with Lemons and so serve it up, and much good do you.*

Dr T.

CHAP. X.

Observations of the Bream, and directions to catch him.

Pisc. The *Bream* being at a full growth is a large and stately Fish: he will breed both in Rivers and Ponds: but loves best to live in ponds, and where, if he likes the water and Air, he will grow not only to be very large, but as fat as a Hog: he is by *Gesner* taken to be more pleasant or sweet than wholesome; this Fish is long in growing, but breeds exceedingly in a water that pleases him; yea, in many Ponds so fast, as to over-store them, and starve the other Fish.

He is very broad with a forked tail, and his scales set in excellent order, he hath large eyes and a narrow sucking mouth; he hath two sets of teeth, and a lozenge-like bone, a bone to help his grinding. The Milter is observed to have two large Milts, and the Female two large bags of eggs or spawn.

Gesner reports, that in *Poland* a certain, and a great, number of large Breams were put into a Pond, which in the next following winter were frozen up into one entire ice, and not one drop of water remaining, nor one of these fish to be found, though they were diligently searched for; and yet the next Spring when the ice was thawed, and the weather warm, and fresh water got into the pond, he affirms they all appeared again. This *Gesner* affirms, and I quote my Author, because it seems almost as incredible as the *Resurrection* to an *Atheist*. But it may win something in point of believing it, to him that considers the breeding or renovation of the Silk-worm and of many insects. And that is considerable which Sir *Francis Bacon* observes in his History of Life and Death (*fol.* 20.) that there be some herbs that die and spring every year, and some endure longer.

But though some do not, yet the *French* esteem this Fish highly, and to that end have this Proverb, *He that hath Breams in his pond is able to bid his friend welcome*. And it is noted, that the best part of a Bream is his belly and head.

Some say, that *Breams* and *Roaches* will mix their eggs, and milt together, and so there is in many places a Bastard breed of *Breams*, that never come to be either large or good, but very numerous.

5 The baits good to catch this *BREAM*

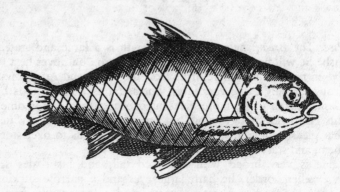

are many. 1. Paste made of brown bread and honey, gentles, or the brood of wasps that be young, (and then not unlike Gentles) and should be hardened in an oven, or dried on a tile before the fire to make them tough; or there is at the root of docks, or
10 flags, or rushes in watery places, a worm not unlike a Maggot, at which Tench will bite freely. Or he will bite at a Grasshopper with his legs nipped off in *June* and *July*, or at several flies under water, which may be found on flags that grow near to the water side. I doubt not but that there be many other baits that are
15 good, but I will turn them all into this most excellent one, either for a *Carp* or *Bream*, in any River or Mere: it was given to me by a most honest and excellent Angler, and hoping you will prove both, I will impart it to you.

1. Let your bait be as big a *red worm* as you can find, without
20 a knot. Get a pint or quart of them in an evening in garden walks, or Chalky Commons after a shower of rain; and put them with clean Moss well washed and picked, and the water squeezed out of the Moss as dry as you can, into an earthen pot or pipkin set dry, and change the Moss fresh every three or four
25 days for three weeks or a month together, then your bait will be at the best, for it will be clear and lively.

2. Having thus prepared your baits, get your tackling ready

and fitted for this sport. Take three long Angling Rods, and as
many and more silk, or silk and hair lines, and as many large
Swan or Goose-quill floats. Then take a piece of Lead made
after this manner, and fasten them to the lower ends
of your Lines. Then fasten your link-hook also to the   5
lead, and let there be about a foot or ten inches between the
lead and the hook; but be sure the lead be heavy enough to
sink the float or quill a little under the water, and not the quill
to bear up the Lead, for the lead must lie on the ground. Note,
that your link next the hook may be smaller than the rest of   10
your line, if you dare adventure for fear of taking the *Pike*
or *Perch*, who will assuredly visit your hooks, till they be taken
out (as I will show you afterwards) before either *Carp* or
Bream will come near to bite. Note also, that when the worm
is well baited, it will crawl up and down, as far as the Lead   15
will give leave, which much enticeth the Fish to bite without
suspicion.

3. Having thus prepared your baits, and fitted your tackling,
repair to the River, where you have seen them swim in schools
or shoals in the Summer time in a hot afternoon, about three or   20
four of the clock, and watch their going forth of their deep holes
and returning (which you may well discern) for they return
about four of the clock most of them seeking food at the bottom,
yet one or two will lie on the top of the water, rolling and
tumbling themselves whilst the rest are under him at the bottom,   25
and so you shall perceive him to keep Sentinel; then mark where
he plays most, and stays longest, (which commonly is in the
broadest and deepest place of the River) and there, or, near
thereabouts, at a clear bottom, and a convenient landing place,
take one of your Angles ready fitted as aforesaid, and sound the   30
bottom, which should be about eight or ten foot deep (two
yards from the bank is the best). Then consider with your self,
whether that water will rise or fall by the next morning by
reason of any Water-mills near, and according to your discretion
take the depth of the place, where you mean after to cast your   35
ground-bait, and to fish, to half an inch; that the Lead lying on
or near the ground-bait, the top of the float may only appear
upright half an inch above the water.

Thus you having found and fitted for the place and depth
thereof, then go home and prepare your ground-bait, which is   40
next to the fruit of your labours, to be regarded.

The Ground-Bait.

You shall take a peck, or a peck and a half (according to the greatness of the stream, and deepness of the water, where you mean to Angle) of sweet gross-ground barley-malt, and boil it in a kettle (one or two warms is enough) then strain it through a Bag into a tub (the liquor whereof hath often done my Horse much good) and when the bag and malt is near cold, take it down to the water-side about eight or nine of the clock in the evening, and not before; cast in two parts of your ground-bait, squeezed hard between your hands, it will sink presently to the bottom, and be sure it may rest in the very place where you mean to Angle; if the stream run hard or move a little, cast your malt in handfuls a little the higher, upwards the stream. You may between your hands close the Malt so fast in handfuls, that the water will hardly part it with the fall.

Your ground-bait thus baited, and tackling fitted, leave your bag with the rest of your tackling and ground-bait near the sporting-place all night, and in the morning about three or four of the clock visit the water-side (but not too near) for they have a cunning Watch-man, and are watchful themselves too.

Then gently take one of your three rods, and bait your hook, casting it over your ground-bait, and gently and secretly draw it to you till the Lead rests about the middle of the ground-bait.

Then take a second Rod and cast in about a yard above, and your third a yard below the first Rod, and stay the Rods in the ground, but go your self so far from the water-side, that you perceive nothing but the top of the floats, which you must watch most diligently; then when you have a bite, you shall perceive the top of your float to sink suddenly into the water; yet nevertheless be not too hasty to run to your Rods, until you see that the Line goes clear away; then creep to the water-side, and give as much Line as possibly you can: if it be a good *Carp* or *Bream*, they will go to the farther side of the River; then strike gently, and hold your Rod at a bent a little while; but if you both pull together you are sure to lose your Game, for either your line or hook, or hold will break; and after you have overcome them, they will make noble sport, and are very shy to be landed. The *Carp* is far stronger and more mettlesome than the *Bream*.

Much more is to be observed in this kind of Fish and Fishing, but it is far fitter for experience and discourse than paper. Only thus much is necessary for you to know, and, to be mindful and careful of; That if the *Pike* or *Perch* do breed in that River, they will be sure to bite first, and must first be taken. And for the most part they are very large, and will repair to your ground-bait, not that they will eat of it, but will feed and sport themselves amongst the young Fry, that gather about and hover over the Bait.

The way to discern the *Pike* and to take him, if you mistrust your *Bream*-hook (for I have taken a *Pike* a yard long several times at my *Bream*-hooks, and sometimes he hath had the luck to sheer my line); May be thus:

Take a small *Bleak*, or *Roach*, or *Gudgeon*, and bait it, and set it alive among your Rods two feet deep from the Cork, with a little red worm on the point of the hook, then take a few crumbs of White-bread, or some of the ground-bait, and sprinkle it gently amongst your Rods. If Mr *Pike* be there, then the little Fish will skip out of the water at his appearance but the live-set Bait is sure to be taken.

Thus continue your sport from four in the morning till eight, and if it be a gloomy, windy day, they will bite all day long. But this is too long to stand to your rods at one place, and it will spoil your evening sport that day; which is this:

About four of the clock in the Afternoon repair to your baited place, and as soon as you come to the water side, cast in one half of the rest of your ground-bait, and stand off: then whilst the Fish are gathering together (for there they will most certainly come for their supper) you may take a pipe of Tobacco; and then in with your three rods as in the morning: You will find excellent sport that evening till eight of the clock; then cast in the residue of your ground-bait, and next morning by four of the clock visit them again for four hours, which is the best sport of all; and after that let them rest till you and your friends have a mind to more sport.

From St *James'* Tide until *Bartholomew* Tide is the best; when they have had all the Summer's food, they are the fattest.

Observe lastly, That after three or four days' fishing together, your Game will be very shy and wary, and you shall hardly get above a bite or two at a baiting; then your only way is to desist from your sport about two or three days; and in the mean time (on the place you late baited, and again intend to bait) you shall take a turf of green, but short grass, as big or bigger than a round Trencher; to the top of this turf, on the green side, you shall with a Needle and green thread fasten one by one as many little red worms as will near cover all the turf: Then take a round board or Trencher, make a hole in the middle thereof, and through the turf placed on the board or Trencher, with a string or cord as long as is fitting, tied to a pole, let it down to the bottom of the water for the Fish to feed upon without disturbance about two or three days; and after that you have drawn it away, you may fall to, and enjoy your former recreation.

B.A.

CHAP. XI.

Observations of the Tench, *and advice how to Angle for him.*

Pisc. The *Tench*, the Physician of Fishes, is observed to love Ponds better than Rivers, and to love pits better than either; yet *Camden* observes there is a River in *Dorset-shire* that abounds with *Tenches*, but doubtless they retire to the most deep and quiet places in it.

This fish hath very large Fins, very small and smooth Scales, a red circle about his Eyes, which are big and of a gold colour, and from either Angle of his mouth there hangs down a little Barb; in every *Tench's* head there are two little stones, which foreign Physicians make great use of, but he is not commended for wholesome meat, though there be very much use made of them, for outward applications. *Rondelitius* says, That at his being at *Rome, he saw a great cure done by applying a Tench to the feet of a very sick man.* This he says was done after an unusual manner by certain Jews. And it is observed that many of those people have many secrets, yet unknown to Christians; secrets that have never yet been written, but have been since the days of their *Solomon* (who knew the nature of all things, even from the Cedar to the Shrub) delivered by tradition from the Father to the Son, and so from generation to generation without writing, or (unless it were casually) without the least communicating them to any other Nation or Tribe: for to do that they account a profanation. And yet it is thought that they, or some Spirit worse than they, first told us, that Lice swallowed alive were a certain cure for the Yellow-Jaundice. This, and many other medicines were discovered by them or by revelation, for, doubtless we attained them not by study.

Well, this fish, besides his eating, is very useful both dead and alive for the good of mankind. But I will meddle no more with that, my honest humble Art teaches no such boldness; there are too many foolish meddlers in Physick and Divinity, that think themselves fit to meddle with hidden secrets, and so bring destruction to their followers. But I'll not meddle with them any

farther than to wish them wiser; and shall tell you next (for, I hope, I may be so bold) that the *Tench* is the Physician of fishes, for the *Pike* especially, and that the *Pike*, being either sick or hurt, is cured by the touch of the *Tench*. And it is observed, that
5 the Tyrant *Pike* will not be a Wolf to his Physician, but forbears to devour him though he be never so hungry.

This fish that carries a natural Balsam in him to cure both himself and others, loves yet to feed in very foul water, and amongst weeds. And yet I am sure he eats pleasantly, and
10 doubtless, you will think so too, if you taste him. And I shall therefore proceed to give you some few, and but a few directions how to catch this *Tench*,

of which I have given you these observations.

He will bite at a Paste made of brown bread and honey, or at
15 a marsh worm, or a Lob-worm; he inclines very much to any paste with which Tar is mixed, and he will bite also at a smaller worm, with his head nippled off, and a Cod-worm put on the hook before that worm; and I doubt not but that he will also in the three hot months (for in the nine colder he stirs not much)
20 bite at a Flag-worm, or at a green Gentle, but can positively say no more of the *Tench*, he being a Fish that I have not often Angled for; but I wish my honest Scholar may, and be ever fortunate when he fishes.

CHAP. XII.

Observations of the Perch, and directions how to fish for him.

Pisc. The *Perch* is a very good, and a very bold biting fish; He is one of the Fishes of prey, that like the *Pike* and *Trout*, carries his teeth in his mouth: which is very large, and he dare venture to kill and devour several other kinds of fish: he has a hooked or hog back, which is armed with sharp and stiff bristles, and all his skin armed or covered over with thick, dry, hard scales, and hath (which few other Fish have) two Fins on his back. He is so bold, that he will invade one of his own kind, which the *Pike* will not do so willingly, and, you may therefore easily believe him to be a bold biter.

The *Perch* is of great esteem in *Italy* saith *Aldrovandus*, and especially the least are there esteemed a dainty dish. And *Gesner* prefers the *Perch* and *Pike* above the *Trout*, or any fresh-water-Fish: he says the *Germans* have this Proverb, *More wholesome than a Perch of Rhine*: and he says the River-*Perch* is so wholesome, that Physicians allow him to be eaten by wounded men or by men in Fevers, or by Women in Child-bed.

He spawns but once a year, and is by Physicians held very nutritive: yet by many to be hard of digestion: They abound more in the River *Po* and in *England* (says *Rondelitius*) than other parts, and have in their brain a stone, which is in foreign parts sold by Apothecaries, being there noted to be very medicinable against the stone in the reins: These be a part of the commendations which some Philosophical brains have bestowed upon the fresh-water *Perch*: yet they commend the Sea-*Perch*, which is known by having but one fin on his back (of which they say, we *English* see but a few) to be a much better fish.

The *Perch* grows slowly, yet will grow, as I have been credibly informed, to be almost two foot long; for an honest informer told me, such a one was not long since taken by Sir *Abraham Williams*, a Gentleman of worth, and a Brother of the Angle (that yet lives, and I wish he may): this was a deep bodied Fish: and doubtless durst have devoured a *Pike* of half his own

length: for I have told you, he is a bold Fish, such a one as but
for extreme hunger, the *Pike* will not devour: for to affright the
Pike and save himself, the *Perch* will set up his fins, much like
as a *Turkey-Cock* will sometimes set up his tail.

5   But, my Scholar, the *Perch* is not only valiant to defend
himself, but he is (as I said) a bold biting fish, yet he will not
bite at all seasons of the year; he is very abstemious in Winter,
yet will bite then in the midst of the day if it be warm: and note
that all Fish bite best about the midst of a warm day in Winter,

10   and he hath been observed by some not usually to bite till the
Mulberry-tree buds; that is to say, till extreme frosts be past
that Spring; for when the *Mulberry-tree* blossoms, many Gar-
deners observe their forward fruit to be past the danger of
Frosts, and some have made the like observation of the *Perch's*

15   biting.
But bite the *Perch* will, and that very boldly: and as one has
wittily observed, if there be twenty or forty in a hole, they may
be at one standing all catched one after another; they being, as
he says, like the wicked of the world, not afraid though their

20   fellows and companions perish in their sight. And you may
observe, that they are not like the solitary *Pike*, but love to
accompany one another, and march together in troops.
And the baits for this bold Fish

are not many; I mean, he will bite as well at some, or at any of

25   these three, as at any, or all others whatsoever: a *Worm*, a
Minnow, or a little *Frog* (of which you may find many in hay-
time); and of *worms*, the Dunghill-worm called a *Brandling* I
take to be best, being well scoured in Moss or Fennel; or he will
bite at a worm that lies under a cow-turd with a bluish head.

30   And if you *rove* for a *Perch* with a *Minnow*, then it is best to be

alive, you sticking your hook through his back-fin; or a *Minnow*
with the hook in his upper lip, and letting him swim up and
down about mid-water, or a little lower, and you still keeping
him to about that depth, by a Cork, which ought not to be a
very little one: and the like way you are to Fish for the *Perch*,   5
with a small frog, your hook being fastened through the skin of
his leg, towards the upper part of it: And lastly, I will give you
but this advice, that you give the *Perch* time enough when he
bites, for there was scarce ever any Angler that has given him
too much. And now I think best to rest my self, for I have   10
almost spent my spirits with talking so long.

Venat. Nay, good Master, one fish more, for you see it rains
still, and you know our Angles are like money put to usury;
they may thrive though we sit still and do nothing but talk and
enjoy one another. Come, come the other fish, good Master.   15

Pisc. But Scholar, have you nothing to mix with this discourse,
which now grows both tedious and tiresome? shall I have
nothing from you that seem to have both a good memory, and
a cheerful Spirit?

Ven. Yes, Master, I will speak you a Copy of Verses that were   20
made by Doctor *Donne*, and made to show the world that he
could make soft and smooth Verses when he thought smoothness worth his labour; and I love them the better, because they
allude to Rivers, and fish and fishing. They be these:

> Come live with me, and be my Love,   25
> And we will some new pleasures prove,
> Of golden sands, and Crystal brooks,
> With silken lines, and silver hooks.

> There will the River whispering run,
> Warmed by thy eyes more than the Sun;   30
> And there the enamelled fish will stay,
> Begging themselves they may betray.

> When thou wilt swim in that live bath,
> Each fish, which every channel hath,
> Most amorously to thee will swim,   35
> Gladder to catch thee, than thou him.

> If thou, to be so seen, beest loath
> By Sun or Moon, thou darkenest both;

And if mine eyes have leave to see,
I need not their light, having thee.

Let others freeze with Angling reeds,
And cut their legs with shells and weeds,
Or treacherously poor fish beset,
With strangling snares, or windowy net.

Let coarse bold hands, from slimy nest,
The bedded fish in banks outwrest,
Let curious Traitors sleave silk flies,
To 'witch poor wandering fishes' eyes.

For thee, thou need'st no such deceit,
For thou thy self art thine own bait:
That fish that is not catched thereby,
Is wiser far, alas, than I.

Pisc. Well remembered, honest Scholar, I thank you for these choice Verses, which I have heard formerly, but had quite forgot, till they were recovered by your happy memory. Well, being I have now rested my self a little, I will make you some requital, by telling you some observations of the *Eel*, for it rains still, and because (as you say) our *Angles* are as money put to Use that thrives when we play, therefore we'll sit still and enjoy our selves a little longer under this *honey-suckle-hedge*.

CHAP. XIII.

Observations of the Eel, and other fish that want scales, and how to fish for them.

Pisc. It is agreed by most men, that the *Eel* is a most dainty fish; the Romans have esteemed her the *Helena* of their feasts, and some *The Queen of palate pleasure*. But most men differ about their breeding: some say they breed by generation as other fish do, and others, that they breed (as some worms do) of mud, as Rats and Mice, and many other living creatures are bred in *Egypt*, by the Sun's heat when it shines upon the overflowing of the River *Nile*: or out of the putrefaction of the earth, and divers other ways. Those that deny them to breed by generation as other fish do; ask: if any man ever saw an *Eel* to have a Spawn or Milt? and they are answered, that they may be as certain of their breeding as if they had seen Spawn: for they say, that they are certain that *Eels* have all parts fit for generation, like other fish, but so small as not to be easily discerned, by reason of their fatness; but that discerned they may be, and that the He and the She *Eel* may be distinguished by their fins. And *Rondelitius* says, he has seen *Eels* cling together like *Dew-worms*.

And others say, that *Eels* growing old breed other *Eels* out of the corruption of their own age, which Sir *Francis Bacon* says, exceeds not ten years. And others say, that as *Pearls* are made of glutinous dew-drops, which are condensed by the Sun's heat in those Countries, so *Eels* are bred of a particular dew falling in the months of *May* or *June* on the banks of some particular Ponds or Rivers (apted by nature for that end) which in a few days are by the Sun's heat turned into *Eels*, and some of the Ancients have called the *Eels* that are thus bred, *The Off-spring of Jove*. I have seen in the beginning of *July*, in a River not far from *Canterbury*, some parts of it covered over with young *Eels*, about the thickness of a straw; and these *Eels* did lie on the top of that water, as thick as motes are said to be in the Sun: and I have heard the like of other Rivers, as namely in *Severn*, (where they are called *Yelvers*) and in a *pond* or *mere* near unto

Stafford-shire, where about a set time in Summer, such small
Eels abound so much, that many of the poorer sort of people,
that inhabit near to it take such *Eels* out of this Mere, with
sieves or sheets, and make a kind of Eel-cake of them, and eat it
5   like as Bread. And *Gesner* quotes venerable *Bede* to say, that in
England there is an Island called *Ely*, by reason of the innumer-
able number of *Eels* that breed in it. But that *Eels* may be bred
as some worms, and some kind of *Bees* and *Wasps* are, either of
dew, or out of the corruption of the earth, seems to be made
10 probable by the *Barnacles* and young *Goslings* bred by the Sun's
heat, and the rotten planks of an old Ship, and hatched of trees ;
both which are related for truths by *Dubartas* and *Lobel*, and
also by our learned *Camden*, and laborious *Gerard* in his
Herbal.

15 It is said by *Rondelitius*, that those *Eels* that are bred in Rivers
that relate to, or be nearer to the Sea, never return to the fresh
waters (as the *Salmon* does always desire to do) when they have
once tasted the salt water ; and I do the more easily believe this,
because I am certain that powdered Beef is a most excellent bait
20 to catch an *Eel* : and though Sir *Francis Bacon* will allow the
Eel's life to be but ten years ; yet he in his History of Life and
Death, mentions a *Lamprey* belonging to the *Roman* Emperor
to be made tame, and so kept for almost threescore years : and
that such useful and pleasant observations were made of this
25 *Lamprey*, that *Crassus* the Orator (who kept her) lamented her
Death. And we read (in Doctor *Hakewill*) that *Hortensius* was
seen to weep at the death of a *Lamprey* that he had kept long,
and loved exceedingly.

It is granted by all, or most men, that *Eels*, for about six
30 months (that is to say, the six cold months of the year) stir not
up and down, neither in the Rivers, nor in the Pools in which
they usually are, but get into the soft earth or mud, and there
many of them together bed themselves, and live without feeding
upon any thing (as I have told you some *Swallows* have been
35 observed to do in hollow trees for those six cold months) : and
this the *Eel* and *Swallow* do, as not being able to endure winter
weather : For *Gesner* quotes *Albertus* to say, that in the year
1125. (that year's winter being more cold than usually) *Eels* did
by nature's instinct get out of the water into a stack of hay in a
40 Meadow upon dry ground, and there bedded themselves, but
yet at last a frost killed them. And our *Camden* relates, that in

Lancashire Fishes were digged out of the earth with Spades, where no water was near to the place. I shall say little more of the Eel, but that, as it is observed he is impatient of cold; so it hath been observed, that in warm weather an *Eel* has been known to live five days out of the water.   5

And lastly, let me tell you that some curious searchers into the natures of Fish, observe that there be several sorts or kinds of *Eels*, as the *silver Eel*, and green or *greenish Eel* (with which the River of *Thames* abounds, and those are called *Grigs*); and a *blackish Eel*, whose head is more flat and bigger than ordinary   10 *Eels*; and also an *Eel* whose Fins are reddish, and but seldom taken in this Nation, (and yet taken sometimes): These several kinds of *Eels* are (say some) diversely bred; as namely, out of the corruption of the earth, and some by dew, and other ways, (as I have said to you): and yet it is affirmed by some for a certain,   15 that the *silver Eel* is bred by generation, but not by Spawning as other Fish do, but that her brood come alive from her, being then little live Eels no bigger nor longer than a pin; and I have had too many testimonies of this to doubt the truth of it my self, and if I thought it needful I might prove it, but I think it is needless.   20

And this Eel of which I have said so much to you, may be caught with divers kinds of Baits: as namely with powdered Beef, with a *Lob* or *Garden-worm*, with a *Minnow*, or gut of a *Hen*, *Chicken*, or the guts of any Fish, or with almost any thing, for he is a greedy Fish; but the Eel may be caught especially   25 with a little, a very little *Lamprey* which some call a *Pride*, and may in the hot months be found many of them in the River *Thames*, and in many mud-heaps in other Rivers, yea, almost as usually as one finds worms in a dunghill.

Next note, that the Eel seldom stirs in the day, but then hides   30 himself, and therefore he is usually caught by night with one of these baits of which I have spoken, and may be then caught by laying hooks, which you are to fasten to the bank or twigs of a tree; or by throwing a string across the stream with many hooks at it, and those baited with the aforesaid Baits, and a clod, or   35 plummet, or stone, thrown into the River with this line, that so you may in the morning find it near to some fixed place, and then take it up with a Drag-hook or otherwise: but these things are indeed too common to be spoken of, and an hour's fishing with any Angler will teach you better, both for these and many   40 other common things in the practical part of *Angling*, than a week's discourse. I shall therefore conclude this direction for taking the *Eel*, by telling you, that in a warm day in Summer I have taken many a good Eel by *sniggling* and have been much pleased with that sport.

5   And because you that are but a young Angler know not what sniggling is, I will now teach it to you. You remember I told you that Eels do not usually stir in the day time, for then they hide themselves under some covert, or under boards or planks about Flood-gates, or Weirs, or Mills, or in holes in the River banks;

10   so that you observing your time in a warm day, when the water is lowest, may take a strong small hook tied to a strong line, or to a string about a yard long, and then into one of these holes, or between any boards about a Mill, or under any great stone or plank, or any place where you think an Eel may hide or

15   shelter her self, you may with the help of a short stick put in your bait, but leisurely, and as far as you may conveniently: and it is scarce to be doubted, but that if there be an Eel within the sight of it, the Eel will bite instantly, and as certainly gorge it: and you need not doubt to have him if you pull him not out

20   of the hole too quickly, but pull him out by degrees, for he lying folded double in his hole, will with the help of his tail break all, unless you give him time to be wearied with pulling, and so get him out by degrees; not pulling too hard.

And to commute for your patient hearing this long Direction

25   I shall next tell you how to make this *EEL*

a most excellent dish of meat:

First, wash him in water and salt, then pull off his skin below his vent or navel, and not much further: having done that, take out his guts as clean as you can, but wash him not: then give

him three or four scotches with a knife, and then put into his
belly and those scotches, sweet herbs, an Anchovy, and a little
Nutmeg grated or cut very small, and your herbs and Anchovies
must also be cut very small, and mixed with good butter and
salt; having done this, then pull his skin over him all but his 5
head, which you are to cut off, to the end you may tie his skin
about that part where his head grew, and it must be so tied as
to keep all his moisture within his skin: and having done this,
tie him with Tape or Pack-thread to a spit, and roast him
leisurely, and baste him with water and salt till his skin breaks, 10
and then with Butter: and having roasted him enough, let what
was put into his belly, and what he drips be his sauce.

S.F.

When I go to dress an Eel thus, I wish he were as long and big,
as that which was caught in *Peterborough* River in the year 15
1667. which was a yard and three quarters long. If you will not
believe me ? then go and see at one of the *Coffee-houses* in *King-
street* in *Westminster*.

But now let me tell you, that though the Eel thus dressed be
not only excellent good, but more harmless than any other way, 20
yet it is certain, that Physicians account the Eel dangerous meat ;
I will advise you therefore, as *Solomon* says of Honey, Prov. 25.
Hast thou found it, eat no more than is sufficient, lest thou
surfeit, for it is not good to eat much honey. And let me add this
that the uncharitable *Italian* bids us, *Give Eels, and no wine to* 25
our Enemies.

And I will beg a little more of your attention to tell you that
Aldrovandus and divers Physicians commend the Eel very much
for medicine though not for meat. But let me tell you one
observation ; That the Eel is never out of season, as *Trouts* and 30
most other fish are at set times, at least most Eels are not.

I might here speak of many other Fish whose shape and nature
are much like the Eel, and frequent both the *Sea* and fresh
Rivers ; as namely the *Lamprel*, the *Lamprey* and the *Lampern* :
as also of the mighty *Conger*, taken often in *Severn*, about 35
Gloucester ; and might also tell in what high esteem many of
them are for the curiosity of their taste ; but these are not so
proper to be talked of by me, because they make us Anglers no
sport, therefore I will let them alone as the Jews do, to whom
they are forbidden by their Law. 40

And Scholar, there is also a Flounder, a Sea-fish, which will wander very far into fresh Rivers, and there lose himself, and dwell and thrive to a hand's breadth, and almost twice so long, a fish without scales, and most excellent meat, and a fish that
5 affords much sport to the Angler, with any small worm, but especially a little bluish worm, gotten out of Marsh ground or Meadows, which should be well scoured; but this though it be most excellent meat, yet it wants scales, and is as I told you therefore an abomination to the Jews.

10 But Scholar, there is a fish that they in *Lancashire* boast very much of, called a *Char*, taken there, (and I think there only) in a Mere called *Windermere*; a Mere, says *Camden*, that is the largest in this Nation, being ten miles in length, and some say as smooth in the bottom as if it were paved with polished marble:
15 this fish never exceeds fifteen or sixteen inches in length; and 'tis spotted like a *Trout*, and has scarce a bone but on the back: but this, though I do not know whether it make the Angler sport, yet I would have you take notice of it, because it is a rarity, and of so high esteem with persons of great note.

20 Nor would I have you ignorant of a rare fish called a *Gwyniad*, of which I shall tell you what *Camden*, and others speak. The River *Dee* (which runs by *Chester*) springs in *Merionethshire*, and as it runs toward *Chester* it runs through *Pemble-Mere*, which is a large water. And it is observed, that
25 though the River *Dee* abounds with *Salmon*, and *Pemble-Mere* with the *Gwyniad*, yet there is never any *Salmon* caught in the *Mere*, nor a *Gwyniad* in the River. And now my next observation shall be of the *Barbel*.

CHAP. XIV.

Observations of the Barbel, and directions how to fish for him.

Pisc. The *Barbel* is so called (says *Gesner*) by reason of his Barb or Wattles at his mouth, which are under his nose or chaps. He is one of those leather-mouthed Fishes that I told you of, that does very seldom break his hold if he be once hooked: but he is so strong, that he will often break both rod or line if he proves to be a big one.

But the *Barbel*, though he be of a fine shape, and looks big, yet he is not accounted the best fish to eat, neither for his wholesomeness nor his taste: But the Male is reputed much better than the Female, whose Spawn is very hurtful, as I will presently declare to you.

They flock together like sheep, and are at the worst in *April*, about which time they Spawn, but quickly grow to be in season. He is able to live in the strongest swifts of the Water (and in Summer they love the shallowest and sharpest streams); and loves to lurk under weeds, and to feed on gravel against a rising ground, and will root and dig in the sands with his nose like a hog, and there nests himself: yet sometimes he retires to deep and swift Bridges, or Flood-gates, or Weirs, where he will nest himself amongst piles, or in hollow places, and take such hold of moss or weeds, that be the water never so swift, it is not able to force him from the place that he contends for. This is his constant custom in Summer, when he and most living creatures sport themselves in the Sun, but at the approach of Winter, then he forsakes the swift streams and shallow waters, and by degrees retires to those parts of the River that are quiet and deeper; in which places (and I think about that time) he Spawns, and as I have formerly told you, with the help of the Milter, hides his Spawn or eggs in holes, which they both dig in the gravel, and then they mutually labour to cover it with the same sand, to prevent it from being devoured by other fish.

There be such store of this fish in the River *Danube*, that *Rondelitius* says, that may in some places of it, and in some

months of the year, be taken by those that dwell near to the
River, with their hands, eight or ten load at a time; he says, they
begin to be good in *May*, and that they cease to be so in *August*,
but it is found to be otherwise in this Nation: but thus far we
5   agree with him, that the Spawn of a *Barbel*, if it be not poison
as he says, yet that it is dangerous meat, and especially in the
month of *May*; which is so certain, that *Gesner* and *Gasius*
declare, it had an ill effect upon them even to the endangering
of their lives.
10   This fish is of a fine cast and handsome shape, with small
scales, which are placed after a most exact and curious manner,

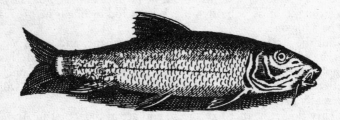

and, as I told you, may be rather said not to be ill, than to be
good meat; the *Chub* and he have (I think) both lost part of
their credit by ill cookery, they being reputed the worst or
15   coarsest of fresh-water-fish: but the *Barbel* affords an *Angler*
choice sport, being a lusty and a cunning Fish: so lusty and
cunning as to endanger the breaking of the Angler's line, by
running his head forcibly towards any covert, or hole, or bank:
and then striking at the line, to break it off with his tail (as is
20   observed by *Plutarch*, in his Book *de industria animalium*) and
also so cunning as to nibble and suck off your worm close to
the hook, and yet avoid the letting the hook come into his
mouth.
    The *Barbel* is also curious for his baits, that is to say, that
25   they be clean and sweet; that is to say, to have your worms well
scoured, and not kept in sour and musty moss, for he is a
curious feeder; but at a well-scoured Lob-worm, he will bite as
boldly as at any bait, and specially, if the night or two before
you fish for him, you shall bait the places where you intend to
30   fish for him with big worms cut into pieces: and note, that none
did ever over-bait the place, nor fish too early or too late for a

Barbel. And the *Barbel* will bite also at Gentles, which (not being too much scoured, but green) are a choice bait for him; and so is cheese, which is not to be too hard, but kept a day or two in a wet linen cloth to make it tough: with this you may also bait the water a day or two before you fish for the *Barbel*, and be much the likelier to catch store: and if the cheese were laid in clarified honey a short time before (as namely, an hour or two) you were still the likelier to catch Fish: some have directed to cut the cheese into thin pieces, and toast it, and then tie it on the hook with fine silk: and some advise to fish for the *Barbel* with Sheep's tallow and soft cheese beaten or worked into a Paste, and that it is choicely good in *August*, and I believe it: but doubtless the Lob-worm well scoured, and the Gentle not too much scoured, and cheese ordered as I have directed, are baits enough, and I think will serve in any month; though I shall commend any Angler that tries conclusions, and is industrious to improve the Art. And now, my honest Scholar, the long shower, and my tedious discourse are both ended together: and I shall give you but this Observation, that when you fish for a *Barbel*, your Rod and Line be both long, and of good strength, for (as I told you) you will find him a heavy and a dogged fish to be dealt withal, yet he seldom or never breaks his hold if he be once strucken. And if you would know more of fishing for the *Umber* or *Barbel*, get into favour with Doctor *Sheldon*, whose skill is above others'; and of that the Poor that dwell about him have a comfortable experience.

And now let's go and see what interest the *Trouts* will pay us for letting our *Angle-rods* lie so long, and so quietly in the water for their use. Come, Scholar, which will you take up?

Ven. Which you think fit, Master.

Pisc. Why, you shall take up that; for I am certain by viewing the Line, it has a Fish at it. Look you, Scholar: well done. Come now, take up the other too; well, now you may tell my brother *Peter* at night, that you have caught a leash of *Trouts* this day. And now let's move toward our lodging, and drink a draught of *Red-Cow's Milk*, as we go, and give pretty *Maudlin* and her honest mother a brace of *Trouts* for their supper.

Venat. Master, I like your motion very well and I think it is now about milking time, and yonder they be at it.

Pisc. God speed you, good woman, I thank you both for our Songs last night; I and my companion have had such fortune a-fishing this day, that we resolve to give you and *Maudlin* a brace of *Trouts* for supper, and we will now taste a draught of your *Red-Cow's milk*.

Milkw. Marry, and that you shall with all my heart, and I will be still your debtor when you come this way: if you will but speak the word, I will make you a good *Sillabub*, of new Verjuice, and then you may sit down in a *hay-cock* and eat it, and *Maudlin* shall sit by and sing you the good old Song of the *Hunting in Chevy Chase*, or some other good Ballad, for she hath good store of them; *Maudlin*, my honest *Maudlin* hath a notable memory, and she thinks nothing too good for you, because you be such honest men.

Venat. We thank you, and intend once in a month to call upon you again, and give you a little warning, and so good night: good night *Maudlin*. And now, good Master, let's lose no time; but tell me somewhat more of Fishing, and if you please, first something of Fishing for a *Gudgeon*.

Pisc. I will, honest Scholar.

CHAP. XV.

Observations of the Gudgeon, the Ruff and the Bleak, and how to fish for them.

The *Gudgeon* is reputed a Fish of excellent taste, and to be very wholesome: he is of a fine shape, of a silver colour, and beautified with black spots on his body and tail. He breeds two or three times in the year, and always in Summer. He is commended for a Fish of excellent nourishment: the *Germans* call him *Groundling*, by reason of his feeding on the ground: and he there feasts himself in sharp streams, and on the gravel. He and the *Barbel* both feed so, and do not hunt for flies at any time, as most other Fishes do: he is an excellent fish to enter a young Angler, being easy to be taken with a small red worm, on or very near to the ground. He is one of those leather-mouthed fish that has his teeth in his throat, and will hardly be lost off from the hook if he be once strucken: they be usually scattered up and down every River in the shallows, in the heat of Summer: but in *Autumn*, when the weeds begin to grow sour or rot, and the weather colder, then they gather together, and get into the deeper parts of the water: and are to be Fished for there, with your hook always touching the ground, if you Fish for him with a float, or with a cork: But many will Fish for the *Gudgeon* by hand, with a running-line upon the ground, without a cork, as a *Trout* is fished for, and it is an excellent way, if you have a gentle rod and as gentle a hand.

There is also another Fish called a *Pope*, and by some a *Ruff*, a Fish that is not known to be in some Rivers; he is much like the *Perch* for his shape, and taken to be better than the *Perch*, but will not grow to be bigger than a *Gudgeon*; he is an excellent Fish, no Fish that swims is of a pleasanter taste, and he is also excellent to enter a young *Angler*, for he is a greedy biter, and they will usually lie abundance of them together in one reserved place where the water is deep, and runs quietly; and an easy Angler, if he has found where they lie, may catch forty or fifty, or sometimes twice so many at a standing.

You must Fish for him with a small red-worm, and if you bait the ground with earth, it is excellent.

There is also a *Bleak*, or fresh-water-Sprat, a Fish that is ever in motion, and therefore called by some the *River-Swallow*; for just as you shall observe the *Swallow* to be most evenings in Summer ever in motion, making short and quick turns when he
5 flies to catch Flies in the air (by which he lives) so does the *Bleak* at the top of the water. *Ausonius* would have him called *Bleak* from his whitish colour: his back is of a pleasant sad or Sea-water-green, his belly white and shining as the Mountain-snow: and doubtless though he have the fortune (which virtue has in
10 poor people) to be neglected, yet the *Bleak* ought to be much valued, though we want *Allamot* salt, and the skill that the *Italians* have to turn them into Anchovies. This fish may be caught with a *Pater-noster* line, that is, six or eight very small hooks tied along the line one half a foot above the other: I have
15 seen five caught thus at one time, and the bait has been Gentles, than which none is better.

Or this fish may be caught with a fine small artificial fly, which is to be of a very sad, brown colour, and very small, and the hook answerable. There is no better sport than whipping for
20 *Bleaks* in a boat, or on a bank in the swift water in a Summer's evening, with a Hazel top about five or six foot long, and a line twice the length of the Rod. I have heard Sir *Henry Wotton* say, that there be many that in *Italy* will catch *Swallows* so, or especially *Martins* (this *Bird-angler* standing on the top of a
25 Steeple to do it, and with a line twice so long as I have spoken of): And let me tell you, Scholar, that both *Martins* and *Bleaks* be most excellent meat.

And let me tell you, that I have known a *Heron* that did constantly frequent one place, caught with a hook baited with a
30 big Minnow or a small *Gudgeon*. The line and hook must be strong, and tied to some loose staff so big as she cannot fly away with it, a line not exceeding two Yards.

Is of nothing; or, that which is nothing worth.

My purpose was to give you some directions concerning *Roach* and *Dace*, and some other inferior Fish, which make the Angler excellent sport, for you know there is more pleasure in Hunting the *Hare* than in eating her: but I will forbear at this time to say any more, because you see yonder come our brother *Peter* and honest *Corydon*: but I will promise you, that as you and I fish and walk tomorrow towards *London*, if I have now forgotten any thing that I can then remember, I will not keep it from you.

Well met, Gentlemen, this is lucky that we meet so just together at this very door. Come Hostess, where are you? is Supper ready? come, first give us drink, and be as quick as you can, for I believe we are all very hungry. Well, brother *Peter* and *Corydon*, to you both; come drink, and then tell me *what luck of fish*: we two have caught but ten Trouts, of which my Scholar caught three; look here's eight, and a brace we gave away: we have had a most pleasant day for fishing and talking, and are returned home both weary and hungry, and now meat and rest will be pleasant.

Pet. And *Corydon* and I have not had an unpleasant day, and yet I have caught but five Trouts: for indeed we went to a good honest Ale-house, and there we played at Shovel-board half the day; all the time that it rained we were there, and as merry as they that fished, and I am glad we are now with a dry house over our heads, for hark how it rains and blows. Come Hostess, give us more Ale, and our supper with what haste you may; and when we have supped let us have your Song, *Piscator*, and the Catch that your Scholar promised us, or else *Corydon* will be dogged.

Pisc. Nay, I will not be worse than my word, you shall not want my Song, and I hope I shall be perfect in it.

Venat. And I hope the like for my Catch, which I have ready too, and therefore let's go merrily to supper, and then have a gentle touch at singing and drinking: but the last with moderation.

Cor. Come, now for your Song, for we have fed heartily. Come Hostess, lay a few more sticks on the fire, and now sing when you will.

Pisc. Well then, here's to you *Corydon*; and now for my
5 Song.

Oh the gallant Fisher's life,
It is the best of any,
'Tis full of pleasure, void of strife,
And 'tis belov'd of many:
10   Other joys
        are but toys,
        only this
        lawful is,
        for our skill
15   breeds no ill,
but content and pleasure.

In a morning up we rise,
Ere Aurora's peeping,
Drink a cup to wash our eyes,
20 Leave the sluggard sleeping:
        Then we go
        to and fro,
        with our knacks
        at our backs,
25   to such streams
        as the Thames,
if we have the leisure.

When we please to walk abroad
For our recreation,
30 In the fields is our abode,
Full of delectation.
        Where in a brook
        with a book,
        or a Lake,
35   fish we take,
        there we sit,
        for a bit,
till we fish entangle.

We have Gentles in a horn,
40 We have paste and worms too,

We can watch both night and morn,
Suffer rain and storms too:
   None do here
   use to swear,
   oaths do fray   5
   fish away,
   we sit still,
   and watch our quill;
Fishers must not wrangle.

If the Sun's excessive heat   10
Make our bodies swelter,
To an Osier *hedge we get*
For a friendly shelter,
   Where in a dike
   Perch *or* Pike,   15
   Roach *or* Dace
   we do chase,
   Bleak *or* Gudgeon
   without grudging,
we are still contented.   20

Or we sometimes pass an hour
Under a green Willow,
That defends us from a shower,
Making earth our pillow,
   Where we may   25
   think and pray,
   before death
   stops our breath:
   other joys
   are but toys,   30
and to be lamented.
               John Chalkhill.

Venat. Well sung, Master, this day's fortune and pleasure, and this night's company and song, do all make me more and more in love with *Angling*. Gentlemen, my Master left me alone for 35 an hour this day, and I verily believe he retired himself from talking with me, that he might be so perfect in this song; was it not Master?

   Pisc. Yes indeed, for it is many years since I learned it, and having forgotten a part of it, I was forced to patch it up by the 40

help of mine own Invention, who am not excellent at Poetry, as my part of the song may testify: But of that I will say no more, lest you should think I mean by discommending it to beg your commendations of it. And therefore without replications let's
5 hear your Catch, Scholar, which I hope will be a good one, for you are both Musical, and have a good fancy to boot.

Venat. Marry and that you shall, and as freely as I would have my honest Master tell me some more secrets of fish and Fishing as we walk and fish towards *London* tomorrow. But
10 Master, first let me tell you, that, that very hour which you were absent from me, I sat down under a *Willow-tree* by the water-side, and considered what you had told me of the Owner of that pleasant Meadow in which you then left me; that he had a plentiful estate, and not a heart to think so; that he had at this
15 time many Law-suits depending, and that they both dampened his mirth, and took up so much of his time and thoughts, that he himself had not leisure to take the sweet content that I (who pretended no title to them), took in his fields; for I could there sit quietly, and looking on the water, see some Fishes sport
20 themselves in the silver streams, others, leaping at Flies of several shapes and colours; looking on the Hills, I could behold them spotted with Woods and Groves; looking down the Meadows, could see here a Boy gathering *Lilies* and *Lady-smocks*, and there a Girl cropping *Culverkeys* and *Cow-slips*, all
25 to make Garlands suitable to this present Month of *May*: these and many other Field-flowers, so perfumed the Air, that I thought that very Meadow like that Field in *Sicily* (of which *Diodorus* speaks) where the perfumes arising from the place, make all Dogs that hunt in it, to fall off, and to lose their hottest
30 scent. I say, as I thus sat joying in my own happy condition, and pitying this poor rich man, that owned this and many other pleasant Groves and Meadows about me, I did thankfully remember what my Saviour said, that the *meek possess the Earth*; or rather, they enjoy what the other possess and enjoy
35 not, for Anglers and meek quiet-spirited-men, are free from those high, those restless thoughts which corrode the sweets of life; and they, and they only can say as the Poet has happily expressed it:

        Hail blest estate of lowliness!
40   *Happy enjoyments of such minds,*

> As rich in self-contentedness,
>   Can, like the reeds in roughest winds
>   By yielding make that blow but small
>   At which proud Oaks and Cedars fall.

There came also into my mind at that time, certain Verses in
praise of a mean estate, and an humble mind, they were written
by *Phineas Fletcher*: an excellent Divine, and an excellent
Angler, and the Author of excellent piscatory Eclogues, in which
you shall see the picture of this good man's mind, and I wish
mine to be like it.

> No empty hopes, no Courtly fears him fright,
>   No begging wants, his middle fortune bite,
> But sweet content exiles both misery and spite.
>
> His certain life, that never can deceive him,
> Is full of thousand sweets, and rich content;
> The smooth-leaved beeches in the field receive him,
> With coolest shade, till noon-tide's heat be spent:
>   His life, is neither tossed in boisterous Seas,
>   Or the vexatious world, or lost in slothful ease;
> Pleased and full blest he lives, when he his God can please.
>
> His bed, more safe than soft, yields quiet sleeps,
> While by his side his faithful Spouse hath place,
>   His little son, into his bosom creeps,
>   The lively picture of his father's face.
> His humble house, or poor state ne'er torment him,
> Less he could like, if less his God had lent him,
> And when he dies, green turfs do for a tomb content him.

Gentlemen, these were a part of the thoughts that then possessed
me, and I there made a conversion of a piece of an old Catch,
and added more to it, fitting them to be sung by us Anglers:
come Master, you can sing well, you must sing a part of it as it
is in this paper.

> Man's life, is but vain: for, 'tis subject to pain
>   And sorrow, and short as a bubble;
> 'Tis a Hodge-podge of business, and money, and care,
>   And care, and money, and trouble.
> But we'll take no care, when the weather proves fair:
>   Nor will we vex now tho' it rain;

> We'll banish all sorrow, and sing till tomorrow,
>   And Angle, and Angle again.

Pet. Aye marry Sir, this is Music indeed, this has cheered my heart, and made me to remember six Verses in praise of Music, which I will speak to you instantly.

> Music, miraculous Rhetoric, that speakest sense
> Without a tongue, excelling eloquence;
> With what ease might thy errors be excused
> Wert thou as truly loved as th'art abused?
> But though dull souls neglect, and some reprove thee,
> I cannot hate thee, 'cause the Angels love thee.

Ven. And the repetition of these last Verses of music have called to my memory what Mr. *Edmund Waller* (a Lover of the Angle) says of Love and Music:

> Whilst I listen to thy voice
> (Chloris) I feel my heart decay:
>   That powerful voice,
> Calls my fleeting Soul away;
> Oh! suppress that magic sound
> Which destroys without a wound.
>
> Peace Chloris, peace, or singing die,
>   That together you and I
>   To Heaven may go:
>   For all we know
>   Of what the blessed do above
> Is, that they sing, and that they love.

Pisc. Well remembered brother *Peter*, these Verses came seasonably, and we thank you heartily. Come, we will all join together, my Host and all, and sing my Scholar's Catch over again, and then each man drink the tother cup and to bed, and thank God we have a dry house over our heads.

Pisc. Well now, good night to every body.

Pet. And so say I.

Ven. And so say I.

Cor. Good night to you all, and I thank you.

*

The ANGLERS Song.

CANTUS.

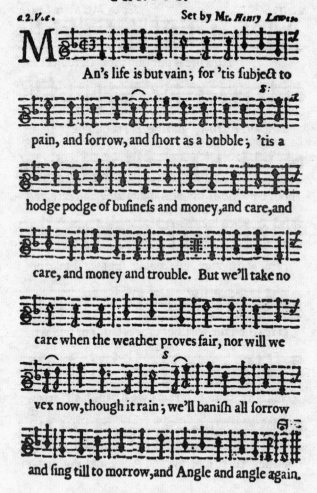

a.2.V.c.   Set by Mr. *Henry Lawes.*

An's life is but vain; for 'tis subject to

pain, and sorrow, and short as a bubble; 'tis a

hodge podge of busines and money, and care, and

care, and money and trouble. But we'll take no

care when the weather proves fair, nor will we

vex now, though it rain; we'll banish all sorrow

and sing till to morrow, and Angle and angle again.

The ANGLERS Song.

BASSUS.

a.2.Voc.   Set by Mr. *Henry Lawes:*

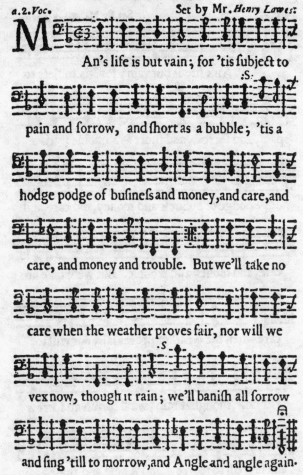

An's life is but vain; for 'tis subject to

pain and sorrow, and short as a bubble; 'tis a

hodge podge of business and money, and care, and

care, and money and trouble. But we'll take no

care when the weather proves fair, nor will we

vex now, though it rain; we'll banish all sorrow

and sing 'till to morrow, and Angle and angle again.

Pisc. Good morrow brother *Peter*, and the like to you honest *Corydon* : come, my Hostess says there is seven shillings to pay, let's each man drink a pot for his morning's draught, and lay down his two shillings, that so my Hostess may not have occasion to repent her self of being so diligent, and using us so kindly.

Pet. The motion is liked by every body, and so Hostess, here's your money ; we Anglers are all beholding to you, it will not be long ere I'll see you again. And now brother *Piscator* I wish you and my brother your Scholar a fair day, and good fortune. Come *Corydon*, this is our way.

CHAP. XVII.

Of Roach and Dace, & how to fish for them.
And of Caddis.

Ven. Good Master, as we go now towards *London*, be still so
courteous as to give me more instructions, for I have several
boxes in my memory, in which I will keep them all very safe,
there shall not one of them be lost.

Pisc. Well Scholar, that I will, and I will hide nothing from
you that I can remember, and can think may help you forward
towards a perfection in this Art; and because we have so much
time, and I have said so little of *Roach* and *Dace*, I will give you
some directions concerning them.

Some say the *Roach* is so called, from *Rutilus*, which they
say, signifies red fins. He is a Fish of no great reputation for his
dainty taste, and his Spawn is accounted much better than any
other part of him. And you may take notice, that as the *Carp* is
accounted the *Water-fox*, for his cunning; so the *Roach* is
accounted the *Water-sheep* for his simplicity or foolishness. It is
noted that the *Roach* and *Dace* recover strength, and grow in
season in a fortnight after Spawning, the *Barbel* and *Chub* in a
month, the *Trout* in four months, and the *Salmon* in the like
time, if he gets into the Sea, and after into fresh water.

Roaches be accounted much better in the River than in a
Pond, though ponds usually breed the biggest. But there is a
kind of bastard small *Roach* that breeds in ponds, with a very
forked tail, and of a very small size, which some say is bred by
the *Bream* and right *Roach*, and some Ponds are stored with
these beyond belief; and knowing-men that know their differ-
ence call them *Ruds*; they differ from the true *Roach* as much
as a Herring from a Pilchard, and these bastard breed of *Roach*
are now scattered in many Rivers, but I think not in *Thames*,
which I believe affords the largest and fattest in this Nation,
especially below *London-bridge*: the *Roach* is a leather-
mouthed Fish, and has a kind of saw-like teeth in his throat.
And lastly let me tell you, the *Roach* makes an Angler excellent
sport, especially the great Roaches about *London*, where I think

there be the best Roach-Anglers, and I think the best *Trout-Anglers* be in *Derby-shire*, for the waters there are clear to an extremity.

Next, let me tell you, you shall fish for this *Roach* in Winter with Paste or Gentles, in *April* with worms or Caddis; in the very hot months with little white snails, or with flies underwater, for he seldom takes them at the top, though the Dace will. In many of the hot months, Roaches may also be caught thus: Take a *May-fly* or *Ant-fly*, sink him with a little lead to the bottom near to the Piles or Posts of a Bridge, or near to any posts of a *Weir*, I mean any deep place where Roaches lie quietly, and then pull your fly up very leisurely, and usually a Roach will follow your bait to the very top of the water and gaze on it there, and run at it and take it lest the fly should fly away from him.

I have seen this done at *Windsor* and *Henley-Bridge*, and great store of *Roach* taken; and sometimes a *Dace* or *Chub*; and in *August* you may fish for them with a Paste made only of the crumbs of Bread, which should be of pure fine Manchet; and that paste must be so tempered betwixt your hands till it be both soft and tough too; a very little water, and time and labour, and clean hands will make it a most excellent paste: But when you fish with it, you must have a small hook, a quick eye, and a nimble hand, or the bait is lost and the fish too (if one may lose that which he never had); with this paste, you may, as I said, take both the Roach and the Dace or Dare, for they be much of a kind, in matter of feeding, cunning, goodness, and usually in size. And therefore take this general direction for some other baits which may concern you to take notice of. They will bite almost at any fly, but especially at *Ant-flies*; concerning which, take this direction, for it is very good.

Take the blackish *Ant-fly* out of the Mole-hill or Ant-Hill, in which place you shall find them in the month of *June*, or if that be too early in the year, then doubtless you may find them in *July*, *August*, and most of *September*; gather them alive with both their wings, and then put them into a Glass that will hold a quart or a pottle; but first put into the Glass a handful or more of the moist earth, out of which you gather them, and as much of the roots of the grass of the said hillock, and then put in the flies gently, that they lose not their wings, lay a clod of earth over it, and then so many as are put into the glass without bruising will live there a month or more, and be always in a readiness for you to fish with; but if you would have them keep longer, then get any great earthen pot, or barrel of three or four gallons (which is better) then wash your barrel with water and honey; and having put into it a quantity of earth and grass roots, then put in your flies, and cover it, and they will live a quarter of a year; these in any stream and clear water, are a deadly bait for *Roach* or *Dace*, or for a *Chub*; and your rule is, to fish not less than a handful from the bottom.

I shall next tell you a winter bait for a *Roach*, a *Dace* or *Chub*, and it is choicely good. About *All-hallowtide* (and so till Frost comes) when you see men ploughing up heath ground, or sandy ground, or green-swards, then follow the plough, and you shall find a white worm as big as two Maggots, and it hath a red head (you may observe in what ground most are, for there the Crows will be very watchful and follow the Plough very close) it is all soft, and full of whitish guts; a worm that is in *Norfolk*, and some other Counties called a *Grub*, and is bred of the Spawn or Eggs of a Beetle, which she leaves in holes that she digs in the ground under Cow or Horse dung, and there rests all Winter, and in *March* or *April* comes to be first a red, and then a black Beetle: gather a thousand or two of these, and put them with a peck or two of their own earth into some tub or firkin, and cover and keep them so warm, that the frost or cold air, or winds kill them not; these you may keep all winter, and kill fish with them at any time: and if you put some of them into a little earth and honey a day before you use them, you will find them an excellent bait for *Bream*, *Carp*, or indeed for almost any fish.

And after this manner you may also keep Gentles all winter, which are a good bait then, and much the better for being lively and tough: or you may breed and keep Gentles thus: Take a piece of Beast's liver, and with a cross stick, hang it in some corner over a pot or barrel half full of dry clay, and as the Gentles grow big, they will fall into the barrel and scour themselves, and be always ready for use whensoever you incline to fish; and these Gentles may be thus created till after *Michael-mas*. But if you desire to keep Gentles to fish with all the year, then get a dead Cat or a Kit and let it be fly-blown, and when the Gentles begin to be alive and to stir, then bury it and them in soft, moist earth, but as free from frost as you can, and these you may dig up at any time when you intend to use them; these will last till *March*, and about that time turn to be Flies.

But if you be nice to foul your Fingers, (which good Anglers seldom are) then take this Bait: Get a handful of well-made
5 Malt, and put it into a dish of water, and then wash and rub it betwixt your hands till you make it clean, and as free from husks as you can; then put that water from it, and put a small quantity of fresh water to it, and set it in something that is fit for that purpose over the Fire, where it is not to boil apace, but
10 leisurely and very softly, until it become somewhat soft, which you may try by feeling it betwixt your Finger and Thumb, and when it is soft, then put your water from it, and then take a sharp Knife, and turning the sprout end of the Corn upward, with the point of your Knife take the back part of the husk off
15 from it, and yet leaving a kind of inward husk on the Corn, or else it is marred, and then cut off that sprouted end (I mean a little of it) that the white may appear, and so pull off the husk on the cloven side (as I directed you) and then cutting off a very little of the other end, that so your hook may enter; and if your
20 hook be small and good, you will find this to be a very choice Bait either for Winter or Summer, you sometimes casting a little of it into the place where your float swims.

And to take the *Roach* and *Dace*, a good Bait is the young brood of Wasps and Bees, if you dip their heads in blood;
25 especially good for *Bream*, if they be baked or hardened in their husks in an Oven, after the bread is taken out of it; or hardened on a Fire-shovel; and so also is the thick blood of *Sheep*, being half dried on a Trencher, that so you may cut it into such pieces as may best fit the size of your hook, and a little salt keeps it
30 from growing black, and makes it not the worse but better: This is taken to be a choice Bait if rightly ordered.

There be several Oils of a strong smell that I have been told of, and to be excellent to tempt Fish to bite, of which I could say much, but I remember I once carried a small Bottle from Sir
35 *George Hastings* to Sir *Henry Wotton*, (they were both chemical men) as a great Present; it was sent, and received, and used with great confidence; and yet upon enquiry I found it did not answer the expectation of Sir *Henry*, which with the help of this and other circumstances, makes me have little belief in such things
40 as many men talk of: not but that I think Fishes both smell and hear (as I have expressed in my former discourse) but there is a

mysterious Knack, which (though it be much easier than the Philosopher's Stone), yet is not attainable by common capacities, or else lies locked up in the brain or breast of some chemical man, that like the *Rosicrucians* will not yet reveal it. But let me nevertheless tell you, that *Camphor* put with moss into your worm-bag with your worms, makes them (if many Anglers be not very much mistaken) a tempting bait, and the Angler more fortunate. But I stepped by chance into this discourse of Oils and Fishes smelling, and though there might be more said, both of it and of Baits for *Roach* and *Dace*, and other float-Fish, yet I will forbear it at this time, and tell you in the next place how you are to prepare your Tackling: concerning which I will for sport sake give you an old Rhyme out of an old Fish-book, which will prove a part and but a part of what you are to provide.

> My Rod and my Line, my Float and my Lead,
> My Hook and my Plummet, my whetstone and knife,
> My Basket, my Baits both living and dead,
> My Net and my Meat, for that is the chief:
> Then I must have Thread, and Hairs green and small,
> With mine Angling purse, and so you have all.

But you must have all these Tackling, and twice so many more, with which if you mean to be a Fisher, you must store your self; and to that purpose I will go with you either to Mr *Margrave* who dwells amongst the Booksellers in St *Paul's* Church-Yard, or to Mr *John Stubs* near to the *Swan in Golden-lane*; they be both honest men, and will fit an *Angler* with what *Tackling* he lacks.*

Venat. Then, good Master, let it be at——for he is nearest to my dwelling, and I pray let's meet there the ninth of *May* next, about two of the clock, and I'll want nothing that a Fisher should be furnished with.

Pisc. Well, and I'll not fail you, God willing, at the time and place appointed.

Venat. I thank you, good Master, and I will not fail you: and, good Master, tell me what Baits more you remember, for it will not now be long ere we shall be at *Tottenham-high-Cross*, and

* *I have heard, that the tackling hath been prized at fifty pounds in the Inventory of an Angler.*

when we come thither I will make you some requital of your pains, by repeating as choice a copy of Verses, as any we have heard since we met together; and that is a proud word for we have heard very good ones.

5   *Pisc.* Well, Scholar, and I shall be then right glad to hear them; and I will as we walk tell you whatsoever comes in my mind, that I think may be worth your hearing. You may make another choice Bait thus, Take a handful or two of the best and biggest *Wheat* you can get, boil it in a little milk (like as
10 *Frumenty* is boiled) boil it so till it be soft, and then fry it very leisurely with Honey and a little beaten Saffron dissolved in milk, and you will find this a choice Bait, and good I think for any Fish, especially for *Roach*, *Dace*, *Chub*, or *Grayling*: I know not but that it may be as good for a River-*carp*, and
15 especially if the ground be a little baited with it.

And you may also note, that the spawn of most Fish is a very tempting bait, being a little hardened on a warm Tile, and cut into fit pieces. Nay, Mulberries and those Blackberries, which grow upon Briars, be good baits for *Chubs* or *Carps*, with these
20 many have been taken in Ponds, and in some Rivers where such Trees have grown near the water and the fruit customarily dropped into it, and there be a hundred other baits more than can be well named, which, by constant baiting the water will become a tempting bait for any Fish in it.

25 You are also to know, that there be divers kinds of *Caddis*, or *Case-worms*, that are to be found in this Nation in several distinct Counties, and in several little Brooks that relate to bigger Rivers; as namely, one *Caddis* called a *Piper*, whose husk or case is a piece of reed about an inch long or longer, and as
30 big about as the compass of a twopence; these worms being kept three or four days in a woollen bag with sand at the bottom of it, and the bag wet once a day, will in three or four days turn to be yellow; and these be a choice bait for the *Chub* or *Chavender*, or indeed for any great Fish, for it is a large Bait.

35 There is also a lesser *Caddis-worm*, called a *Cock-spur*, being in fashion like the spur of a Cock, sharp at one end; and the case or house in which this dwells is made of small husks, and gravel, and slime, most curiously made of these, even so as to be wondered at, but not to be made by man no more than a *King-*
40 *fisher's* nest can, which is made of little Fishes' bones, and have such a Geometrical inter-weaving and connexion, as the like is

not to be done by the art of man: This kind of *Caddis* is a choice bait for any float-Fish, it is much less than the *Piper-Caddis*, and to be so ordered, and these may be so preserved ten, fifteen, or twenty days, or it may be longer.

There is also another *Caddis*, called by some a *Straw-worm*, and by some a *Rough-coat*, whose house or case is made of little pieces of bents, and rushes, and straws, and water-weeds, and I know not what, which are so knit together with condensed slime, that they stick about her husk or case, not unlike the bristles of a *Hedge-hog*; these three *Caddises* are commonly taken in the beginning of Summer, and are good indeed to take any kind of fish with float or otherwise. I might tell you of many more, which as these do early, so those have their time also of turning to be flies later in Summer; but I might lose my self, and tire you by such a discourse; I shall therefore but remember you, that to know these, and their several kinds, and to what flies every particular *Caddis* turns, and then how to use them first as they be *Caddis*, and after as they be *flies*, is an art, and an art that every one that professes to be an Angler has not leisure to search after, and if he had is not capable of learning.

I'll tell you, Scholar, several Countries have several kinds of *Caddises*, that indeed differ as much as dogs do: That is to say, as much as a very *Cur* and a *Greyhound* do. These be usually bred in the very little rills or ditches that run into bigger Rivers, and I think a more proper bait for those very Rivers, than any other. I know not how or of what this *Caddis* receives life, or what coloured fly, it turns to; but doubtless, they are the death of many *Trouts*, and this is one killing way.

Take one (or more if need be) of these large yellow *Caddis*, pull off his head, and with it pull out his black gut, put the body (as little bruised as is possible) on a very little hook, armed on with a Red hair (which will show like the *Caddis-head*) and a very little thin lead, so put upon the shank of the hook that it may sink presently; throw this bait thus ordered (which will look very yellow) into any great still hole where a Trout is, and he will presently venture his life for it, 'tis not to be doubted if you be not espied; and that the bait first touch the water, before the line; and this will do best in the deepest stillest water.

Next let me tell you, I have been much pleased to walk quietly by a Brook with a little stick in my hand, with which I might easily take these, and consider the curiosity of their composure;

and if you shall ever like to do so, then note, that your stick
must be a little Hazel or Willow cleft, or have a nick at one end
of it, by which means you may with ease take many of them in
that nick out of the water, before you have any occasion to use
5 them. These, my honest Scholar, are some observations told to
you as they now come suddenly into my memory, of which you
may make some use: but for the practical part, it is that, that
makes an Angler: it is diligence, and observation, and practice,
and an ambition to be the best in the Art that must do it. I will
10 tell you, Scholar, I once heard one say, *I envy not him that eats
better* meat *than I do, nor him that is* richer, *or that wears better*
clothes *than I do. I envy no body but him, and him only, that
catches more* fish *than I do.* And such a man is like to prove an
Angler, and this noble emulation I wish to you and all young
15 Anglers.

CHAP. XVIII.

Of the Minnow or Pink, of the Loach, and of the Bull-head, or Miller's-thumb.

Pisc. There be also three or four other little fish that I had almost forgot, that are all without scales, and may for excellency of meat be compared to any fish of greatest value, and largest size. They be usually full of eggs or spawn all the months of Summer; for they breed often, as 'tis observed *mice* and many of the smaller four-footed Creatures of the earth do; and as those, so these come quickly to their full growth and perfection. And it is needful that they breed both often and numerously, for they be (besides other accidents of ruin) both a prey, and baits for other fish. And first, I shall tell you of the *Minnow* or *Pink*.

The *Minnow* hath, when he is in perfect season, and not sick (which is only presently after spawning) a kind of dappled or waved colour, like to a *Panther*, on his sides, inclining to a greenish and sky-colour, his belly being milk-white, and his back almost black or blackish. He is a sharp biter at a small worm, and in hot weather makes excellent sport for young Anglers, or boys, or women that love that Recreation, and in the spring they make of them excellent *Minnow-Tansies*; for being washed well in salt, and their heads and tails cut off, and their guts taken out, and not washed after, they prove excellent for that use, that is, being *fried with yolks of eggs, the flowers of* Cowslips, *and of* Primroses, *and a little Tansy*, thus used they make a dainty dish of meat.

The Loach is, as I told you, a most dainty dish, he breeds and feeds in little and clear swift brooks or rills; and lives there upon the gravel, and in the sharpest streams: He grows not to be above a finger-long, and no thicker than is suitable to that length. This *LOACH*,

is not unlike the shape of the Eel: He has a beard or wattles like a *Barbel*. He has two fins at his sides, four at his belly and one at his tail; he is dappled with many black or brown spots, his mouth is Barbel-like under his nose. This Fish is usually full of eggs or spawn, and is by *Gesner* and other learned Physicians commended for great nourishment, and to be very grateful both to the palate and stomach of sick persons; he is to be fished for with a very small worm at the bottom, for he very seldom or never rises above the Gravel, on which I told you he usually gets his Living.

The *Miller's-thumb* or *Bull-head*, is a Fish of no pleasing shape. He is by *Gesner* compared to the *Sea-toad-fish*, for his similitude and shape. It has a head big and flat, much greater than suitable to his Body; a mouth very wide and usually gaping. He is without teeth, but his lips are very rough, much like to a File. He hath two Fins near to his gills, which be roundish or crested, two Fins also under the Belly, two on the back, one below the Vent, and the Fin of his tail is round. Nature hath painted the Body of this Fish with *whitish*, *blackish*, *brownish* spots. They be usually full of eggs or spawn all the Summer (I mean the Females) and those eggs swell their Vents almost into the form of a dug. They begin to spawn about *April*, and (as I told you) spawn several months in the Summer; and in the winter the Minnow, and Loach and Bull-head dwell in the mud as the Eel doth, or we know not where: no more than we know where the Cuckoo and Swallow, and other half-year-birds (which first appear to us in *April*) spend their six cold winter melancholy months. This *Bull-head*

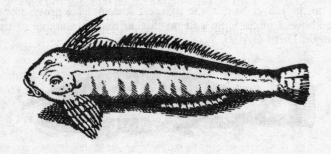

does usually dwell and hide himself in holes or amongst stones in clear water; and in very hot days will lie a long time very still, and sun himself, and will be easy to be seen upon any flat stone, or any gravel, at which time, he will suffer an Angler to put a hook baited with a small worm very near unto his very mouth, and he never refuses to bite, or indeed to be caught with the worst of Anglers. *Matthiolus* commends him much more for his taste and nourishment, than for his shape or beauty.

There is also a little Fish called a *Stickleback*: a Fish without scales, but hath his body fenced with several prickles. I know not where he dwells in winter, nor what he is good for in summer, but only to make sport for boys and women-Anglers, and to feed other Fish that be Fish of prey, as Trouts in particular, who will bite at him as at a Pink, and better, if your hook be rightly baited with him, for he may be so baited, as his tail turning like the sail of a wind-mill will make him turn more quick than any *Pink* or *Minnow* can. For note, that the nimble turning of that or the *Minnow* is the perfection of *Minnow-Fishing*. To which end, if you put your hook into his mouth, and out at his tail, and then having first tied him with white thread a little above his tail, and placed him after such a manner on your hook as he is like to turn, then sew up his mouth to your line, and he is like to turn quick, and tempt any *Trout*: but if he do not turn quick, then turn his tail a little more or less towards the inner part; or towards the side of the hook, or put the *Minnow* or *Stickleback* a little more crooked or more straight on your hook, until it will turn both true and fast; and then doubt not but to tempt any great *Trout* that lies in a swift stream. And the *Loach* that I told you of will do the like: no bait is more tempting, provided the *Loach* be not too big.

And now *Scholar*, with the help of this fine morning, and your patient attention, I have said all that my present memory will afford me concerning most of the several Fish that are usually fished for in fresh waters.

Venat. But Master, you have by your former civility made me hope that you will make good your promise, and say something of the several Rivers that be of most note in this Nation; and also of *Fish-ponds*, and the ordering of them; and do it I pray good Master, for I love any Discourse of Rivers, and Fish and fishing, the time spent in such discourse passes away very pleasantly.

CHAP. XIX.

Of several Rivers, and some Observations of Fish.

Pisc. Well Scholar, since the ways and weather do both favour us, and that we yet see not *Tottenham-Cross*, you shall see my willingness to satisfy your desire. And first, for the Rivers of this Nation, there be (as you may note out of Doctor *Heylin's* Geography, and others) in number 325. but those of chiefest note he reckons and describes as followeth.

The chief is *Thames*, compounded of two Rivers, *Thame* and *Isis*; whereof the former rising somewhat beyond *Thame* in *Buckingham-shire*, and the latter in *Cirencester* in *Gloucestershire* meet together about *Dorchester* in *Oxford-shire*, the issue of which happy conjunction is the *Thamisis* or *Thames*. Hence it flieth betwixt *Berks*, *Buckingham-shire*, *Middlesex*, *Surrey*, *Kent*, and *Essex*, and so weddeth himself to the Kentish *Medway* in the very jaws of the Ocean; this glorious River feeleth the violence and benefit of the Sea more than any River in *Europe*, ebbing and flowing twice a day, more than sixty miles: about whose banks are so many fair Towns, and Princely Palaces that a *German Poet* thus truly spake:

> *Tot Campos, &c.*
> *We saw so many* Woods *and Princely* bowers,
> *Sweet* Fields, *brave* Palaces, *and* stately Towers,
> *So many* Gardens *dressed with curious care,*
> *That* Thames *with* royal Tiber *may compare.*

2. The second River of note, is *Sabrina* or *Severn*: it hath its beginning in *Pumlumon Fawr-Hill* in *Montgomery-shire*, and his end seven miles from *Bristol*, washing in the mean space the walls of *Shrewsbury*, *Worcester*, and *Gloucester* and divers other places and palaces of note.

3. *Trent*, so called for thirty kind of Fishes that are found in it, or for that it receiveth thirty lesser Rivers, who having his fountain in *Staffordshire*, and gliding through the Countries of

Nottingham, *Lincoln*, *Leicester*, and *York*, augmenteth the turbulent current of *Humber*, the most violent stream of all the Isle. This *Humber* is not, to say truth, a distinct River, having a spring head of his own, but it is rather the mouth or *Aestuarium* of divers Rivers here confluent and meeting together; namely, *Ure*, *Derwent*, and especially of *Ouse* and *Trent*; and (as the *Danube*, having received into its *channel*, the River *Drave*, *Save*, *Theiss*, and divers others) changeth his name into *Humber*, as the old Geographers call it.

4. *Medway*, a Kentish River, famous for harbouring the Royal Navy.

5. *Tweed*, the north-east bound of *England*, on whose northern banks is seated the strong and impregnable Town of *Berwick*.

6. *Tyne*, famous for *Newcastle*, and her inexhaustible Coal-pits. These and the rest of principal note, are thus comprehended in one of Mr *Drayton's* Sonnets.

> *The floods' queen*, Thames, *for ships and swans is crowned*
> *And stately* Severn *for her shore is praised*,
> *The Crystal* Trent *for fords and fish renowned*,
> *And* Avon's *fame to* Albion's *cliffs is raised*,
> Carlegion Chester *vaunts her holy* Dee,
> York *many wonders of her* Ouse *can tell*,
> *The* Peak *her* Dove, *whose banks so fertile be*,
> *And* Kent *will say her* Medway *doth excel*.
> Cotswold *commends her* Isis *to the* Tame,
> *Our Northern borders boast of* Tweed's *fair flood*,
> *Our Western parts extol their* Wylye's *fame*,
> *And the* Old Lea *brags of the* Danish *blood*.

These Observations are out of learned Dr *Heylyn*, and my old deceased friend *Michael Drayton*; and because you say, you love such discourses as those of *rivers* and *fish* and *fishing*, I love you the better, and love the more to impart them to you: nevertheless, *Scholar*, if I should begin but to name the several sorts of strange Fish that are usually taken in many of those Rivers that run into the Sea, I might beget wonder in you, or unbelief, or both; and yet I will venture to tell you a real truth concerning one lately dissected by Dr *Wharton*, a man of great learning and experience, and of equal freedom to communicate it; one that loves me and my Art, one to whom I have been beholding for many of the choicest observations that I have imparted to you. This good man, that dares do any thing rather than tell an untruth, did (I say) tell me, he lately dissected one strange fish and he thus described it to me.

The Fish was almost a yard broad, and twice that length; his 5
mouth wide enough to receive or take into it the head of a man,
his stomach seven or eight inches broad: he is of a slow motion,
and usually lies or lurks close in the mud, and has a moveable
string on his head about a span, or near unto a quarter of a yard
long, by the moving of which (which is his natural bait) *when* 10
he lies close and unseen in the mud, he draws other smaller fish
so close to him that he can suck them into his mouth, and so
devours and digests them.

And, Scholar, do not wonder at this, for besides the credit of the Relator, you are to note, many of these, and Fishes which 15 are of the like and more unusual shapes, are very often taken on the mouths of our Sea-Rivers, and on the Sea-shore; and this will be no wonder to any that have travelled *Egypt*, where 'tis known the famous River *Nile* does not only breed Fishes that yet want names, but by the overflowing of that River and the 20 help of the Sun's heat on the fat slime which that River leaves on the Banks (when it falls back into its natural channel) such strange fish and beasts are also bred, that no man can give a name to, as *Grotius* (in his *Sophampaneas*) and others have observed. 25

But whither am I strayed in this discourse? I will end it by telling you, that at the mouth of some of these Rivers of ours, Herrings are so plentiful, as namely, near to *Yarmouth* in *Norfolk*, and in the West-Country, Pilchards so very plentiful, as you will wonder to read what our learned *Camden* relates of 30 them in his *Britannia*, p. 178, 186.

Well, Scholar, I will stop here, and tell you what by reading and conference I have observed concerning Fish-ponds.

CHAP. XX.

Of fish-ponds, and how to order them.

Doctor *Liebault* the learned French man, in his large discourse of *Maison Rustique*, gives this direction for making of *Fish-ponds*, I shall refer you to him to read it at large, but I think I shall contract it, and yet make it as useful.

He adviseth, that when you have drained the ground, and made the earth firm where the head of the Pond must be, that you must then in that place drive in two or three rows of Oak or Elm Piles, which should be scorched in the fire, or half burned before they be driven into the earth, (for being thus used it preserves them much longer from rotting) and having done so, lay Faggots or Bavins of smaller wood betwixt them, and then earth betwixt and above them, and then having first very well rammed them and the earth, use another pile in like manner as the first were : and note that the second pile is to be of or about the height that you intend to make your Sluice or Flood-gate, or the vent that you intend shall convey the overflowings of your Pond in any flood that shall endanger the breaking of the Pond dam.

Then he advises that you plant Willows or Owlers about it, or both, and then cast in Bavins in some places not far from the side, and in the most sandy places, for Fish both to spawn upon, and to defend them and the young Fry from the many Fish, and also from Vermin that lie at watch to destroy them, especially the spawn of the *Carp* and *Tench*, when 'tis left to the mercy of ducks or Vermin.

He and *Dubravius* and all others advise, that you make choice of such a place for your Pond, that it may be refreshed with a little rill, or with rain water running or falling into it ; by which Fish are more inclined both to breed, and are also refreshed and fed the better, and do prove to be of a much sweeter and more pleasant taste.

To which end it is observed; that such Pools as be large and have most gravel, and shallows where *fish* may sport themselves,

do afford Fish of the purest taste. And note, that in all Pools it
is best for fish to have some retiring place, as namely hollow
banks, or shelves, or roots of trees to keep them from danger;
and when they think fit from the extreme heat of Summer; as
5 also, from the extremity of cold in Winter. And note, that if
many trees be growing about your Pond, the leaves thereof
falling into the water, make it nauseous to the Fish, and the Fish
to be so to the eater of it.

'Tis noted that the *Tench* and *Eel* love mud, and the *Carp*
10 loves gravelly ground, and in the hot months to feed on grass:
You are to cleanse your Pond, if you intend either profit or
pleasure, once every three or four Years, (especially some Ponds)
and then let it lie dry six or twelve months, both to kill the
water-weeds, as *Water-lilies*, *Candocks*, *Reate* and *Bull-rushes*
15 that breed there; and also that as these die for want of water,
so grass may grow in the Pond's bottom, which *Carps* will eat
greedily in all the hot months if the Pond be clean. The letting
your Pond dry and sowing Oats in the bottom is also good, for
the fish feed the faster: and being sometime let dry, you may
20 observe what kind of Fish either increases or thrives best in that
water; for they differ much both in their breeding and feeding.

Liebault also advises, that if your Ponds be not very large and
roomy, that you often feed your fish by throwing into them
chippings of Bread, Curds, Grains, or the entrails of Chickens,
25 or of any fowl or beast that you kill to feed your selves; for
these afford Fish a great relief. He says that Frogs and Ducks do
much harm, and devour both the Spawn and the young Fry of
all Fish, especially of the *Carp*. And I have, besides experience,
many testimonies of it. But *Liebault* allows Water-frogs to be
30 good meat, especially in some Months, if they be fat: but you
are to note, that he is a *French-man*, and we *English* will hardly
believe him, though we know frogs are usually eaten in his
Country: however he advises to destroy them and King-fishers
out of your ponds; and he advises, not to suffer much shooting
35 at wild fowl, for that (he says) affrightens, and harms, and
destroys the Fish.

Note, that Carps and Tench thrive and breed best when no
other fish is put with them into the same Pond; for all other fish
devour their spawn, or at least the greatest part of it. And note,
40 that clods of grass thrown into any Pond feed any Carps in
Summer: and that garden earth and parsley thrown into a Pond,

recovers and refreshes the sick fish. And note, that when you
store your pond, you are to put into it two or three Milters for
one Spawner, if you put them into a breeding Pond: but if into
a nurse-pond, or feeding pond, in which they will not breed,
then no care is to be taken, whether there be most Male or   5
Female Carps.

It is observed, that the best ponds to breed Carps are those
that be stony or sandy, and are warm, and free from wind, and
that are not deep, but have willow trees and grass on their sides,
over which the water does sometimes flow: and note, that Carps   10
do more usually breed in marl pits, or pits that have clean clay
bottoms, or in new ponds, or ponds that lie dry a winter season,
than in old ponds, that be full of mud and weeds.

Well *Scholar*, I have told you the substance of all that either
observation or *discourse*, or a diligent *Survey* of *Dubravius* and   15
Liebault hath told me. Not that they in their long discourses
have not said more, but the most of the rest are so common
observations, as if a man should tell a good Arithmetician, that
twice two, is four. I will therefore put an end to this discourse,
and we will here sit down and rest us.   20

CHAP. XXI.

Directions for making of a Line, and for the colouring of both Rod and Line.

Pisc. Well, Scholar, I have held you too long about these *Caddis*, and smaller *fish*, and *rivers*, and *Fish-ponds*, and my spirits are almost spent, and so I doubt is your patience; but being we are now almost at *Tottenham*, where I first met you, and where we are to part, I will lose no time, but give you a little direction how to make and order your Lines, and to colour the hair of which you make your Lines, for that is very needful to be known of an Angler; and also how to paint your Rod; especially your top, for a right grown top is a choice Commodity, and should be preserved from the water soaking into it, which makes it in wet weather to be heavy, and fish ill-favouredly, and not true, and also it rots quickly for want of painting: and I think a good top is worth preserving, or I had not taken care to keep a top above twenty years.

But first for your line.

First, note, That you are to take care, that your hair be round and clear, and free from galls or scabs, or frets; for a well-chosen, even, clear, round hair, of a kind of glass-colour, will prove as strong as three uneven, scabby hairs, that are ill chosen, and full of galls or unevenness. You shall seldom find a black hair but it is round, but many white are flat and uneven; therefore if you get a lock of right, round, clear, glass-colour hair make much of it.

And for making your *Line*, observe this rule, First, let your hair be clean washed ere you go about to twist it: and then choose not only the clearest hair for it, but hairs that be of an equal bigness, for such do usually stretch all together, and break altogether, which hairs of an unequal bigness never do, but break singly, and so deceive the Angler that trusts to them.

When you have twisted your links, lay them in water for a quarter of an hour, at least, and then twist them over again before you tie them into a Line: for those that do not so, shall usually find their Line to have a hair or two shrink, and be shorter than the rest at the first fishing with it, which is so much of the strength of the Line lost for want of first watering it, and then re-twisting it; and this is most visible in a seven-hair line, one of those which hath always a black hair in the middle.

5   And for dyeing of your hairs do it thus:

Take a pint of strong Ale, half a pound of soot, and a little quantity of the juice of *Walnut*-tree leaves, and an equal quantity of Alum; put these together into a pot, pan, or pipkin, and boil them half an hour, and having so done, let it cool, and being
10 cold, put your hair into it, and there let it lie; it will turn your hair to be a kind of water or glass colour, or greenish, and the longer you let it lie, the deeper coloured it will be; you might be taught to make many other colours, but it is to little purpose; for doubtless the water-colour, or glass-coloured hair is the
15 most choice and most useful for an *Angler*; but let it not be too green.

But if you desire to colour hair greener; then do it thus: Take a quart of small Ale, half a pound of Alum, then put these into a pan or pipkin, and your hair into it with them; then put it
20 upon a fire, and let it boil softly for half an hour, and then take out your hair, and let it dry; and having so done, then take a pottle of water, and put into it two handful of Marigolds, and cover it with a tile (or what you think fit) and set it again on the Fire, where it is to boil again softly for half an hour, about
25 which time the scum will turn yellow; then put into it half a pound of Copperas beaten small, and with it the hair that you intend to colour, then let the hair be boiled softly till half the liquor be wasted, and then let it cool three or four hours with your hair in it: and you are to observe, that the more Copperas
30 you put into it, the greener it will be, but doubtless the pale green is best; But if you desire yellow hair, (which is only good when the weeds rot) then put in the more *Marigolds*, and abate most of the Copperas, or leave it quite out, and take a little Verdigris instead of it.

35 This for colouring your hair. And as for painting your Rod, which must be in Oil, you must first make a size with glue and water, boiled together, until the glue be dissolved, and the size of a Lye-colour; then strike your size upon the wood with a Bristle, or a Brush, or Pencil, whilst it is hot: that being quite
40 dry, take white Lead, and a little red Lead, and a little coal-black, so much as all together will make an ash-colour; grind

these all together with Linseed Oil, let it be thick, and lay it thin upon the wood with a Brush or Pencil; this do for the ground of any colour to lie upon wood.

For a Green.

Take Pink and Verdigris, and grind them together in Linseed Oil, as thin as you can well grind it, then lay it smoothly on with your Brush, and drive it thin; once doing for the most part will serve, if you lay it well; and if twice be sure your first colour be thoroughly dry, before you lay on a second.

Well Scholar; having now taught you to paint your Rod: and, we having still a mile to Tottenham High-Cross, I will, as we walk towards it, in the cool shade of this sweet Honey-suckle-Hedge, mention to you some of the thoughts and joys that have possessed my Soul since we two met together. And, these thoughts shall be told you, that you also may join with me in thankfulness to the giver of every good and perfect gift for our happiness. And, that our present happiness may appear to be the greater, and we the more thankful for it: I will beg you to consider with me, how many do, even at this very time, lie under the torment of the Stone, the Gout, and Tooth-ache; and, this we are free from. And, every misery that I miss is a new mercy, and therefore let us be thankful. There have been since we met, others, that have met disasters of broken Limbs, some have been blasted, others Thunder-strucken; and we have been freed from these, and all those many other miseries that threaten human nature: let us therefore rejoice and be thankful. Nay, which is a far greater mercy, we are free from the unsupportable burden of an accusing, tormenting Conscience: a misery that none can bear, and therefore let us praise him for his preventing grace; and say, every misery that I miss, is a new mercy: Nay, let me tell you there be many that have forty times our Estates, that would give the greatest part of it to be healthful and cheerful like us; who with the expense of a little money have eat, and drank, and laughed, and Angled, and sung, and slept securely: and rose next day, and cast away care, and sung, and laughed, and Angled again: which are blessings, rich men cannot purchase with all their money. Let me tell you Scholar: I have a rich Neighbour, that is always so busy, that he has no leisure to laugh; the whole business of his life, is to get money,

and more money, that he may still get more and more money;
he is still drudging on; and says, that Solomon *says, the diligent*
hand maketh rich: *and 'tis true indeed, but he considers not,*
that 'tis not in the power of riches to make a man happy: for, it
5   *was wisely said by a man of great observation,* that there be as
many miseries beyond riches, as on this side them: *and yet God*
deliver us from pinching poverty; and grant, that having a
competency, we may be content and thankful. Let us not repine,
or so much as think the gifts of God unequally dealt, if we see
10 *another abound with riches, when as God knows, the cares that*
are the keys that keep those riches, hang often so heavily at the
rich man's girdle, that they clog him with weary days and
restless nights, even when others sleep quietly. We see but the
outside of the rich man's happiness: few consider him to be like
15 the Silk-worm, *that when she seems to play, is at the very same*
time spinning her own bowels, and consuming her self. And this
many rich men do; loading themselves with corroding cares, to
keep what they have (probably) unconscionably got. Let us
therefore be thankful for health and a competence; and above
20 *all, for a quiet Conscience.*

   Let me tell you, Scholar, that Diogenes *walked on a day with*
his friend to see a Country Fair; *where he saw,* Ribbons, *and*
Looking-glasses, *and* Nut-crackers, *and* Fiddles, *and* Hobby-
horses, *and many other gim-cracks; and having observed them,*
25 *and, all the other* finnimbruns *that make a complete Country*
Fair: *He said to his friend,* Lord! How many things are there in
this world of which *Diogenes hath no need? And truly, it is so,*
or might be so, with very many who vex, and toil themselves, to
get what they have no need of. Can any man charge God, that
30 *he hath not given him enough to make his life happy? no*
doubtless: for, nature is content with a little: and yet, you shall
hardly meet with a man, that complains not of some want,
though he indeed wants nothing but his will, it may be, nothing
but his will of his poor Neighbour, for not worshipping, or not
35 *flattering him, and thus, when we might be happy and quiet, we*
create trouble to our selves. I have heard of a man, that was
angry with himself because he was no taller, and of a Woman,
that broke her Looking-glass *because it would not show her*
face to be as young and handsome as her next Neighbour's was.
40 *And, I knew another, to whom God had given health, and*
plenty, but, a Wife that nature had made peevish, and, her

Husband's riches had made Purse-proud, *and must because she was rich (and for no other virtue) sit in the highest Pew in the Church: which being denied her; she engaged her Husband into a contention for it, and at last, into a Law-suit with a dogged Neighbour, who was as rich as he, and had a Wife as peevish and* Purse-proud *as the other: and this Law-suit, begot higher oppositions, and actionable words, and more vexations, and Law-suits: for you must remember that both were rich, and must therefore have their wills. Well, this wilful* Purse-proud *Law-suit lasted during the life of the first Husband: after which his wife vexed, and chid, and chid and vexed, till she also chid and vexed herself into her grave, and so the wealth of these poor rich people was cursed into a punishment, because they wanted meek and thankful hearts; for those only can make us happy. I knew a man that had health and riches, and several houses all beautiful and ready furnished, and would often trouble himself and Family to be removing from one house to another; and being asked by a friend, why he removed so often from one house to another? replied, it was to find content in some one of them: but, his friend knowing his temper, told him, if he would find content in any of his houses? he must leave himself behind him; for, content will never dwell but in a meek and quiet soul. And this may appear if we read and consider what our Saviour says in* St Matthew's *Gospel: for he there says,*—Blessed be the merciful for they shall obtain mercy.—Blessed be the pure in heart; for they shall see God.—Blessed be the poor in Spirit; for theirs is the Kingdom of Heaven. *And*—blessed be the meek; for they shall possess the earth.—*not that the* meek *shall not also obtain mercy, and see God, and be comforted, and at last come to the Kingdom of Heaven; but in the mean time he (and he only) possesses the earth as he goes towards that Kingdom of Heaven, by being humble and cheerful, and content with what his good God has allotted him: he has no turbulent, repining, vexatious thoughts that he deserves better: nor is vexed when he sees others possessed of more honour or more riches than his wise God has allotted for his share; but he possesses what he has with a meek and contented quietness: such a quietness as makes his very dreams pleasing both to God and himself.*

My honest Scholar, all this is told to incline you to thankfulness; and to incline you the more, let me tell you, that though the Prophet David *was guilty of* Murder *and* Adultery, *and*

*many other of the most deadly sins; yet he was said to be a man
after God's own heart, because he abounded more with thankfulness than any other that is mentioned in holy Scripture, as
may appear in his book of Psalms; where there is such a*
5 *Commixture of his confessing of his sins and unworthiness, and
such thankfulness for God's pardon and mercies, as did make
him to be accounted even by God himself, to be* a man after his
own heart, *and let us in that, labour to be as like him as we
can; let not the blessings we receive daily from God, make us*
10 *not to value, or not praise him because they be common; let us
not forget to praise him for the innocent mirth and pleasure, we
have met with since we met together. What would a blind man
give to see the pleasant Rivers and meadows and flowers and
fountains, that we have met with since we met together? I have*
15 *been told, that if a man that was born blind could obtain to
have his sight for but only one hour, during his whole life, and
should at the first opening of his eyes, fix his sight upon the Sun
when it was in his full glory, either at the rising or setting of it;
he would be so transported, and amazed, and so admire the*
20 *glory of it, that he would not willingly turn his eyes from that
first ravishing object, to behold all the other various beauties
this world could present to him. And this, and many other like
blessings we enjoy daily; and for most of them, because they be
so common, most men forget to pay their praises but let not*
25 *us, because it is a Sacrifice so pleasing to him that made that
Sun, and us, and still protects us, and gives us flowers and
showers and stomachs and meat and content and leisure to go
a-fishing.*

Well Scholar, I have almost tired my self, and I fear more
30 *than almost tired you: but I now see* Tottenham High-Cross,
*and our short walk thither shall put a period to my too long
discourse, in which, my meaning was, and is, to plant that in
your mind, with which I labour to possess my own Soul: that
is; a meek and thankful heart. And, to that end, I have showed*
35 *you, that riches without them, do not make any man happy. But
let me tell you, that riches with them remove many fears, and
cares, and therefore my advice is, that you* endeavour to be
honestly rich; or, contentedly poor: *but, be sure, that your
riches be justly got, or you spoil all. For, it is well said by*
40 Caussin, *he that loses his Conscience, has nothing left that is
worth keeping. Therefore be sure you look to that. And, in the*

next place, look to your health: and if you have it praise God,
and value it next to a good Conscience; for, health is the second
blessing that we Mortals are capable of: a blessing, that money
cannot buy, and therefore value it, and be thankful for it. As for
money (which may be said to be the third blessing) neglect it   5
not: but note, that there is no necessity of being rich: for I told
you, there be as many miseries beyond riches as on this side
them: *and, if you have a competence, enjoy it with a meek,*
cheerful, thankful heart. I will tell you Scholar, I have heard a
grave Divine say, that God has two dwellings; one in Heaven;   10
and, the other in a meek and thankful heart. *Which Almighty*
God grant to me, and to my honest Scholar: and so, you are
welcome to Tottenham High-Cross.

Venat. Well Master, I thank you for all your good directions,
but, for none more than this last of thankfulness, which I hope I   15
shall never forget. And pray let's now rest our selves in this
sweet shady Arbour, which nature her self has woven with her
own fine fingers; 'tis such a contexture of *Woodbines, Sweet-*
briar, Jasmine, and *Myrtle*; and so interwoven, as will secure us
both from the Sun's violent heat; and from the approaching   20
shower, and being sat down I will requite a part of your
courtesies with a bottle of *Sack, Milk, Oranges,* and *Sugar*;
which all put together, make a drink like *Nectar,* indeed too
good for any body but us *Anglers*: and so Master, here is a full
glass to you of that liquor, and when you have pledged me, I   25
will repeat the Verses which I promised you; it is a Copy printed
amongst some of Sir *Henry Wotton's*: and doubtless made
either by him, or by a lover of Angling: Come Master, now
drink a glass to me, and then I will pledge you, and fall to my
repetition; it is a description of such *Country-Recreations* as I   30
have enjoyed since I had the happiness to fall into your
company.

    Quivering fears, *heart-tearing* cares,
    Anxious sighs, *untimely* tears,
      Fly, fly to Courts,   35
      Fly to fond worldlings' sports
Where strained Sardonic smiles are glosing still,
And grief is forced to laugh against her will.
      Where mirth's but mummery,
      And sorrows only real be.   40

Fly from our Country-pastimes, fly,
Sad troops of human misery,
   Come serene looks,
   Clear as the crystal Brooks,
5   Or the pure azured heaven that smiles to see
The rich attendance on our poverty;
   Peace and a secure mind,
   Which all men seek, we only find.

Abused Mortals, did you know
10 Where joy, hearts-ease and comforts grow?
   You'd scorn proud Towers,
   And seek them in these Bowers,
Where winds sometimes our woods perhaps may shake,
But blustering care could never tempest make,
15   Nor murmurs e'er come nigh us,
   Saving, of fountains that glide by us.

Here's no fantastic Masque nor Dance,
But of our Kids that frisk and prance;
   Nor wars are seen,
20   Unless upon the green
Two harmless Lambs are butting one the other,
Which done, both bleating run each to his Mother.
   And wounds are never found,
   Save what the plough-share gives the ground.

25 Here are no entrapping baits
To hasten too, too hasty fates,
   Unless it be
   The fond credulity
Of silly fish, which (worldling like) still look
30 Upon the bait, but never on the hook:
   Nor envy, 'nless among
   The birds for prize of their sweet song.

Go, let the diving Negro seek
For Gems hid in some forlorn creek:
35   We all pearls scorn,
   Save what the dewy morn
Congeals upon each little spire of grass,
Which careless shepherds beat down as they pass:
   And gold ne'er here appears,
40   Save what the yellow Ceres bears.

Blest silent groves, oh may you be
For ever mirth's best nursery!
  May pure contents
  For ever pitch their tents
Upon these downs, these meads, these rocks, these mountains,　5
And Peace still slumber by these purling fountains:
  Which we may every year
  Meet when we come a-fishing here.

Pisc. Trust me (Scholar) I thank you heartily for these Verses, they be choicely good, and doubtless made by a lover of　10 Angling: Come, now, drink a glass to me, and I will requite you with another very good Copy: it is a Farewell to the vanities of the World, and some say written by Sir *Harry Wotton*, who I told you was an excellent Angler. But let them be writ by whom they will, he that writ them had a brave soul, and must needs be　15 possessed with happy thoughts at the time of their composure:

Farewell ye gilded follies, pleasing troubles;
Farewell ye honoured rags, ye glorious bubbles:
Fame's but a hollow echo, Gold, pure clay;
Honour the darling but of one short day.　20
Beauty (th'eyes idol) but a damasked skin;
State but a golden prison, to live in
And torture free-born minds: embroidered Trains
Merely but pageants for proud swelling veins:
And Blood Allied to Greatness is alone　25
Inherited, not purchased, nor our own.
  Fame, Honour, Beauty, State, Train, Blood and Birth
  Are but the fading Blossoms of the earth.

I would be great, but that the Sun doth still
Level his rays against the rising hill:　30
I would be high, but see the proudest Oak
Most subject to the rending Thunder-stroke:
I would be rich, but see men (too unkind)
Dig in the bowels of the richest mind:
I would be wise, but that I often see　35
The Fox suspected, whilst the Ass goes free:
I would be fair, but see the fair and proud,
(Like the bright Sun) oft setting in a cloud:
I would be poor, but know the humble grass
Still trampled on by each unworthy Ass:　40
Rich hated: wise suspected: scorned if poor:

Great *feared :* fair *tempted :* high *still envied more :*
  I have wished all ; but now I wish for neither ;
  Great, high, rich, wise, *nor* fair ; poor *I'll be rather.*

     Would the world now adopt me for her heir,
5   Would Beauty's Queen entitle me the Fair,
     Fame speak me Fortune's Minion : *could I vie*
     Angels with India, *with a speaking eye*
     Command bare heads, bowed knees, strike Justice dumb
     As well as blind and lame, *or give a tongue*
10   To stones by Epitaphs ; *be called* great Master
     In the loose Rhymes of every Poetaster :
     Could I be more than any man that lives,
     Great, fair, rich, wise, all in Superlatives :
     Yet I more freely would these gifts resign,
15   Than ever fortune would have made them mine,
       And hold one minute of this holy leisure
       Beyond the riches of this empty pleasure.

     Welcome pure thoughts, welcome ye silent Groves,
     These guests, these courts my soul most dearly loves :
20   Now the winged people of the sky shall sing
     My cheerful Anthems to the gladsome Spring :
     A Prayer-Book *now,* shall be my looking-glass,
     In which I will adore sweet Virtue's face.
     Here dwell no hateful looks, no Palace cares,
25   No broken Vows dwell here, nor pale-faced Fears :
     Then here I'll sit, and sigh my hot love's folly,
     And learn t'affect an holy melancholy,
       And if Contentment be a stranger then,
       I'll ne'er look for it, but in heaven again.

30 *Venat.* Well Master ! these Verses be worthy to keep a room
in every man's memory. I thank you for them ; and I thank you
for your many instructions, which (God willing) I will not
forget : and as St *Augustine* in his Confessions (*book* 9. *chap.*
3.) commemorates the kindness of his friend *Verecundus,* for
35 lending him and his companion a *Country-house,* because there
they rested and enjoyed themselves free from the troubles of the
world ; so, having had the like advantage, both by your conver-
sation, and the Art you have taught me, I ought ever to do the
like : for indeed, your company and discourse have been so
40 useful and pleasant, that I may truly say, *I have only lived since*

I enjoyed them, and turned Angler, and not before. Nevertheless, here I must part with you, here in this now sad place where I was so happy as first to meet you: But I shall long for the ninth of *May*, for then I hope again to enjoy your beloved company at the appointed time and place. And now I wish for some 5 *somniferous potion*, that might force me to sleep away the intermitted time, which will pass away with me as tediously, as it does with men in sorrow; nevertheless I will make it as short as I can by my *hopes* and *wishes*. And my good Master, I will not forget the doctrine which you told me *Socrates* taught his 10 Scholars, *That they should not think to be honoured so much for being* Philosophers, *as to honour* Philosophy *by their virtuous lives*. You advised me to the like concerning *Angling*, and I will endeavour to do so, and to live like those many *worthy men*, of which you made mention in the former part of your 15 discourse. This is my firm resolution; and as a pious man advised his friend, *That to beget* Mortification *he should frequent* Churches; *and view* Monuments, *and* Charnel-houses, *and then and there consider, how many dead bones time had piled up at the gates of death*. So when I would beget *content*, 20 and increase confidence in the *Power*, and *Wisdom*, and *Providence* of Almighty God, I will walk the *Meadows* by some gliding stream, and there contemplate the *Lilies* that take no care, and those very many other various little living *creatures*, that are not only created but fed (man knows not how) by the 25 goodness of the God of *Nature*, and therefore trust in him. This is my purpose: and so, *Let every thing that hath breath praise the Lord*. And let the blessing of St Peter's Master be with mine.

Pisc. And upon all that are lovers of *Virtue*; and dare trust in his *providence*, and be *quiet*, and go a-*Angling*.   30

Study to be quiet, 1 Thes. 4. 11.

FINIS.

APPENDIX

1. The tune for 'Come live with me' (57: 37) and 'If all the world' (58: 35)

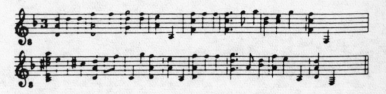

'Come live with me, and be my Love' William Corkine, *The Second Book of Ayres*

2. The tune for 'I married a Wife of late' (59: 33)

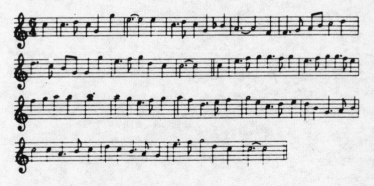

'The Merry Merry Milke Maids' *The English Dancing Master* (1651)

NOTES

Abbreviations

Camden   William Camden, *Britain, or a Chorographicall Description*, translated by Philemon Holland (1610); the 1637 edition is the one used

DNB   *Dictionary of National Biography*

Gesner   Conrad von Gesner, *Historia Animalium* (Frankfurt, 1620); unless otherwise stated, Book iv (of fish) is the volume referred to

Hakewill   George Hakewill, *Apologie of the Power and Providence of God* (1627)

OD Proverbs   *Oxford Dictionary of Proverbs*, compiled by W. G. Smith and edited and revised by F. P. Wilson (3rd edition, 1970)

OED   *The Compact Edition of the Oxford English Dictionary ... Reproduced Micrographically* (Oxford, 1971)

TLS   *Times Literary Supplement*

3:2–3 **John Offley of Madeley Manor** (d. 1658) Great-grandson of Sir Thomas Offley, Lord Mayor of London (1557). There is an engraving of Madeley Manor in Robert Plot's *Staffordshire* (1686). Walton's large family came from Staffordshire, and the families may have been connected.

3:32 **Sir Henry Wotton** (1568–1639) Ambassador, poet, and writer on architecture and garden design, he played an important part in introducing new ideas about painting, optics, and aesthetics from Italy to England. Walton knew him, and wrote his *Life* (1651).

5:31 **Nat. and R. Roe** Robert Roe is mentioned in the will of Izaak Walton's sister, Anne Grinsell; Walton inscribed a copy of the *Lives* (1670) to his 'Cozen Roe', and Robert Roe's name appears as that of a witness on Walton's property deeds after 1655. One of Walton's Grinsell nephews was named Nathaniel.

6:9 **Camden** William Camden (1551–1623), headmaster of Westminster School, published *Britannia* in Latin in 1586; an English translation appeared in 1610.

6:16 **Mr Hales**   George Hales, *A Private School of Defence* (1614).

9:11–13 **PISCATOR. VENATOR. AUCEPS**   Latin for Angler, Huntsman, and Falconer.

9:26 **Theobalds**   The three men are travelling north along the road which follows the River Lea from Tottenham to Ware. The turning off the road which Auceps plans to take is about seven miles from Tottenham. Venator's road lies with Piscator much further: Hoddesdon is about twelve miles from Tottenham, and only four short of Ware itself. The Thatched House was near the High Street in Hoddesdon. Theobalds Palace, built by the Cecils in the most magnificent style of the 1570s, was exchanged for Hatfield House with James I; by 1652 open-air religious meetings were taking place in the park, and Parliament largely demolished the palace. Charles II gave the estate to Albemarle.

10:5 **Good company etc.**   This proverb occurs in Latin; see *OD Proverbs*, p. 527.

10:23 **Mr Sadler**   Ralph Sadler of Standon had both Staffordshire and Kent connections, and Walton knew the family.

11:14 **Lucian well skilled** etc.   From *Certain Select Dialogues of Lucian*, tr. Francis Hickes (Oxford, 1634).

11:18 **Solomon**   Proverbs 24:9.

11:33 **Montaigne**   Montaigne, *Essayes*, tr. Florio (2nd edn, 1613), II, xii, p. 250. Izaak Walton's copy of this edition survives.

13:19 **Jove's servant in ordinary**   Juvenal calls the eagle 'one of Jove's household' (Satire XIV). In Ordinary: belonging to the regular staff.

13:21 **the son of Dædalus**   Icarus, who flew from Crete with his father, with wings of feathers and wax. Despite his father's warnings, Icarus flew too near the sun; the wax melted and he fell into the sea and was drowned.

14:2–3 **breath of life**   Genesis 2:7 and Psalm 104:29.

14:29 **alive and dead**   Cf. Webster, *The White Devil* (1612), V. iv. 89–92:

> Call for the Robin Redbreast and the Wren
> Since o'er shady groves they hover
> And with leaves and flowers do cover
> The friendless bodies of unburied men.

14:40 **Varro his Aviary**   Marcus Terentius Varro (116–27 BC) discusses the price of birds and describes his aviary in *De Re Rustica*, iii.4.8 ff.

15:9–10 **Mr G. Sandys**   George Sandys, *A Relation of a Journey* (1615), p. 206.

15:12 **the Dove**   Genesis 8:8–12.

15:15 **the Sacrifices of the Law** Leviticus 12:6-8; Luke 2:24.

15:17 **Elijah** 1 Kings 17:4-6.

15:21 **a Dove** Luke 3:22, Matthew 3:16, Mark 1:10 and John 1:32.

15:35 **two kinds** There were various methods of classifying hawks, although some writers dispensed with classification. Walton is nearest to the *Book of St Albans* tradition, as found in its various reprints of the sixteenth century.

17:12-13 **one Supper** Walton has conflated two passages in Plutarch: it was Antony, not Cleopatra, who had eight wild boars roasted 'for one only supper', and that not a feast but an ordinary dinner (Plutarch, *Lives of the Noble Grecians and Romans*, tr. North (1603), p. 923).

17:25 **Haddocks** Perhaps proverbial: '[I will] give thy flesh boy for haddocks meate', Giles and Phineas Fletcher, *Poetical Works*, ed. F. S. Boas (1908, 1970), i, p. 245.

17:31 **Xenophon** *Cyrupaedia: The institution and Life of Cyrus*, tr. Holland (1632), pp. 4-5.

18:15 **Moses** Leviticus 11:1-8.

18:29 **we protest** 'If you swear you'll catch no fish', *OD Proverbs*, p. 792.

19:2 **friend of God** It was Abraham who was called the friend of God (James 2:23); Walton may have been thinking of Exodus 33:11.

19:20 **wood back again to water** I can find no source for this experiment; perhaps it was described to Walton in his conference with Dr Wharton (see below, note to 20:19).

20:1 **plenty of Fish** After the Reformation the obligation to abstain from meat on certain days was not religious but legal; some Protestant writers did, however, advocate abstinence for religious reasons.

20:4 **the chief diet** Leviticus 11 and Deuteronomy 14 lay down the Mosaic regulations for diet; Walton's interpretation is somewhat one-sided.

20:14 **incredible value** Walton probably derives this from Hakewill, pp. 356-60.

20:19 **Dr Wharton** Dr Thomas Wharton (1614-74) was a Fellow of the Royal College of Physicians and was one of the few physicians who stayed in London throughout the Plague of 1665. He was a noted anatomist and published an important treatise on the glands, *Adenographia* (1656). He discovered the sub-maxillary (Wharton's) gland.

20:40 **Tully** i.e. Cicero.

21:6 **Rome** Walton's descriptions of Rome (with some inaccuracies) are derived from John Raymond, *An Itinerary* (1648); Walton's annotated copy of this book is in the Bodleian Library (Antiq. f. E. 1648/1).

21:11 **Jerusalem**   Walton's account of the Holy Land derives from George Sandys's *A Relation of a Journey*; see above, note to 15:9–10.

21:20 **spoken to a fish**   Jonah 2:10.

22:5 **five miles to the Thatched-House**   They were now just past Waltham Cross; Auceps had turned aside at Theobalds.

22:27 **Virtue, a reward to it self**   *OD Proverbs*, p. 861.

22:31 **the antiquity of Angling**   This paragraph is derived from Gervase Markham, *The Pleasure of Princes* (1614), p. 3. Markham was the uncle of the Ralph Sadler who owned the otter-dogs; see above, note to 10:23.

22:33 **Belus**   Son of Poseidon.

22:36 **Seth**   Josephus, *Antiquities of the Jews*, I. ii. 3, says that the descendants of Seth inscribed their discoveries upon two pillars.

23:7 **Amos** etc.   Amos 4:2; Job 41:1, 2. See also Isaiah 19:8 and Habakkuk 1:15.

23:32 **God enjoys himself only** etc.   'All the pleasure of God is in God himself: . . . he alone is an infinite good to himself' (Nicolas Caussin, *The Holy Court*, tr. Sir T. H[awkins]. (edition of 1663), p. 579).

23:36 **the fathers**   See Cornelius a Lapide, s.j., *Commentarium in quattuor Evangelia* (Lyons, 1638), ii, pp. 129–33, who cites Basil, Titus, Augustine, Bede, Cassian, Bernard, and others.

24:16 **Peter du Moulin**   In his *Accomplishment of the Prophecies*, tr. J. Heath (Oxford, 1613), A3ʳ.

24:30 **an ingenuous Spaniard**   He has not been identified.

25:4 **a River in Epirus** etc.   Most of the following rivers are described in Josuah Sylvester's translation of Du Bartas's *Divine Weeks and Works*, 3rd Day of 1st Week, ll. 235–72. See below, note to 27:14. The English rivers are variously discussed by Camden in his *Britannia* (see above, note to 6:9), Drayton, *Poly-Olbion*, xxii, ll. 11–14, and Mercator, *Historia Mundi or Mercator's Atlas* (1635), p. 46. The River Sabbaticus is described in Josephus, *De Bello Judaico*, vii. 24.

25:29 **Pliny the Philosopher**   Pliny the Elder (23–79), author of the *Natural History*, one of Walton's favourite sources.

25:31 **Balæna or Whirl-Pool**   The Balaena is described in Pliny, *Natural History*, Book ix, chapters 3, 8, and 22, though Walton has cut down Pliny's estimation of its size from four acres. 'Whirl-pool' is another name for the whale: cf. Spenser, *The Faerie Queene*, II. xii. 23.

26:5–6 **Dr Casaubon**   Dr Meric Casaubon, whom Walton probably knew, as he was a friend of Sir Henry Wotton, published two treatises *Of Credulity and Incredulity*, the first, *in Things Natural*

Civil and Divine, in 1668, the second, *in Things Divine and Spiritual*, in 1670. It is to the first of these that Walton refers (pp. 235–51).

26:10–11 **John Tradescant, Elias Ashmole Esq** The John Tradescants, father and son, collected plants and other marvels, some in their physic garden at Lambeth, and others in their museum; travellers were commissioned to bring rarities back from foreign parts, and John Tradescant the younger (1608–62) made his own collection in Virginia, which he brought home, publishing, in 1656, a catalogue of the complete collection, *Musaeum Tradescantium*; Walton's list is based on p. 8. After Tradescant's death, the collection passed to Elias Ashmole (1617–92), to become the nucleus of the Ashmolean Museum, Oxford, where part of the original Tradescant collection can still be seen. Ashmole, who had wide scholarly and antiquarian interests, was born in Lichfield; his godfather was named Offley, probably a member of the family of the dedicatee of *The Complete Angler*. We owe to Ashmole our knowledge of Walton's rescue of the Lesser George after the battle of Worcester (see Introduction, p. xvi).

26:28 **Mr George Herbert** Walton published his *Life* of George Herbert (1593–1633) in 1670. What follow are stanzas 36, 8, and 7 from Herbert's 'Providence'.

27:8 **Pliny says** *Natural History*, Book ix, chapter 2.

27:12 **Gesner** Conrad von Gesner (1516–65) was the author of *Historia Animalium* (Zurich, 1558), of which the fourth book, on fishes, is one of Walton's principal sources. It is a scholarly and scientific book, and reprints a number of earlier writers on fish, such as the whole of Rondelet (Walton's Rondeletius), and much of Bellonius, Aristotle, Pliny, Aelian, and Salvian. Walton draws upon Gesner for these writers, as well as for Gesner's own original writings.

27:14 **Divine Dubartas** Guillaume de Saluste, Sieur du Bartas (1544?–90), author of *Divine Weeks and Works* (see above, note to 25:4), tr. Josuah Sylvester. The standard edition of the translation is that by Susan Snyder (Oxford, 1979). The quotation here is from the 5th Day of the 1st Week, ll. 29–48, slightly altered by Walton.

28:6 **devours her** Quoted from Montaigne, *Essayes*, tr. Florio (1613), p. 256.

28:8 **Hermit** Du Bartas, ed. cit., 5th Day of 1st Week, ll. 389–408.

28:14 **Adonis** Although Gesner refers to Aelian (a third-century Roman who wrote in Greek), he does not give a reference. Walton probably saw a copy of Aelian's *De Animalium Natura*, in which a chapter is devoted to the Adonis: IX. 36.

28:21 **Sargus** Sea-bream; see Du Bartas, ed. cit., 5th Day of 1st Week, ll. 195–200.

28:33 **Cantharus** Black sea-bream; see ibid., ll. 201–4.

29:9 **Thracian women** See ibid., ll. 209–11.

29:22 **Mullet**   See ibid., ll. 205–8.

29:37 **Job**   See James 5:11.

30:16 **wonderful works of God**   Psalm 107: 23, 24.

40–1 Walton here follows much tradition, including sermons by Donne. See *The Compleat Angler*, ed. Jonquil Bevan (Oxford, 1983), p. 383.

31:17 **an ingenuous and learned man**   Apparently Donne: see his *Sermons*, ed. Potter and Simpson (Berkeley and Los Angeles, 1953–62), i, Sermon 5, pp. 236, 237.

32:7–8 **Ferdinand Mendez Pinto**   See his *Voyages and Adventures*, tr. Henry Cogan (1653), chapter 79.

32:11 **Mark Antony and Cleopatra**   North's translation (1603), p. 924, tells how Antony, ashamed of catching nothing, sought to deceive Cleopatra by instructing his servants to dive and fasten fish to his hooks. Cleopatra 'found it straight, yet seemed not to see it, but wondered at his excellent fishing'. The following day she instructed her own servants to anticipate Antony's, so that when he drew up his line the fish on his hook was salted.

32:20 **a harmless Recreation**   The issue of clergymen hunting was still a live one; in 1621 George Abbot, Archbishop of Canterbury, when out hunting accidentally shot and killed a keeper. He was then deemed to have become disqualified for his office. The controversy is discussed in Peter Heylyn, *Life of Laud* (1668), pp. 86–8.

32:23 **learned Perkins**   There seems no evidence that William Perkins (1558–1602), an eminent Puritan theologian, was fond of fishing, and I can find no reference to the sport in his *Workes* (1626–31).

32:24 **Whitaker**   Dr William Whitaker (1548–95), a nephew of Dean Alexander Nowel (see following note) is described as an angler by Thomas Fuller in his *Holy State* (1648), p. 172.

32:29 **Doctor Nowel**   The life of this scholar (1507?–1602) was recounted by Thomas Fuller in his *Abel Redevivus* (of which Walton's copy of the 1651 edition is preserved in Salisbury Cathedral Library) and in his *Worthies* (1662). Walton's account, which first appeared in the 1661 edition of the *Angler*, is close to the second version. His portrait is described in Rachel Lane Poole, *Catalogue of Portraits in Oxford* (1912–25), i, p. 249. Walton could have copied the inscription on the portrait when he was staying at Christ Church in 1660.

33:31 **Sir Henry Wotton**   See above, note to 3:32.

34:16 **This day dame Nature**   This poem appears in *Reliquiae Wottonianae* (1651), p. 524, in a slightly variant form. The volume was probably edited by Walton; it is prefaced by the first edition of Walton's *Life* of Sir Henry.

35:2 **Jo. Davors Esq**   This quotation is from *The Secrets of Angling* (1613) by John Dennys. Walton's ascription to 'Jo. Davors' is probably based on identification of Jo. Davies, who signed a commendatory verse, with the 'I.D.' of the title-page. Dennys's name, however, is given in the Stationers' Register (see Sir Henry Ellis, *Catalogue of Books on Angling*, 1811). The stanzas Walton quotes are on B7ʳ–B7ᵛ.

35:26 **Tithonus** Aurora, the dawn-goddess, was the wife of Tithonus. He is described as old because, although he had been granted the gift of eternal life, he had not been granted the gift of eternal youth.

37:35 **her tail is Fish** Here, and throughout the passage dealing with the otter, up to 38:33, Walton is confused about the creature's sex. It is clear that the otter in the hunt is female, while in the earlier editions Walton's remarks about otters in general used the masculine gender. Processes of revision have compounded the muddle. Walton's comments on the classification of otters derive from Edward Topsell, *Historie of Four-Footed Beastes* (1658), pp. 444–6. Topsell's book is largely based on the volume of Gesner's *Historia* which deals with quadrupeds.

38:12 **he can smell** Gesner, Book i, *De Quadrupedibus*, p. 685, declares that otters can smell.

38:15 **Ottery** This river is in Devonshire, not Cornwall.

39:1–2 **Mr Nich. Seagrave** Sir Nicholas Harris Nicolas, in his edition of *The Complete Angler* (1836), suggests the fourth son of Charles Seagrave of Scalford, Leics., and Alice, daughter of John Flower of Whitwell, Rutland. This family was related to James Duport, of Trinity College, Cambridge, who wrote commendatory verses for the *Life of Herbert* (1670) and for the fifth edition of *The Complete Angler* (1676).

39:6 **Old Rose** Nicolas (see preceding note) quotes:

> Now we're met like jovial fellows,
> Let us do as wise men tell us,
> Sing Old Rose and burn the bellows;
> Let us do as wise men tell us.

40:4–5 **13 of Edw. the I and the like in Rich. the III** These statutes make it illegal to take salmon between the midle of April and the Nativity of John the Baptist (24 June); they are 13th Edw. I, stat. I, cap. 47, and 13th Rich. II (not Rich. III), stat. I, cap. 19, which confirms the earlier statute.

40:10 **. . . nobody's business** *OD Proverbs*, p. 231.

40:17 **Levitical Law** Deuteronomy 22:6–7.

40:36 **Trout-hall** The atmosphere of the 'honest Ale-house' chosen by the huntsmen is well contrasted with that of the inns patronised by the anglers. Piscator's plan to sleep at Trout-hall did not materialise, because they chose instead to sleep at Bleak-hall, after hearing from its hostess at midday that Peter and his friend had sent word that they would lodge there that night. (See p. 55 for the change of plan, p. 57 for the name of the inn.) Trout-hall cannot be identified.

41 :5 **the Poet**   unidentified.

42 :20 **Come Hostess**   We are now to imagine them at Bleak-hall.

45 :4 **The Chub**   This first paragraph is largely derived from Rondelet, quoted in Gesner, pp. 182–4.

46 :10 **Thus was the Cheven dressed**   These recipes are simpler than those usual in contemporary cooking books. For a more elaborate sauce, see below, 106 :29.

48 :41 **Seneca**   The following passage comes from Hakewill, pp. 358–9.

52 :4 **Fordwich Trout**   A species of sea trout, these have enjoyed a considerable local celebrity. Fordwich is a few miles downstream from Canterbury (the home of Walton's first wife); the Royal Museum, Canterbury, owns a stuffed Fordwich trout, and a portrait in oils of a Fordwich trout with the following inscription: 'TAKEN. AT. FORDWICH. IN. KENT. IN. THE. YEAR. 1672. WEIGH'D. 27. POUNDS : . . .' The fish looks as if it had been bolted together; but it is a very early example of its kind.

52 :9 **Sir George Hastings**   Mentioned again at 97 :20–1 and 154 :35 as a 'chemical' man and friend of Sir Henry Wotton. Perhaps the son and heir of the famous huntsman Henry Hastings of Woodlands Park, Dorset, second son of George, fourth Earl of Huntingdon (*DNB*, 'Henry Hastings').

52 :22–3 Psalm 147 :9.

53 :4 **Albertus**   Quoted by Topsell, *Historie of Serpents* (1608), p. 180.

53 :26 **Sir Francis Bacon**   *The History Natural and Experimental of Life and Death* (1638), pp. 59–60.

55 :4 **Royal Society**   Founded 1660. A catalogue of thirty-three sorts of English spiders was contributed by Martin Lister to the Royal Society's *Philosophical Transactions*, no. 72 (19 June 1671), pp. 2170–5.

55 :27 **Landing Net**   Cf. William Samuel, *Arte of Angling* (1577), facsimile edition by C. E. Bentley (Princeton, 1956), B1–B2, where Viator helps Piscator land a fish.

56 :26 **bleating Dams**   The preceding paragraph is reminiscent of a passage in Sir Philip Sidney's *Arcadia*: see the Penguin edition of Maurice Evans (Harmondsworth, 1977), p. 69. For a discussion of the significance of this and the other three 'Arcadian' passages in the *Angler*, see Jonquil Bevan, *Izaak Walton's The Compleat Angler: The Art of Recreation* (Brighton and New York, 1988), pp. 50–6, 128–11, 128–9.

56 :28 **the Poet**   Unidentified.

56 :37 **Kit. Marlowe**   The main source for Marlowe's 'Come live with

me' is *England's Helicon* (1600). Walton added the sixth stanza
('Thy silver dishes . . .') to his second edition of the *Angler* (1655); it
is otherwise known only from a broadside in the Roxburghe Collection, which also contains 'If all the world' (*Roxburghe Ballads*, ed.
William Chappell and J. W. Ebsworth (London and Hertford,
1871–99), ii, pp. 1–6). For the tune, see the Appendix, p. 183 above.

56:39 **Sir Walter Raleigh**   Ralegh's authorship of this poem is doubt-
ful; the matter is discussed in my Oxford edition of *The Compleat
Angler* (1983), pp. 390–1. The textual situation is similar to that of
Marlowe's 'Come live with me' (see preceding note).

57:24–5 **Troy Town**   The ballads in the Milkmaid's repertory are
discussed in Claude M. Simpson, *The British Broadside Ballad and
its Music* (New Brunswick, 1966), on pp. 126–7 ('Come Shepherds'); pp. 201–5 ('As at noon'); pp. 576–8 ('Phillida flouts me');
pp. 96–101, 369–70 ('Chevy Chase'); and pp. 284, 587–90 ('Troy
Town').

58:27 **Queen Elizabeth**   The story is recounted by Holinshed, *Chron-
icles of England* (1808), iv, p. 133.

58:31 **Sir Thomas Overbury**   In *The Wife, with Additions of New
Characters*, enlarged edition (1622), L7^r.

59:33 **I married a Wife**   These stanzas are really half-stanzas and
come from separate ballads which were sung to the tune. They may
be found in Claude M. Simpson (see above, note to 57:24–5), pp.
490–3. For the tune, see the Appendix, p. 183 above.

62:19 **barren ground**   See Matthew 13 : 3–9.

62:35 **'Tis merry**   *OD Proverbs*, p. 528.

62:38 **Mr. William Basse**   A servant of Sir Richard Wenman of Thame
Park, Oxon. (a member of the Great Tew circle). Basse's verses
survive in MS collections, and a number were printed in his lifetime.
They were collected and edited by R. W. Bond in 1893. See Claude
M. Simpson (see above, note to 57:24–5), pp. 37–9, 710–13.

63:17 **Corydon's Song**   John Chalkhill was identified by P. J. Croft,
TLS, 27 June 1958; he is also the author of the poem on pp. 142–3,
and of *Thealma and Clearchus*, a poem edited by Izaak Walton in
1683. His sister Martha was the stepmother of Anne Ken, Walton's
second wife. He went up to Trinity College, Cambridge, in 1610,
and died in 1642; he is buried in St Margaret's, Westminster. For
Thealma and Clearchus, see George Saintsbury, *Minor Poets of the
Caroline Period* (Oxford, 1921), ii, pp. 367–443.

65:3 **'Tis the company**   *OD Proverbs*, p. 138.

65:9 **The Angler's Song**   By William Basse: see above, note to 62:38.

71:12 **Pliny holds**   *Natural History* xi. 112. Francis Bacon agrees:
Sylva Sylvarum (1650), p. 153.

72:21 **as one has observed**   Most of Walton's account of caterpillars is taken from Edward Topsell's *History of Serpents* (1608). The detailed description which follows is almost word for word from *Serpents* (1658 edition), p. 666.

75:22 **Lessius** Leonard Lessius, *Hygiasticon: or, the Right Course of Preserving Life and Health unto Extream Old Age*, advocates temperance throughout. It was published at Cambridge in 1634 in a translation by George Herbert's friend Nicholas Ferrar, together with another treatise on temperance translated by Herbert himself.

75:38–39 **an ingenuous brother of the Angle** In fact the paragraph that follows comes from Leonard Mascall's *A Booke of Fishing with Hooke and Line* (1590), pp. 16–18. The ultimate source is the *Treatyse of Fysshynge wyth an Angle*, part of the second edition of *The Book of St Albans* (1496).

76:39 **Mr. Thomas Barker** His *Art of Angling* first appeared in 1651, reappearing in 1653. In 1657 it reappeared as *Barker's Delight*, showing Walton's influence, just as Walton had been influenced by Barker. He was a cook by trade, and lived in Westminster.

78:30 **Witches, that sell so many winds** Lapland was famous for its witches (see *Paradise Lost*, ii. 665), and witches in general were supposed to sell winds (see *Macbeth*, I. ii. 11). The wind-raising technique practised by the Lapland witches is described in Richard Eden, *History of Travayle* (1577), but Giles Fletcher, *The Russe Commonwealth* (1591), observes: 'Though for enchanting of ships that saile along their [the Laplanders'] coast . . . and their giving of winds good to their friends, and contrary to other . . . [it] is a very fable' (f. 77).

78:39 **When the wind is South** *OD Proverbs*, p. 893.

79:3 **Solomon** Ecclesiastes 11:4.

79:7 **good Horse** *OD Proverbs*, p. 320.

79:16–17 **May-butter** *OD Proverbs*, p. 94; see also the Glossary, below.

79:27 **fish down the stream** Walton has often been censured for this advice; he derives it from Barker, *The Art of Angling* (1653), p. 2; the whole paragraph, and the following one, are close to Barker.

80:24–25 **Mr. Herbert** George Herbert's 'Vertue' was first printed in *The Temple* (1633). See above, note to 26:28.

82:13 **Ch. Harvie** (1595–1663) 'Common-prayer' did not appear in the first edition of Harvey's *The Synagogue* (1640), but was added in 1647. It first appears in *The Complete Angler* in the edition of 1655, together with a commendatory verse from Harvey. Walton repaid the compliment by contributing a commendatory verse to the 1657 edition of *The Synagogue*.

82:22–23 A reference to the first line of Virgil's 'First Eclogue', which recalls the Beech Tree of the earlier 'Arcadian' passage which precedes the meeting with the Milkmaid and her mother. See above, 56:26. Just as the meditation under the Beech Tree conjures up the interlude of the Milkmaid, so this meditation under the Sycamore conjures up the interlude of the Gipsies and Beggars. For the significance of the Sycamore see George Herbert, *The English Poems*, ed. C. A. Patrides (Everyman, 1974), p. 100.

82:30 **Dr. Butler** Probably Dr William Butler (1535–1618), an eminent physician long remembered for a medical drink, 'Dr Butler's Ale'.

82:38 **only on Holy-days** From John Raymond, *An Itinerary* (1648), a1ʳ. See above, note to 21:6.

83:12 **Kenna** Walton's second wife, Anne Ken.

83:12 footnote **Like Hermit poor** This well-known song, attributed to Sir Walter Ralegh, appeared in *Brittons bowre of Delight* (1591) and *The Phoenix Nest* (1593). It was set to music by Ferrabosco in *Ayres* (1609) and by Nicholas Lanier in Playford's *Select Musicall Ayres and Dialogues*. To judge from other quotations and references, Walton had the 1659 edition of Playford's collection; see below, notes to 145:28 and 146:6.

83:20 **Bryan** Unknown; it has been conjectured that this was Walton's dog.

83:21 **Shawford-brook** That part of the River Sow that runs through Shallowford, or Shawford, the small estate Walton bought in 1655, near his native Stafford. Shallowford is now the home of the Izaak Walton Cottage Museum Trust.

85:1 **English Gusman** The life of Guzman d'Alfarache was written by Mattheo and translated into English and most other European languages. Walton refers to *The English Gusman* (1652), by George Fidge, an account of the highwayman James Hind. Hind was apprehended while staying 'over against St. *Dunstans* Church in Fleet-street', the parish in which Walton had lived until the outbreak of the Civil War; St Dunstan's Churchyard continued to be the address of his friend and publisher, Richard Marriot.

85:18–19 **Beggars-bush** To be found in Beaumont and Fletcher's *Comedies and Tragedies* (1647), this play is the work of Beaumont and Massinger. Walton is perhaps thinking of Ben Jonson's masque *The Gypsies Metamorphos'd* (1621).

85:28 **Frank Davison** A distant relation of Walton's first wife, Rachel Floud, Davison (1575–1619) published his *Poetical Rhapsody* in 1602. The authorship of this poem is discussed by H. E. Rollins in his edition of *A Poetical Rhapsody* (1931), ii, p. 170.

86:31–32 **within the bent of my Rod** I would have kept my rod and line at an angle (bent), that is, I would not have allowed the fish to pull the rod down into a straight line with the fishing-line.

87:4 **Hares change Sexes** See, for example, Hakewill, p. 10.

87:8 **Mer. Casaubon** See above, note to 26:5–6. The reference is in the first volume (1668), p. 252.

87:9 **Gasper Peucerus**   Gaspar Peucer (1525–1602).

87:26 **some poor body**   For the anglers' charity see below, note to 137:25.

88:33 **Gesner**   See above, note to 38:12. It seems a little illogical to suppose that because otters can smell trout, trout can smell; perhaps we have to bear in mind the uncertain classification of otters themselves as half beast, half fish.

88:35 **Bacon**   *Sylva Sylvarum, or a Naturall History* (1650), p. 167.

89:3 **Eels unbed themselves**   A common belief; see, for example, *Pericles*, IV. ii. 140–1.

89:16 **Hakewill**   See above, note to 87:9. Walton's reference here is correct.

89:19 **chap. I. and 7**   Actually James 3:7.

89:27 **Martial**   Walton's reference is correct. He has taken his translation from Hakewill, p. 360. He supplied the first line of the epigram (*Baiano procul a lacu monemus*) in manuscript in the copy of the 1661 edition of the *Angler* which he presented to Anne King, daughter-in-law of Henry King. The Sovereign in the poem is the Emperor Domitian and the fish are lampreys.

89:39 **Leominster**   Proverbial for the quality of its wool; see *OD Proverbs*, p. 455.

90:15 **Solomon**   Ecclesiastes 3:11.

91:7 **Aldrovandus**   *De Piscibus* (Bologna, 1613), p. 593. Ulysses Aldrovandus (1524?–1607) wrote a *Natural History* in thirteen volumes.

91:8 **Gesner**   p. 982.

91:11 **The French**   Rondelet (in Gesner, p. 1004) calls the umbla, a species of salmon, the 'Umble Chevalier'. Gesner tells us that the French believe the umber (thymallus, a different fish from the umbla) to eat gold, and that they find them in the Loire (p. 981).

91:17 **Water-thyme**   It is generally stated that the umber or thymallus smells of thyme. See Gesner, p. 980.

91:30 **Salvian**   Ippolito Salviani (1514–72), physician to Pope Julius III, quoted by Gesner, p. 983.

91:33 **St. Ambrose**   Gesner, p. 980, quoting from Ambrose's *Hexaemeron*, v. 2.

92:20 **River Dove**   Walton often visited the Dove, which he fished with his friend Charles Cotton, the author, at Walton's request, of *The Complete Angler Part II* (1676).

93:4 **The Salmon**   The account of the breeding and migration is largely derived from Gesner, pp. 827–9.

93:33 **cast his bill**   The eagle does not cast his bill; but Francis Bacon (*History of Life and Death* (1638), p. 53) assumes that it does.

93:35–6 **as one has wittily observed**   Several writers make this observation, among them William Worship in his sermon *The Fisher* (1612), G7ᵛ.

94:4 **History of Life and Death** pp. 59–60.

94:15 **eight foot** Gesner, p. 282, says eight cubits; for another example of Walton cutting down what he thought an excessive estimate, see above, 26:5–6.

94:16 **in his Britannia** pp. 654–5.

94:23 **Michael Drayton** Drayton (1563–1631) was one of the Mermaid Tavern poets; see Introduction, note 7. He ended his life at his lodgings in Fleet Street, where he was a near neighbour of Walton, and they shared various Staffordshire and Derbyshire connections, among them Ralph Sadler (see above, note to 10:23). The quotation here is from Song vi of *Poly-Olbion*, ll. 39–55.

95:3 **Gesner** p. 826.

95:34 **Camden** p. 633.

96:19 **some use a wheel** The first mention of the angling-reel.

96:23 **Oliver Henley** Nothing seems to be known about him.

97:1 **Bacon's Natural History** See above, note to 88:35.

97:3 **Gesner says** See above, notes to 88:33 and 95:3.

97:11 **Polypody** A fern of the genus *Polypodium*, which grows on oaks and other trees.

97:14 **Vulnera hederæ** 'When a large piece of ivy is bruised, it exudes a gum congealed from its oil, which is very similar to whitewash, and smells very sweet for a long time.' Pungent oils placed on bait to attract fish enjoyed a considerable mystique in both printed and manuscript sources. Secrecy seems to be part of the tradition: Walton's comment that this recipe is 'in a learned language, lest it should be made common' almost suggests that fish can read English, but not Latin! In fact, the Latin of this recipe, coherent in the 1676 edition, is mumbo-jumbo in earlier editions: an indication that Walton was unable to read Latin without considerable help.

97:20–1 **Sir George Hastings** See above, note to 52:9.

99:7 **learned Gesner** Gesner (p. 503) quotes Cardanus, who expresses the view that pike appear in ponds without apparent natural source. Gesner himself suggests that perhaps the spawn of pike might be devoured by herons, who later secrete the spawn in ponds, where they are able to grow. Walton, in his first edition, shares Gesner's scepticism, but by the fifth edition his view has veered round. He was attacked for this passage by his most hostile critic, Richard Franck, in his *Northern Memoirs* (1694). Franck describes a meeting in which he taxed Walton with this opinion, advancing Gesner's own argument, that the appearance of pike in ponds where they had previously been unknown could be due to the droppings of birds: 'which my Compleat Angler no sooner deliberated, but drop'd his argument, and leaves Gesner to defend it ; so huff'd away' (*Northern Memoirs*, ed. [Sir Walter Scott] (1821), p. 177).

99:14 **Bacon** *History of Life and Death* (1638), pp. 59–60.

99:18 **Pike taken in Swedeland** This story is in Gesner's Preface to *De Piscium Natura* (edition of 1620), a3ᵛ. It seems possible, though, that Walton obtained it from William Samuel, *The Arte of Angling* (1577), since Gesner says the incident happened in Swabia, while Samuel says it happened in 'Swethland', which may provide Walton with 'Swedeland'. See D. E. Rhodes, 'A New Line for the Angler, 1577', *The Library*, 5th ser., x (1955), pp. 123–4.

99:33 **Gesner relates** Gesner, p. 503. Many writers comment on the pike's ferocity .

100:5 **Mr. Seagrave** See above, note to 39:1–2.

100:12 **it has no ears** *OD Proverbs*, p. 45.

100:35–36 **Gesner affirms** This paragraph and the next two come from Gesner, pp. 503, 505.

101:32 **Dubravius** Johann Dubraw (d. 1553), Bishop of Olmutz in Moravia. The story occurs in his *De Piscinis*, translated as *A New Booke of Good Husbandry* (1599), where it occurs at ff. 5ᵛ–6. Walton seems to have used the translation.

104:25 **Pliny** *Natural History*, ix. 159.

104:25 **Cardanus** (1501–76); in his *De Subtilitate* (1550), he describes how frogs and fish are carried off by the wind and fall as rain (xvi. 262).

106:29 **First open your Pike** Although none of Walton's recipes are to be found word-for-word in any of the contemporary cooking books that have survived, the recipes for roasting or stewing fish do not vary much. There is a pike recipe very similar to Walton's in W.M.'s *The Queens Closet Opened* (1658), pp. 102–3. I have not been able to identify M.B.

107:27 **Gesner tells us** pp. 501–2, 536.

109:7 **Mr. Mascall** L[eonard]. M[ascall]., *A Booke of Fishing with Hooke and Line* (1590), p. 7.

109:13 **Sir Richard Baker** Baker (1568–1645) shared rooms at Oxford with Sir Henry Wotton. The verses quoted come in *A Chronicle of the Kings of England* (1643), iii, p. 66.

109:18–19 **the Carp endures most hardness** 'The Carpe of all pond fish will abide most hardnesse in carriage' (John Taverner, *Certaine Experiments concerning Fish and Fruit* (1600), p. 24).

110:3 **Aristotle and Pliny** In Gesner, p. 312.

110:9 **Jovius** Paolo Giovio (1483–1552), Bishop of Nocera, wrote a life of Sannazzaro. A book on Roman fish was compiled in the early sixteenth century from his commentaries. In this book, *De Piscibus Romanis* (Basle, 1561), he does not mention carp, saying merely that there are very large fish in Lake Como (p. 70).

110:11–17 **the Bear ... the Elephant ... the Crocodile** Bacon, *History of Life and Death* (1638), pp. 46, 45–6, 60.

111 footnote **Mr. Fr. Ru.** Probably Francis Russell of Strensham, Worcestershire, brother-in-law of Charles Cotton and of Henry King. See above, notes to 89:27 and 92:20.

111:19–20 **History of Life and Death** 1638 edition, pp. 59–60.

111:21–5 **Gesner says** pp. 312, 310.

111:34 **Janus Dubravius** See above, note to 101:32. This passage is not to be found in Dubravius; Walton has adapted it from Taverner, *Certaine Experiments concerning Fish and Fruit* (1600), p. 18.

112:19 **The Physicians** This information comes from Gesner, p. 313.

112:23 **Caviare** Aldrovandus, *De Piscibus* (Bologna, 1613), p. 639.

113:18 **And some have been so curious** All writers agree that the carp is a difficult fish to catch, but I have not found one who specifies a particular day of the year. Mascall says: 'at certaine times to wit, at foure a clock in the morning, and eight at night be his chief byting times' (*A Booke of Fishing with Hooke and Line* (1590), p. 8).

115:10 **Dr. T.** Unidentified. Robert May, *The Accomplisht Cook* (2nd edn, 1665), gives a similar recipe for stewing carp in claret, but does not suggest the fish should be stuffed; he puts the same ingredients into the sauce. See also William Rabisha, *The Whole Body of Cookery Dissected* (1661) and M.B., *The Ladies Cabinet Enlarged and Opened* (1655).

117:8 **Gesner** In fact, Rondelet, quoted by Gesner, p. 317.

117:24–5 **This Gesner affirms** p. 317.

117:30 **History of Life and Death (fol. 20.)** It is this reference which enables us to identify the edition (of 1638) that Walton used.

117:33 **this Proverb** 'Qui a brasme, peut bien brasmer ses amis', Gesner, p. 316.

118:10 **Tench** An error for 'bream'.

118:16 **a most honest and excellent angler** The rest of this chapter seems to be derived from B.A., who remains unidentified.

121:35 **From St. James' Tide until Bartholomew Tide** That is, from 25 July to 24 August (old style, ten days later than today).

123:4 **the Physician of Fishes** Gesner, p. 986.

123:6 **Camden** 'the most famous river *Stoure* passing full of tenches and Eeles especially' (p. 214).

123:15 **Rondelitius** The first part of this paragraph, including the quotation from Rondelet, comes from Gesner, p. 985.

123:21 **Solomon** 1 Kings 4:29–33.

123:28 **Yellow-Jaundice** There seems to be no evidence that this cure for jaundice was especially associated with the Jews. It is recommended by William Salmon in his amplified translation of the *Pharmacopoeia Londinensis* (1678), and by Johann Schroeder in *The*

Compleat Chymical Dispensatory, translated by William Rowland (1699): 'the Louse ... The country-people eat them against the Jaundies' (p. 544). I am indebted to my colleague Malcolm Nicolson for the last two references.

124:2 **the Physician of fishes**   See above, note to 123:4.

125:13 **Aldrovandus**   *De Piscibus* (Bologna, 1613), p. 624.

125:15 **Gesner**   pp. 701, 698.

125:23 **Rondelitius**   These opinions may be found in Gesner, pp. 701, 700, 702, and 696, but they are not attributed to Rondelet. Perhaps Walton assumed that here, as so often, the first entry Gesner gives is from Rondelet.

125:35–4 **Sir Abraham Williams**   Agent in England for the Queen of Bohemia, and an acquaintance of Sir Henry Wotton. (See *The Life and Letters of Sir Henry Wotton*, ed. Logan Pearsall Smith (1907), ii, pp. 369, 470.)

127:21 **Doctor Donne**   John Donne (1573–1631), Dean of St Paul's. This poem may be found in *Elegies and Songs and Sonnets* of John Donne, ed. Helen Gardner (Oxford, 1965), p. 156; there are eight variants between Walton's text and that in the first edition of 1633. It is interesting to note that Venator says he will 'speak' these verses, despite the fact that they are a parody of Marlowe's 'Come live with me' (see above, note to 56:37), which is sung to its well-known tune.

129:4 **It is agreed**   The following paragraph, including the reference to Rondelet, comes from Gesner, pp. 40–2.

129:23 **Bacon**   *History of Life and Death* (1638), pp. 59–60.

129:24–5 **Pearls are made**   Pliny, *Natural History*, tr. Philemon Holland (1634), IX. xxxv. 254.

130:5 **Gesner**   pp. 59–60.

130:12–13 **Dubartas ... Lobel ... Camden ... Gerard**   Walton has already quoted the relevant passage from Du Bartas above (p. 73). Mathieu l'Obel illustrates the British Geese-bearing Shells in his *Icones Stirpium* (1581), ii. 259. Camden mentions the matter in his section on Scotland, p. 204, and Gerard devotes a chapter to the 'Goose-tree' in his *Herbal* (1597), p. 1391.

130:15 **Rondelitius**   Gesner, p. 40.

130:21–2 **History of Life and Death**   1638 edition, pp. 59–60.

130:26 **Hakewill**   p. 360.

130:29 **all, or most men**   Gesner, pp. 44–5; Gesner is not quoting Albertus (who has just been quoted), but the *Annales Augustae Vindelicae* (i.e. the Annals of Augsburg).

130:41 **Camden**   p. 748.

131:15 **it is affirmed**   By Gesner, p. 44.

133:13 **S.F.**   A number of cooking books give recipes for roasting eels: Robert May's *The Accomplisht Cook* (2nd edn, 1665) gives several. However, I have not found another recipe which includes anchovies and nutmeg, and no one else suggests the neat method of dealing with the head. S.F. remains unidentified.

133:17–18 **King-street in Westminster** Walton sometimes stayed with his Grinsell cousins in King Street, Westminster (Bodleian Library, MS Wood 44, fol. 382).

133:22 **Prov. 25** Proverbs 25:16.

133:25 **the uncharitable Italian** Untraced, but the saying is in Gesner, p. 47.

133:28 **Aldrovandus** *De Piscibus* (Bologna, 1613), pp. 551 ff.

134:12 **Camden** p. 755.

134:21 **Camden** p. 666.

134:24 **Pemble-Mere** Bala Lake, or Llyn Tegid.

135:4 **says Gesner** On p. 124.

135:36 **Rondelitius** Not Rondelet, but Albertus, quoted by Gesner, pp. 124–5.

136:7 **Gesner and Gasius** Gesner cites the experience of Antonio Gazi (*c.* 1450–1530), who records in his *De Conservatione Sanitatis* (Venice, 1491) the near-fatal effects upon him of eating barbels' eggs. In the best scientific tradition, Gesner tried the experiment himself, and was likewise very ill. See Gesner, p. 125.

136:20 **Plutarch** *De Sollertia Animalium*, chap. xxiv.

137:24 **Doctor Sheldon** Born in Staffordshire, Gilbert Sheldon (1598–1677) was ordained in 1622. He was opposed alike to Arminianism and Puritanism. In 1630 he was responsible for the preferment of Izaak Walton's nephew-in-law, Henry Valentine, to the living of St Nicholas, Deptford. Like Walton's friend George Morley, he was a member of the Great Tew circle. In 1648 he was ejected from the Wardenship of All Souls, Oxford, and passed his time in Staffordshire, Nottinghamshire, and Derbyshire, organising the survival of the underground Anglican Church, and administering a fund for the families of dispossessed clergy. He seems to have belonged to a 'guild of angling' similar to that described in *The Complete Angler*. In the 1655 edition of the *Angler* he is described as Doctor *Sh.*, his full name not being given until after the Restoration.

137:25 **the Poor** The distribution of fish to the poor is an important theme in *The Complete Angler*.

138:6 **Sillabub** This dish usually calls for equal quantities of cider (or sack: white wine) and cream, beaten together with egg-whites and sugar. There are various recipes. Walton's would be a simple one, such as that in *The Closet of Sir Kenelm Digby Opened* (1669), p. 141: 'Take a pint of Verjuyce [acid juice of fruit] in a bowl; milk the cow to the Verjuyce; take off the Curd; and take sweetcream and beat them together with a little Sack and Sugar; put it into your Syllabub pot; then strew sugar upon it, and so send it to the Table.'

138:8–9 **Chevy Chase**   For the ballad repertoire of the Milkmaid and her mother, see above, 57:22–5.

140:11 **Allamot salt**   Imported salt was often named after its place of origin, e.g. Bay salt from Bourgneuf Bay. No kind of salt will turn a bleak into an anchovy; they are different species. Nevertheless, there were English and Welsh attempts to emulate the secret process of preserving fish so as to imitate Italian anchovies. John Collins, *Salt and Fishery* (1682), describes (pp. 101 ff.) how the Italians preserve their anchovies with Spanish salt and a pickle made of salt, red wine 'or the Lees thereof' and 'powder of Saunders' (i.e. sandalwood). The use of Spanish salt may add some colour to the suggestion that Allamot may be a corruption of Alto Monte, in Calabria, where there were important salt mines. Another possibility is a corruption of *A la mode*, as in 'alamode beef'. (See *OED*, Alamode.)

140:13 **Pater-noster line**   The *OED* gives this as the earliest use of this word; it is derived from the spacing of the paternoster beads on a rosary.

141:5–6 **Hunting the Hare**   This sounds like a proverb, but I have been unable to trace it.

141:8 **let us have your Song etc.**   These promises were made on p. 63, and on p. 86 Piscator explains that he was forced to 'patch up' his song because 'it is so long since I learnt it, that I have forgot a part of it'.

143:5–6 **oaths do fray**   *OD Proverbs*, p. 792, and see above, 18:29.

144:27 **that Field in Sicily**   The field from which Proserpina was carried away by Dis to the underworld; it is described in Diodorus Siculus, *The History*, tr. Henry Cogan (1653), p. 226.

144:33 **the meek possess the Earth**   Matthew 5:5.

144:37 **the Poet**   Unidentified.

145:6 **Phineas Fletcher**   Fletcher (1582–1650) published his *Piscatorie Eclogs* in 1633, but Walton's quotation comes, with slight alteration, from his *Purple Island* (Giles and Phineas Fletcher, *Poetical Works*, ed. F. S. Boas (1908–9), ii, pp. 151–2).

145:28 **a piece of an old Catch**   The words and music of this catch are given in all editions; it is highly unusual to find printed music in a book of this kind. Henry Lawes (1596–1662) is remembered chiefly for his collaboration with Milton over *Comus*. He also wrote the music for masques by Thomas Carew and William Cartwright, who were both known to Walton, and when, at the outbreak of the Civil War, he was ousted from his appointments, he was employed in the Kentish family of Dering, friends of Walton. It is very likely that he set this 'old Catch' at Walton's request. Words and music were printed in Playford's *Select Musical Ayres and Dialogues* (1659), p. 62. See above, note to 83:12 footnote.

146:6 **Music, miraculous Rhetoric** These six lines are a very free version of two quatrains that first appear in John Hilton's *Catch that Catch Can*, published by Playford in 1652. They are signed W.D.; it has been suggested that they are by Sir William Davenant, poet and dramatist, and a friend of Charles Cotton the elder. They are also printed in the 1659 edition of *Select Musical Ayres and Dialogues*; see above, notes to 83:12 footnote and 145:28.

146:15 **Whilst I listen** These verses first appeared in the *Poems* (1645) of Edmund Waller (1608–87). They were set to music by Henry Lawes (see above, note to 145:28), and printed in his *Ayres and Dialogues* (1653). Words and music were added to the 1659 edition of Playford's *Select Musical Ayres and Dialogues*. All versions except Walton's have 'noise' for 'voice' in l. 3.

151:13 **Some say** As usual, Walton begins the description of a new fish with reference to Gesner; here pp. 820–2.

152:1–2 **the best Trout-Anglers be in Derby-shire** Doubtless a compliment to his friend Charles Cotton, of Beresford Hall, Derbyshire, with whom Walton went to stay, and who wrote Part II of *The Complete Angler* at Walton's request.

154:35–6 **chemical men** For the concoction of 'secret' oils for catching fish, see above, note to 97:14; for Sir George Hastings, see note to 52:9 and for Sir Henry Wotton, see note to 3:32.

155:16 **My Rod and my Line** etc.   Source unknown; there are several other indications that there were early fishing books of which no copy now survives.

155:24–6 **Mr. Margrave ... Mr. John Stubs** The names of tackle-merchants vary from one edition of the *Angler* to another; Walton was obviously concerned to keep his information up-to-date. The practical realism of these addresses contrasts with the more 'mythical' characters, such as the Milkmaid (from a character book) and the King of the Beggars (from a play). Other angling books published by Richard Marriot name the same changing group of tackle-merchants, some of whom have inserted formal advertisements in the books.

161:7 **Matthiolus** Pietro Andrea Mattioli (1500–77) was a Sienese physician and botanist, but his remark about the Bull-head has not been traced.

163:7–8 **Doctor Heylin's Geography** Walton's own copy of Peter Heylyn's *Microcosmus* (1621) is in Salisbury Cathedral Library; but the edition used here is either that of the enlarged 1625 *Geography* or a later one.

163:10–164:29 **The chief is Thames ... Danish blood** Verbatim from Heylyn (unusually for Walton, who often modifies his quotations); pp. 461–3 in the 1625 edition of *Geography*.

164:38 **Dr. Wharton** See above, note to 20:19. The description that follows is, perhaps, a description of the Sea-Angler, *Lophius piscatorius*.

165:24 **Grotius (in his Sophampaneas)** This play by Hugo de Groot (1588–1645) was translated from the Latin by Francis Goldsmith in 1652. It is an interesting precursor of Milton's *Samson Agonistes*, in its classical treatment of a biblical theme (the story of Joseph). Milton, who frequently mentions Grotius in his prose works, met him in Paris in 1638; before Milton embarked on his foreign travels, he had sought the advice of Sir Henry Wotton (who was acquainted with Grotius). The play has a chorus at the end of Act II which invokes the Nile: it is to this, and to Goldsmith's notes on it, that Walton refers.

165:26 **But whither am I strayed . . . ?** This is a standard rhetorical device, much employed by Walton in his *Lives*.

165:30 **learned Camden** pp. 477–8, 186.

167:7–168:36 **He adviseth . . . etc.** Estienne and Liebault's *Maison Rustique* was translated by Richard Surflet in 1600, and revised and extended by Gervase Markham in 1616. In what follows, Walton draws on the 1616 edition, and does not distinguish between Markham's additions and the original. For Markham, see above, note to 22:31). Walton, in what follows, has added a few observations from other writers, e.g. John Taverner, *Certaine Experiments concerning Fish and Fruits* (1600) and L[eonard]. M[ascall]., *A Booke of Fishing with Hooke and Line* (1590).

169:15 **Dubravius** Little or no use has been made of this author here.

171:26 **make much of it** Most English writers recommend the hairs from the tail of a white stallion.

173:8 **before you lay on a second** Henry Peacham, *The Compleat Gentleman* (1634), recommends the preparation of the surface with a size; he then says that colours should be ground in linseed oil: white lead, red lead, coal-black (see Glossary, below), and verdigris and pink (see Glossary).

173:9 **Well Scholar** The following passage, in italics, up to 177:13, was added to the fifth edition and presumably set directly from Walton's own manuscript.

173:26 **we are free from** *OD Proverbs*, p. 294. Nicolas Caussin, *The Holy Court*, tr. Sir T. H[awkins]. (edition of 1663), p. 21, similarly lists the misfortunes of others as a cause of gratitude to those who are free of them. Caussin is cited again by Walton below, 176:40.

174:2 **Solomon** Proverbs 10:4.

174:5 **a man of great observation** Either Montaigne: 'I see miserie as neere beyond two thousand crownes rent, as if it were to hand' (*Essayes*, tr. Florio (1613), I. xl. 135) or Sir Henry Wotton: 'Many think there are as many miseries beyond happiness, as on this side of it' (Logan Pearsall Smith (ed.), *The Life and Letters of Sir Henry Wotton* (1907), ii, pp. 490–1).

174:26 **How many things are there**   This story is told of Socrates in Richard Taverner's *The Garden of Wysdome* (1539), B6ᵛ. It derives from Diogenes Laertius (*Vitae Philosophorum*, II. v. 25), hence, doubtless, the confusion of name.

175:21 **he must leave himself behind him**   Cf. Montaigne, *Essayes*, tr. Florio (1613), I. xxxviii. 119.

175:28 **possess the earth**   Matthew 5:7, 8, 3 and 5.

176:2–3 **because he abounded more with thankfulness**   David is said to have been a man after God's own heart in Acts 13:22, but the reason given is Walton's own.

176:40 **Caussin**   'He that loseth his Conscience, hath nothing else to gain nor lose.' Nicolas Caussin, *The Holy Court*, tr. Sir T. H[awkins]. (edition of 1663), a3ʳ.

177:9–10 **a grave Divine**   According to Moses Browne, this was Donne.

177:23 **a drink like Nectar**   There is a similar recipe in *The Queens Closet Opened* (1655), p. 267. It is given there as a recipe for hippocras, a drink which does not usually contain milk.

177:26 **a Copy**   This poem appears in *Reliquiae Wottonianae* (1651), which was edited by Walton. It is there given the title 'A Description of the Countrey's Recreation' and signed 'Ignoto', so Walton was uncertain then of its authorship. It is also in the anthology of poems compiled by the Aston family, whom Walton knew (*Tixall Poetry*, ed. Arthur Clifford (1813), pp. 297–300).

179:18 **Farewell ye gilded follies**   The authorship of this poem is doubtful, as Walton indicates. In his first two editions of the *Angler* he attributed it to Donne, an attribution confirmed in various MSS. He must have had some reason for changing his ascription in his third edition (1661), and mentioning Wotton; but the poem is not in any edition of *Reliquiae Wottonianae*. In *Wits Interpreter* (1671) it is given to Sir Kenelm Digby, an ascription which also finds MS support.

180:8–9 **vie Angels**   Compare wealth; see both words in the Glossary.

180:35–6 **book 9. chap. 3.)**   I have corrected this reference; it was originally, and wrongly, printed as book 4.

181:25–6 **Lilies that take no care**   Matthew 6:28; Luke 12:27.

181:29 **Let every thing**   Psalm 150:6.

181:30 **St. Peter's Master**   The *Treatyse of Fysshynge wyth an Angle* (1496) also ends with a blessing: 'the blessyng of God and saynt Peter'. The unusual expression 'St. Peter's Master be with you' occurs in William Samuel's *Arte of Angling* (1577), A8.

181:33 **1 Thes. 4. 11**   'And that ye study to be quiet, and to do your own business, and to work with your own hands, as we commanded you; That ye may walk honestly toward them that are without, and that ye may have lack of nothing.'

GLOSSARY

(imper : imperative ; met. : metaphorical ; n : noun ; vb : verb)

abate lessen
accidental incidental, subsidiary
activity energy, agility
adventure (vb) take a risk
aerie (1) brood or (2) nest of birds of prey
aestuarium estuary
affect (vb) to be affectionately attached to
against in readiness for
a grace of God by the grace of God
ague malarial fever
allamot unidentified (see note to 140:11)
All-hallowtide season of All Saints (1 November)
amazement stupefaction, bewilderment
amusement gaze in astonishment, puzzle
angel gold coin depicting the archangel Michael defeating the dragon
angle angling rod and line
answerable corresponding
ant-fly winged ant
apace quickly
apt (vb) make suitable
arming barb
asafoetida concreted resinous gum, with pungent smell
at on
aurelia chrysalis
barley-wine strong ale
barnacles barnacle and brent geese
bavin bundle of brushwood
bay-salt salt from the salt-pans of Bourgneuf Bay
bear the bell take first place
bear your charges pay for you
before in front
beholding indebted
bent (1) angle between rod and line (see note to 86:31–2)
bent (2) grass

benzoin aromatic resin from the Indonesian tree *Styrax benzoin*
betwixt between
bottles (of hay) bundles
brace pair
braked (of hemp) combed
brandling red worm with rings or bands of brighter colouring
burden chorus
candock yellow water-lily
care away away with care !
career flight, course
case-worm caddis-worm, larva of the caddis-fly
cast form
casting (1) throwing
casting (2) vomiting
casually by occasion = by chance
catch part-song, round
cave hollow place
chaps jaws
chargeable expensive
charges expenses
cheven chub, chavender
chid chided, scolded
clerk cleric, scholar
coal-black graphite
cod-worm caddis-worm, larva of the caddis-fly
colewort cabbage
comfortable comforting
communicable communicative
commute (vb) exchange
competence, competency sufficient income
complexion nature, temperament
composure composition
comprehend include
conceits witticisms
conclusions, to try engage in trial of skill ; determine by experiment
conference collection
conjure charm, bewitch, raise spirits
considerable worth consideration
constant constantly
contemn despise
copperas sulphate of iron, green vitriol
countries counties ; parts of the countryside
credit reputation
crewel thin worsted yarn
cropper pouter pigeon

cubit 18 or 22 inches
culverkeys bluebell, wild hyacinth, *Hyacinthoides non-scripta*
curiosity pursuit, interest; pedantry
curious made with care or art, excellent; elaborate; particular, careful, cautious
dainty fastidious
dam mother (animal)
damasked like damask (pink) rose
dap (vb) fish by letting bait bob lightly on the water
date end, closing date
degree rank
dew-worm common earthworm
distempered unregulated
ditty song
divers various; several
docibleness docility
dock-worm a grub found on the dock plant
dogged obstinate, reluctant
dor humming beetle: black dung-beetle, cockchafer, rose-beetle, etc.
doubling musical ornamentation of phrases
drag-hook dredge-hook; hook linked to under-water net or lines
draw cuts draw lots with sticks of unequal length
dress (vb) prepare (a dish)
drive spread out thinly
dug udder of female mammal
dug-worm kind of red worm
dun dull greyish-brown
easy without effort
eat be eaten
ell 45 inches
end purpose
engross monopolise
enter begin, initiate
even just, simply
even lay even bet
except (vb) take exception
exceptions objections
excrements outgrowths, e.g. feathers, horns
expiring breathing out
fain would be glad to
falling-sickness epilepsy
false quarter quarter: half of horse's hoof; false quarter: scarred or cracked section of hoof
fancy imagination
fashion method

fat rich

fearful timid

fence month closed season for fish or game

fere companion, mate

filleting ribbon, string

finis the end

finnimbrums nonsenses (word apparently invented by Walton: the context makes it plain)

firkin small cask, one-fourth the size of a barrel

fitchew weasel

flags plants with bladed leaf growing in moist ground: coarse grass; flag irises, etc.

flag-worm worm found in the roots of flags (wild irises)

flesh meat

float-fish fish caught by float-fishing

fond foolish

forbear (vb) desist

force put a strained sense upon

form hare's lurking-place

fountain source (of river)

fray affright, frighten

freely without constraint

frumenty dish of hulled wheat boiled in milk and seasoned with sugar, cinnamon, etc.

fry young fish

fulimart foul-martin, polecat

ganderglass early purple orchid, *Orchis mascula*

generation breeding

gentle maggot, larva, of flesh-fly or bluebottle

get acquire money, property

gillyflower clove-scented pink

gilt-tail unidentified

glosing hypocritical

golden age happy age of time before the Fall of Man

gorge (vb) swallow down

gorrara unidentified; perhaps carara, Hebridean name for the great northern diver

grace *see* a grace

grateful acceptable

green fresh, young

green-sickness chlorosis (anaemic illness of young girls)

green-sward turf

gross-ground coarsely ground

ground (painting) undercoat

hackle long shining feathers at the neck of certain birds

half-year-birds migratory birds
handful (measure) four inches
harl barb, fibre, of feather
haut goût high, piquant flavour
have with you! (imper.) make an attempt!
heads headings
Helena Helen of Troy and thus (met.) the most beautiful person, fish, etc.
helmet pigeon whose head plumage differs in colour from that of its body
hen-driver hen-harrier
high ambitious, grand
hogback crested ridge or hill
hold, holt lurking-place
honest worthy, good
hope expect, trust
horn (vb) make cuckold
humour (n) fluid or juice of animal or plant (thought to govern temperament in humans)
humour (vb) make to a particular character or style
in case if it be the case
ingenuous = ingenious: clever, talented, inventive
inspiring breathing in
invade attack
irreprovable blameless
jealous vigilant, suspicious, watchful
kennel (vb) live in, go to, dwelling of a animal
Killbuck traditional hound name
kirtle outer skirt or petticoat
kit kitten
knack crafty contrivance (e.g. fishing apparatus)
'las alas
laverock lark (perhaps the woodlark)
lead lead weight
leash three (originally of hounds, since there were three hounds to a leash)
lecturer supernumerary parish preacher, maintained by voluntary contribution or by endowment
lee-shore side away from the wind
list (n) selvage or edge
list (vb) be pleasing to
lob-worm common earthworm
logger-headed large-headed
lure (vb) entice
lusty healthy and strong

lye alkaline water made by pouring water over the ashes of wood or other vegetable matter ; it is almost colourless

magazine-bag bag of materials for angling (from magazine, store of ammunition)

mail breast feathers

make conscience of be conscientious about

manchet fine wheaten bread

marl soil consisting of clay and carbonate of lime

marry by Mary ! (exclamation)

marsh-worm bluehead-worm

masque elaborate court entertainment

match bargain, agreement

May-butter butter made in May, when the cows are eating new grass, is held to be especially runny

mean humble

meat food

mew (vb) house (of hawk)

mewing housing (of hawk)

Michaelmas 29 September

middle moderate, medium

milter male fish in spawning time

minion darling

mixtion mixture

mote particle of dust

motion proposal

mould-warp mole

mummery play-acting, hollow pretence

nice precise, fine, exact

oak-worm worm that lives on the oak tree

observable worthy of observation or note

oil of Peter (oil of the rock) rock-oil ; petroleum

order (vb) arrange

other cup second cup

over-store over-stock

owe own

owlers alders

pack-thread stout thread for tying parcels

Palatinate state of the old German Empire under the rule of the Count Palatine of the Rhine

palmer-fly, palmer-(= pilgrim-) worm destructive hairy caterpillar

palm-tree willow

peascod pea-pod

peck two gallons

peckled speckled

pencil paint-brush

perfectly thoroughly, fully

pewit lapwing

philosopher's stone stone sought by alchemists, believed to transmute base metals into gold

physic medicine

pickerel-weed pondweed, a species of *Potamogeton*

pink (1) minnow

pink (2) yellowish, or greenish-yellow pigment

pipkin small earthenware pot or pan

pismire ant

pleasant good-humoured, amusing

pleasure (vb) please

pledge (vb) drink to the health of

plover's top plover's crest

plummet weight attached to fishing-line, to keep float upright

Polonian Polish

pottle two quarts

pouch (vb) swallow

powdered beef dried, salted beef

practice performance

presently immediately, shortly

prest ready

pretend (vb) claim

pretended offered, undertook

prevent anticipate

primitive early

prove experience, try

purling swift-flowing, babbling

purpose (vb) plan, propose

put down (hunting) cause to lie down, lie low

quarter *see* false quarter

quick-fire rapid, hot, fire (in cooking)

rascal young, lean, inferior (of game)

reason, in your in your opinion, according to your reasoning

reate water crowfoot

reclaiming taming

red lead a red oxide of lead

reins kidneys

resolve (vb) settle a question

right true

rill stream

Ringwood traditional hound name

Rosicrucians members of a society credited with secret and magic knowledge

roundelay short song with repetitions; birdsong

rove aim

running-line fishing-line weighted so as to run along the bed of the stream

runt breed of large domestic pigeon

russet coarse cloth

sack white wine

sad (of a colour) dull, neutral-tinted

scotch (vb) slash, score

scour clean

seasonably in good season, well-timed

set up provide an apprentice with tools of his trade

sharp (of a stream) rapid

shift (n) effort

short below standard (of taste)

shovel-board shove-halfpenny: still a traditional English pub game (players hit with their hands small coins or metal discs along a graduated board or table)

sillabub mixture of cream or milk with wine, cider, sherry, etc.

simple stupid

sleave (vb) divide (silk) by separation into filaments

sleight skill, skilful trick

small ale ale weak in alcohol

smoking pelting

snap, at the at the first touch (of the fish)

sniggling fishing with short line, strong hook, and no float, using a stick to push the bait into the prey's (usually eel's) hole

soar (vb) fly, or float, high

softly (of boiling) gently

Solan goose gannet

sometimes formerly, sometime

spawning breeding (fish)

spike lavender (*Lavandula spica*); hence oil of spike, essential oil of lavender

stand in cost, stand in debt

stare starling

still habitually, continually

stomach appetite

stones testicles

store plenty

stroke a sillabub mix sillabub (q.v.) by milking a cow into the sillabub pot

strong lines terse, witty, unmelodious poetry

suddenly immediately, shortly

Swedeland Sweden

sweetbriar wild rose
Sweetlips traditional hound name
tag-tail *unidentified*
threescore sixty (a score = twenty)
throstle song-thrush
tit-lark meadow pipit
titmouse tit (as blue tit, coal tit, great tit)
toil make weary
top upper part of a jointed fishing-rod
tother *see* other cup
touch slight amount
towardly promising
to you here's a health to you
trade (vb) practise
trencher wooden plate
twachel *see* lob-worm
twopence half-groat: hammered silver coin varying in diameter from 14 to 17 mm
unconscionably against (virtuous) conscience
urchin hedgehog
use (n) investing for interest; usury
use (vb) be accustomed
usually habitually
vent outlet
vent, at taking breath above the surface of water
verdigris green or greenish blue dye obtained from dilute acetic acid and copper
verjuice acid liquor from crab-apples or unripe fruit
very true; same; actual
vie compete
virgin wax unadulterated wax
viz (Lat.) *videlicet*: that is to say, namely
want lack
wanton luxuriant, thickly-growing; pleasure-loving
wantonness playfulness; lasciviousness
warrant promise, guarantee
wasted lost, exhausted
watery (met.) vapid, poor, thin
welkin sky, heavens
white lead lead carbonate and hydrated lead oxide
whip (vb) fish stream with whipping motion
win gain, earn
withal with; moreover
wonted accustomed

WALTON AND HIS CRITICS

John Floud, who wrote the poem below, was Walton's brother-in-law; little is known of him. The poem first appeared in *The Complete Angler*, 1655. It sets what will be a long tradition of seeing the *Angler* as a portrayal of idealised nature; it also makes the important point about the book's accessibility to a wide range of readers.

> *To my dear Brother Mr Izaak Walton, upon his*
> Complete Angler.
>
> *Erasmus* in his learned Colloquies
> Has mixed some toys, that by varieties
> He might entice all Readers: for in him
> Each *child* may wade, or tallest *giant* swim.
> And such is this Discourse: there's none so low,
> Or highly learn'd, to whom hence may not flow
> Pleasure and information: both which are
> Taught us with so much art, that I might swear
> Safely, the choicest Critic cannot tell,
> Whether your matchless judgement most excel
> In *Angling* or its *praise*: where commendation
> First charms, then makes an *art* a *recreation*.
>   'Twas so to me: who *saw* the cheerful Spring
> Pictured in every *meadow*, heard *birds* sing
> *Sonnets* in every *grove*, saw *fishes* play
> In the cool *crystal streams*, like *lambs* in *May*:
> And they may play, till *Anglers* read this *book*;
> But after, 'tis a wise *fish* 'scapes a *hook*.
>   Jo. *Floud*, Mr. of Arts.

Richard Franck wrote his *Northern Memoirs* in 1658, although they were not printed until 1696. A Cromwellian trooper, Franck must have been temperamentally inimical to Walton; he took the trouble to seek Walton out in Stafford to tax him with his old-fashioned views about the propagation of pike. That

Walton then 'huff'd away' is scarcely surprising. The following quotation is taken from the edition of *Northern Memoirs* edited (anonymously) by Sir Walter Scott in 1821. This is his opinion of *The Complete Angler*:

Isaac Walton (late author of *The Compleat Angler*) has imposed upon the world this monthly novelty [the twelve flies for trout, which derive from 1496], which he understood not himself; but stuffs his book with morals from Dubravius and others, not giving us one precedent of his own practical experiments, except otherwise where he prefers the trencher before the troling rod; who lays the stress of his arguments upon other men's observations, where with he stuffs his indigested octavo; so brings himself under the angler's censure, and the common calamity of a plagiary, to be pitied (poor man) for his loss of time in scribbling and transcribing other men's notions.

What follows was written in a copy of the fourth edition (1668) in the John Rylands Library, Manchester; it is based on Moses Browne's Introduction to his edition (1750). Browne produced his edition at the suggestion of Dr Johnson.

This is no trifling work, but both entertaining and instructive: whether we consider the Elegant Simplicity of the Style, the Ease and unaffected Humor of the Dialogue, the lovely Scenes which it delineates, the enchanting Pastoral Poetry which it contains, or the fine Morality it so sweetly incloses, [it] has hardly its Fellow in any of the Modern Languages.

Wordsworth's sonnet about *The Complete Angler* is described as written upon a blank leaf of the book. It was first published in 1819.

> While flowing rivers yield a blameless sport,
> Shall live the name of Walton: Sage benign!
> Whose pen, the mysteries of the rod and line
> Unfolding, did not fruitlessly exhort
> To reverend watching of each still report
> That nature utters from her rural shrine.
> Meek, nobly versed in simple discipline –
> He found the longest summer day too short,
> To his loved pastime given by sedgy Lee.
> Or down the tempting maze of Shawford brook –
> Fairer than life itself, in this sweet Book,
> The cowslip-bank and shady willow-tree;
> And the fresh meads – where flowed, from every nook
> Of his full bosom, gladsome Piety!

Sir Walter Scott, in his Preface to his [anonymous] edition of Franck's *Northern Memoirs* (1821), states his own view clearly:

> Probably no reader, while he reads the disparaging passages in which the venerable Isaac Walton is introduced, can forbear wishing that the good old man, who had so true an eye for nature, so simple a taste for her most innocent pleasures, and withal, so sound a judgment, both concerning men and things, had made this northern tour instead of Franck; and had detailed in the beautiful simplicity of his Arcadian language, his observations on the scenery and manners of Scotland.

Byron's brief attack on Walton takes no account of changing perceptions about animals' ability to experience pain; Walton had said, 'I am not of a cruel nature; I love to kill nothing but fish,' which seems to indicate that he did not understand fish as capable of suffering. These lines from *Don Juan* xiii. 106, were first published in 1823:

> Whatever Izaak Walton sings or says;
> The quaint, old, cruel coxcomb in his gullet
> Should have a hook, and a small trout to pull it.

Despite Byron's objection, pleasure in the rural escape of *The Complete Angler* continued during the nineteenth century, while editions of the *Angler* came out apace; during the 1880s in particular these were large, extravagantly illustrated volumes, far removed from the pocket-sized editions of Walton's own time. By the early twentieth century John Buchan is claiming for the *Angler* the status of pastoral. Here is a quotation from his *Introduction* to the (relatively simple) edition of 1901:

> With all his modest intentions he is a past master of the little country idyll ... The pastoral drama, really a lost art since Theocritus, in spite of Roman, Italian and Elizabethan revivals, is here restored in all its fresh and courtly grace.

There has been very little modern attempt to grapple with the critical problems posed by *The Complete Angler*: almost the only book-length study is John R. Cooper's *The Art of the Compleat Angler* (Durham, NC, 1968). He states the fundamental difficulty clearly (pp. 4–5):

> Despite the popularity of the *Angler*, criticism of it has been singularly inadequate. Those critics who have attempted more than mere appreciation have shown a vagueness of purpose and even a

perceptible embarrassment in their attempts to deal with this strange and charming work. The reason seems to have been that *The Compleat Angler* cannot easily be made to fit any of the more familiar critical categories ... *The Compleat Angler* is a prose narrative, and yet it is clearly not a novel or a short story.

SUGGESTIONS FOR FURTHER READING

Despite the fact that, at the last count (1986), there were 456 separate editions of *The Complete Angler* (including translations), critical discussion is sparse. There is a gap here waiting to be filled. In the eighteenth and nineteenth centuries, the book met with somewhat anodyne acclaim; probably the best comments in this period are to be found in the introductions of the numerous editions. In the twentieth century the book has experienced an almost total critical silence. General studies of the prose of the period – e.g. Paul Salzman, *English Prose Fiction 1558–1700* (Oxford, 1985) – ignore it completely.

Bevan, Jonquil, *Izaak Walton's The Compleat Angler: The Art of Recreation* (Brighton and New York, 1988).

Chadwick, Owen, *The Fisherman and his God: Izaak Walton* (The Drawbridge Lecture, King's College, London, 1984). An essay by a Christian writer, with a committed viewpoint; an elegant, acute, and original study.

Chalker, John, *The English Georgic: A Study in the Development of a Form* (1969). Provides a background for one of the many genres to which (it could be argued) *The Complete Angler* belongs.

Cooper, John R., *The Art of The Compleat Angler* (Durham, NC, 1968). Cooper is principally interested in the classical and European traditions of georgic and pastoral, and he provides a useful background for these; he also writes about the book as a dialogue.

Costa, Francisque, *L'œuvre d'Izaak Walton* (Paris, 1973). The basic Izaak Walton *Handbook*, dealing with all aspects of Walton's life and writings; badly flawed by misprints, it nevertheless deserves to be corrected and translated.

Ollard, Richard, *Clarendon and his Friends* (1987). An invaluable account of Great Tew and other circles related to Walton.

Thomas, Keith, *Man and the Natural World: Changing Attitudes in England 1500–1800* (1983; reprinted Harmondsworth, 1984). This magisterial book provides a general context for the study of natural history; it is particularly useful to students of *The Complete Angler* for its discussion of growing perceptions about cruelty to animals.

ACKNOWLEDGEMENTS

All editors of *The Complete Angler* must acknowledge a debt to Sir Nicholas Harris Nicolas, whose edition was first printed in 1836. There have been other important editions since. But I wish here to acknowledge more personal debts: to Chloe Appleby, Eluned M. Brown, the late John Buxton, the late Margaret Crum, Suzanne Eward, Roy Flannagan, the late Helen Gardner, Alastair Fowler, Kathleen M. Lea, D. F. McKenzie, Winifred Maynard, Louise Millard, Desmond Neill, Roger Savage, Christopher Shaddock, and the late William Urry.

The publishers and editor are also grateful to all copyright holders for permission to quote from the extracts reprinted in the 'Walton and His Critics' section of this edition.

CLASSIC NOVELS
IN EVERYMAN

A SELECTION

The Way of All Flesh
SAMUEL BUTLER
A savagely funny odyssey from joy-
less duty to unbridled liberalism **£4.99**

Born in Exile
GEORGE GISSING
A rationalist's progress towards love
and compromise in class-ridden
Victorian England **£4.99**

David Copperfield
CHARLES DICKENS
One of Dickens's best-loved novels,
brimming with humour **£3.99**

The Last Chronicle of Barset
ANTHONY TROLLOPE
Trollope's magnificent conclusion
to his Barsetshire novels **£4.99**

He Knew He Was Right
ANTHONY TROLLOPE
Sexual jealousy, money and
women's rights within marriage –
a novel ahead of its time **£6.99**

Tess of the D'Urbervilles
THOMAS HARDY
The powerful, poetic classic of
wronged innocence **£3.99**

Tom Jones
HENRY FIELDING
The wayward adventures of one of
literatures most likeable heroes
£5.99

Wuthering Heights
and Poems
EMILY BRONTË
A powerful work of genius – one of
the great masterpieces of literature
£3.50

The Master of Ballantrae
and Weir of Hermiston
R. L. STEVENSON
Together in one volume, two great
novels of high adventure and family
conflict **£4.99**

£5.99

AVAILABILITY
All books are available from your local bookshop or direct from
**Littlehampton Book Services Cash Sales, 14 Eldon Way, Lineside Estate,
Littlehampton, West Sussex BN17 7HE.** PRICES ARE SUBJECT TO CHANGE.

To order any of the books, please enclose a cheque (in £ sterling) made payable to
Littlehampton Book Services, or phone your order through with credit card details (Access,
Visa or Mastercard) on 0903 721596 (24 hour answering service) stating card number and
expiry date. Please add £1.25 for package and postage to the total value of your order.

In the USA, for further information and a complete catalogue call 1-800-526-2778.

SHORT STORY COLLECTIONS IN EVERYMAN

A SELECTION

The Secret Self 1: Short Stories by Women
'A superb collection' *Guardian* **£4.99**

Selected Short Stories and Poems
THOMAS HARDY
The best of Hardy's Wessex in a unique selection **£4.99**

The Best of Sherlock Holmes
ARTHUR CONAN DOYLE
All the favourite adventures in one volume **£4.99**

Great Tales of Detection Nineteen Stories
Chosen by Dorothy L. Sayers **£3.99**

Short Stories
KATHERINE MANSFIELD
A selection displaying the remarkable range of Mansfield's writing **£3.99**

Selected Stories
RUDYARD KIPLING
Includes stories chosen to reveal the 'other' Kipling **£4.50**

The Strange Case of Dr Jekyll and Mr Hyde and Other Stories
R. L. STEVENSON
An exciting selection of gripping tales from a master of suspense **£3.99**

The Day of Silence and Other Stories
GEORGE GISSING
Gissing's finest stories, available for the first time in one volume **£4.99**

Selected Tales
HENRY JAMES
Stories portraying the tensions between private life and the outside world **£5.99**

£4.99

AVAILABILITY

All books are available from your local bookshop or direct from
Littlehampton Book Services Cash Sales, 14 Eldon Way, Lineside Estate, Littlehampton, West Sussex BN17 7HE. PRICES ARE SUBJECT TO CHANGE.

To order any of the books, please enclose a cheque (in £ sterling) made payable to Littlehampton Book Services, or phone your order through with credit card details (Access, Visa or Mastercard) on 0903 721596 (24 hour answering service) stating card number and expiry date. Please add £1.25 for package and postage to the total value of your order.

In the USA, for further information and a complete catalogue call 1-800-526-2778.

PHILOSOPHY AND RELIGIOUS WRITING IN EVERYMAN

A SELECTION

Ethics
SPINOZA
Spinoza's famous discourse on the power of understanding £4.99

Critique of Pure Reason
IMMANUEL KANT
The capacity of the human intellect examined £6.99

A Discourse on Method, Meditations, and Principles
RENÉ DESCARTES
Takes the theory of mind over matter into a new dimension £4.99

Philosophical Works including the Works on Vision
GEORGE BERKELEY
An eloquent defence of the power of the spirit in the physical world £4.99

Utilitarianism, On Liberty, Considerations on Representative Government
J. S. MILL
Three radical works which transformed political science £5.99

Utopia
THOMAS MORE
A critique of contemporary ills allied with a visionary ideal for society £3.99

An Essay Concerning Human Understanding
JOHN LOCKE
A central work in the development of modern philosophy £5.99

Hindu Scriptures
The most important ancient Hindu writings in one volume £6.99

Apologia Pro Vita Sua
JOHN HENRY NEWMAN
A moving and inspiring account of a Christian's spiritual journey £5.99

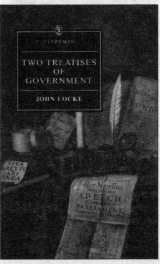

£3.99

AVAILABILITY

All books are available from your local bookshop or direct from
Littlehampton Book Services Cash Sales, 14 Eldon Way, Lineside Estate, Littlehampton, West Sussex BN17 7HE. PRICES ARE SUBJECT TO CHANGE.

To order any of the books, please enclose a cheque (in £ sterling) made payable to Littlehampton Book Services, or phone your order through with credit card details (Access, Visa or Mastercard) on 0903 721596 (24 hour answering service) stating card number and expiry date. Please add £1.25 for package and postage to the total value of your order.

In the USA, for further information and a complete catalogue call 1-800-526-2778.

ESSAYS, CRITICISM AND HISTORY IN EVERYMAN

A SELECTION

The Embassy to Constantinople and Other Writings
LIUDPRAND OF CREMONA
An insider's view of political machinations in medieval Europe **£5.99**

Speeches and Letters
ABRAHAM LINCOLN
A key document of the American Civil War **£4.99**

Essays
FRANCIS BACON
An excellent introduction to Bacon's incisive wit and moral outlook **£3.99**

Puritanism and Liberty: Being the Army Debates (1647-49) from the Clarke Manuscripts
A fascinating revelation of Puritan minds in action **£7.99**

Biographia Literaria
SAMUEL TAYLOR COLERIDGE
A masterpiece of criticism, marrying the study of literature with philosophy **£4.99**

Essays on Literature and Art
WALTER PATER
Insights on culture and literature from a major voice of the 1890s **£3.99**

Chesterton on Dickens: Criticisms and Appreciations
A landmark in Dickens criticism, rarely surpassed **£4.99**

Essays and Poems
R. L. STEVENSON
Stevenson's hidden treasures in a new selection **£4.99**

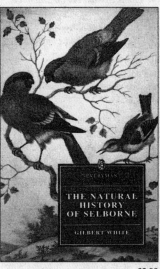

£3.99

POETRY
IN EVERYMAN

A SELECTION

Silver Poets of the Sixteenth Century

EDITED BY

DOUGLAS BROOKS-DAVIES
A new edition of this famous
Everyman collection **£6.99**

Complete Poems

JOHN DONNE
The father of metaphysical verse in
this highly-acclaimed edition **£6.99**

Complete English Poems, Of Education, Areopagitica

JOHN MILTON
An excellent introduction to
Milton's poetry and prose **£6.99**

Selected Poems

JOHN DRYDEN
A poet's portrait of Restoration
England **£4.99**

Selected Poems and Prose

PERCY BYSSHE SHELLEY
'The essential Shelley' in one
volume **£3.50**

Women Romantic Poets 1780-1830: An Anthology

Hidden talent from the Romantic era
rediscovered **£5.99**

Poems in Scots and English

ROBERT BURNS
The best of Scotland's greatest lyric
poet **£4.99**

Selected Poems

D. H. LAWRENCE
A new, authoritative selection
spanning the whole of Lawrence's
literary career **£4.99**

The Poems

W. B. YEATS
Ireland's greatest lyric poet
surveyed in this ground-breaking
edition **£7.99**

£5.99
